To Claire

who is

'MORE PRECIOUS THAN RUBIES'

To me, All love
Duda
xxx

Mary Taylor:
friend of Charlotte Brontë, strong-minded woman

~

Joan Bellamy

Highgate of Beverley

Highgate Publications (Beverley) Limited
2002

Acknowledgements

I am grateful for the assistance of the staffs of the Alpine Club; Bodleian Library, Brontë Parsonage Museum; Brotherton Collection, the University of Leeds Library; Women's Library, Guildhall University, London; Leeds City Reference Library; Leeds Library; John Rylands Library.

The Arts Faculty Research Committee of the Open University and the British Council in New Zealand provided financial assistance. My thanks to Mrs. E. Nussey for permission to consult her late husband's papers, and to Jürg Thommen formerly of the Grand Hotel Kronenhof, Pontresina.

For their encouragement I thank colleagues of the Women in the Humanities Research Group of the Open University; Ms. Helga Hughes B.A., Museum Officer, Red House Museum, Dr. Robert and Mrs. Louise Barnard, Mme. Marie-Thérèse Belmer who travelled with me in Switzerland and Dr. and Mrs. Richard Taylor.

I am indebted to the work of Mrs. Mabel Ferrett; to the work of the late Professor Joan Stevens relating to Mary Taylor in New Zealand. Blackwell Publishing have permitted me to quote from T. J. Wise & J. A. Symington (eds), *The Brontës: Their Lives, Friendships and Correspondence.*

Cover Photograph by kind permission of the Brontë Parsonage Museum.

British Library Cataloguing in Publication Data.
A catalogue record for this book is available from the British Library.

ISBN 1 902645 28 6

Published by

Highgate of Beverley

Highgate Publications (Beverley) Limited
4 Newbegin, Beverley, HU17 8EG. Telephone (01482) 886017

Printed by Highgate Print Limited
4 Newbegin, Beverley, HU17 8EG. Telephone (01482) 886017

Contents

Introduction

Mary Taylor has been called 'Charlotte Brontë's most intelligent school-friend'[1] and 'the most radical feminist Charlotte Brontë knew'.[2] Elizabeth Gaskell described her as 'a cherished associate' of Brontë,[3] while Charlotte herself declared: 'It is vain to limit a character like hers within ordinary boundaries – she will overstep them. I am morally certain Mary will establish her own landmarks'.[4]

In almost any account of Charlotte Brontë's life, we catch momentary glimpses of Mary Taylor (1817-93), but important as her friendship with Brontë was, Taylor has further claims on our interest. She was a feminist theoretician, who contributed to the debates generated by the emergence of the nineteenth-century women's movement; her journalism and novel represent an important strand in those debates. Notable too are the enterprise and courage with which she shaped her own career and achieved personal independence. Today as the search for women's history and achievements gathers pace, adding to our knowledge of women's past, Mary Taylor's own story has powerful claims to be told as fully as surviving evidence allows.

Mary Taylor, born in 1817, was the elder daughter and fourth child of Anne (Tickell) Taylor, and her husband Joshua, of Gomersal, near Leeds in West Yorkshire. The village lies above the valley of the river Spen, between Bradford and Wakefield, Leeds and Halifax. In the nineteenth century it was a developed woollen textile area producing blankets and heavy cloth and was consequently known as the Heavy Woollen District. The locality is rich in Brontë associations. Patrick Brontë had been a curate there, while Charlotte had lifelong friends in the district, notably Ellen Nussey and Mary Taylor and their families.

It was here that Charlotte Brontë (1816-55) situated her novel *Shirley*, drawing on local history for its industrial, condition-of-England features. It was here in 1812 that the Luddite riots erupted, launched by those cloth croppers whose livelihood was being destroyed by technological innovation and economic crisis. Their situation provides the historical framework as well as a central problem of the novel. In her descriptions of scenery, and places, Brontë drew on the local topography and some notable houses, while for some of her characters she recalls traits of actual personalities of the district, some very well known and easily recognised.

Mary Taylor and Ellen Nussey were intimate friends of Charlotte Brontë, whom they had first met at school. It was to them that Mrs. Gaskell turned for help when she began writing *The Life of Charlotte Brontë* in 1855, the year of the novelist's death. It was Nussey who had taken the initiative in suggesting the need for a biography to counteract the numerous inaccuracies appearing in the press.[5] She is credited, too, with the proposal to invite Mrs. Gaskell to write it. From her came a collection of about 350 letters, many from Charlotte herself, others relating to her, including some from Mary Taylor. Unfortunately Nussey exercised quite heavy censorship on the material, with names, and even whole sections, scored out but she also provided a valuable account of her friendship and schooldays with Brontë and Taylor.[6]

Mary, unfortunately, had little to offer Gaskell in the way of correspondence. It is more than likely that Charlotte confided in Mary hopes and emotions she knew were outside Ellen Nussey's range of knowledge and sympathies. She certainly discussed her ambitions with Mary and probably confided in her about her feelings towards M. Heger in letters which Mary had thought it better to destroy because she was unable to guarantee their security from other eyes. She had, however, retained the now famous letter from Charlotte which describes her visit with Anne to the offices of the publishers, Smith, Elder, to prove that Currer, Ellis and Acton Bell (the three sisters' *noms-de-plume*), were indeed three separate people. Taylor placed this letter at Gaskell's disposal and provided reminiscences of her friend.

As Gaskell was at work on the writing of the biography, Mary shrewdly commented from New Zealand:

> I can never think without gloomy anger of Charlotte's sacrifices to the selfish old man [Patrick Brontë]. How well we know that, had she left him entirely and succeeded in gaining wealth, and name and influence, she would have had all the world lauding her to the skies for any trivial act of generosity that would have cost her nothing! But how on earth is all this to be set straight! Mrs. Gaskell seems far too able a woman to put her head into such a wasp nest, as she would raise about her by speaking the truth of living people. How she will get through with it I can't imagine.[7]

Mrs. Gaskell had been forewarned about possible difficulties; Ellen Nussey had passed Mary's opinion on to her. She didn't, as it transpired, get 'through with it'. She provoked threats of libel actions from Mrs. Robinson (by that time Lady Scott), who was the former employer of Branwell and of Anne Brontë, and from the family of the Reverend Carus Wilson who had been connected with the Cowan Bridge school.

There were other protests. J. S. Mill resented Gaskell's repetition of Brontë's comments about an anonymous *Westminster Review* article of 1851, 'The Emancipation of Women', that it seemed like the work of a hard-hearted, jealous woman. She then fixed on J. S. Mill as its author.[8] Harriet Taylor Mill had in fact written it and J. S. Mill protested at what he regarded as an insult to his wife.

Taylor received copies of the first edition of *The Life* direct from Gaskell and the publishers, and in her characteristically frank way expressed her warm appreciation of it while explaining to the author what she saw as its limitations:

> I am unaccountably in receipt by post of two vols. containing the 'Life of C. Brontë'. I have pleasure in attributing this compliment to you; I beg therefore, to thank you for them. The book is a perfect success, in giving a true picture of a melancholy life, and you have practically answered my puzzle as to how you would give an account of her, not being at liberty to give a true description of those around. Though not so gloomy as the truth, it is perhaps as much so as people will accept without calling it exaggerated, and feeling the desire to doubt and contradict it. I have seen two reviews of it. One of them sums it up as 'a life of poverty and self-suppression', the other has nothing to the purpose at all. Neither of them seems to think it a strange or wrong state of things that a woman of first-rate talents, industry and integrity should live all her life in a walking nightmare of 'poverty and self-suppression'. I doubt whether any of them will.
>
> It must upset most people's notions of beauty to be told that the portrait at the beginning is that of an ugly woman. I do not altogether like the idea of publishing a flattered likeness.[9]

To George Smith, her publisher, Gaskell was rather dismissive of Taylor's reservations, even misrepresenting them somewhat:

> ... it [MT's letter] contained little more than a sort of accusation that I had softened the peculiarities and faults of the male portion of the family too much; & a pretty good bit about the portrait saying it was too much flattered, and describing the real face.[10]

Mrs. Gaskell failed to appreciate that Taylor objected to the portrait because it collaborated with the convention which judged women by their appearance while their actual characters and achievements were trivialised or ignored. The *Saturday Review* carried the kind of notice to which Taylor refers so contemptuously:

> If any one wishes to see how a woman possessed of the highest intellectual power can disregard every temptation which intellect throws in the way of women – how generously and nobly a human being can live under the pressure of accumulated misfortunes – the record is at hand in the life of Charlotte Brontë.[11]

Mrs. Gaskell, exhausted by the stress of hostile complaints, got to work to eliminate offending material and gratefully drew extensively, sometimes verbatim, on Taylor's account to fill some of the gaps. Taylor regretted the necessity for the revisions and thought Mrs. Gaskell would appear over-hasty and inconsistent in yielding to the threats of libel. She believed the first edition was all true but 'You know one dare not always say the world moves'.[12] She nevertheless thought the book, though amended, would be valuable.

Perhaps even Mary Taylor, feminist as she was, failed to appreciate the full significance of Gaskell's achievement. The world was accustomed to biographies of 'great' men. Here was one of the earliest biographies of a woman and a woman writer, though *The Life* was not a feminist gesture but a testimony to a friendship. Neither Brontë nor Gaskell was fully sympathetic to the early women's rights movement. Though each experienced the conflicts inherent in the demands of being a professional writer while fulfilling the duties expected of a 'womanly woman' of their times, they had considerable reservations about many of the views then being developed on women's and feminist issues. The very fact of the book's existence, however, apart from its intrinsic qualities, represents an important advance in women's claims for status in the world of letters and literature.

Without Brontë's fame, to which *The Life* contributed, few outside the confines of the industrial community where she was born, brought up and where she ended her days, would ever have heard of Mary Taylor's name. Her life and career, nevertheless, are more significant than a footnote in Brontë studies. Research into the history of the nineteenth-century women's movement is inserting new portraits alongside the already more familiar personalities such as Bodichon, Butler, Davies, Garrett-Anderson and Jex-Blake. As we study the growth of the movement they inspired we are bound to recognise that, impressive as they are as individuals, they did not achieve their successes single-handed and we have to ask: 'Who stood alongside them? 'Who else contributed to the nineteenth-century women's movement?' The pioneers and the leaders needed supporters, who achieved less prominence, perhaps, but were equally dedicated. There were women of all classes active not only in London, but in the provinces, especially in the major industrial centres, who played their part in a wide range of campaigns. They constituted a vital 'second echelon' which expanded and perpetuated the movement. Mary Taylor has claims to be regarded as a member of that second echelon. She contributed significantly to the debates on 'the woman question' in the 1860s and 1870s through her published articles. She also aspired though, regrettably without the same success, to enter the feminist debate through the medium of her novel *Miss Miles*. The story of her own life, her emigration, her success as a businesswoman achieving financial independence, her thirst for reading, knowledge and enjoyment of travel, is in itself a stimulating, even inspiring story. Hers is an articulate voice, lively, witty and well-informed, which brings us yet a little closer to the nineteenth-century women's movement, a voice loved and admired by her devoted friend Charlotte Brontë.

Red House, 1890s. Kirklees Cultural Services.

Chapter 1

'Our house of violent dissent and radicalism'[13]

The Taylor family, which could trace its recorded origins back to the sixteenth century, was closely identified first with the village of Gomersal, and later with Hunsworth, only a mile below in the valley of the river Spen where in the eighteenth century they established their mill. They were considered a leading family in the area, well known for their strong radical political views and dissenting religious beliefs, a tradition transmitted to succeeding generations until late into the nineteenth century.

Their home was built in the seventeenth century and was occupied continuously by successive generations of the Taylor family until 1887. It came to be known as Red House perhaps because it was built of red brick, unlike most of the houses in the locality which were stone. The elegant building has survived largely intact and is now a period house museum.

The Taylors were typical of many families in the district. In the seventeenth and early eighteenth centuries they combined small-scale farming with the manufacture and the merchanting of cloth. The textile industry was then a cottage industry, with spinning and weaving being done by home-based workers processing the raw materials provided by local merchants such as the Taylors, who took the white cloth for sale in the tightly regulated market at Leeds, some seven miles distant.

The family steadily improved and expanded their property around Red House and bought land which sloped down the hillside to the valley and the mill. Mary Taylor's grandfather, John (1736/7–1805), moving with the times which saw the development of water-powered machinery and the growth of the factory system, had shifted production from the family home to Hunsworth on the riverside. There, heavy cloth was manufactured and dyed red for army uniforms. The early generations of Taylors seem to have been active innovators, at the forefront in introducing steam-driven power and, later, in bringing gas-lighting to the mill; two of Mary's brothers were regarded as first-rate industrial chemists.

The same John Taylor who transferred his production to the mill on the river was an active Dissenter and said to be proud to be host to John Wesley, who often preached in the district.

Dissent was widespread and militant. There were active Moravian, Methodist and Wesleyan Methodist chapels and communities in the district, frequently split by doctrinal disputes, proliferating new sects and constructing yet more chapels with names such as Bethel, Mount Tabor, Providence and Zion. John Taylor finally adhered to the New Connexion Methodists, founded in 1796–7. Near his home he built a small chapel and even established a graveyard for the sect on land near Red House.

His eldest son, Joshua II (1766–1840), was Mary's father. He inherited

1

the Hunsworth mill and established his own bank to facilitate the complex commercial transactions involved in textile production. He was intelligent and forceful, a Dissenter in religion and a fierce Republican. He seems to have been well-educated and, indeed, highly cultivated. He travelled abroad on business. We know that he took advantage of the brief period of peace between the French and the English in 1802 and travelled as far as Italy. Like many tourists, before and since, he bought souvenirs, including pictures which hung in Red House, and he had his miniature portrait painted. He is said to have been a fluent French and Italian speaker.

As with so many families, much of the knowledge we have of them generally concerns the male members. We know practically nothing of Mary's grandmother Anne Waring (1739-1817) and very little of the facts of her mother's life. She was Anne Tickell (1781-1856) from Workington in Cumbria, daughter of a sea-captain.

Joshua and Anne were married in 1810 when he was already 44 years old. For a man of the period this was a late marriage, especially as he must have been already fully independent, his father having died five years before. Theirs was typical of nineteenth-century marriages in producing children, at short, indeed perilously short, intervals. Anne bore six children in about seven years. They were Joshua III (1812-80), John (1813-1901), Joseph (1816-57) Mary (1817-93), Martha (1819-42) and William Waring (1819-1903). The family's dynastic sense is expressed in the frequency of the names Joshua, John, Joseph and William, given to successive generations of sons.

In February 1826, when Mary was 9 years old, the family sustained a heavy blow. Like a number of manufacturers who also owned private banks, Taylor tied up too many assets in his mill, and when a crisis came, the bank failed. 'The bankruptcy hearing emphasised "over-engagements in woollen manufactures" as the reason for the bank's demise.'[14] A contributory factor was the failure of a firm with whom Taylor did business and which was owned by a relative, Abraham Dixon, who had married Joshua's sister.

1825 had seen the first major economic slump in the history of industrial capitalism, bringing bank failures and bankruptcy to manufacturers and trades people of all kinds. A letter in the local *Leeds Mercury* of February 25th 1826, which announced Taylor's failure, opens: 'Commercial distress is now the burden of our song'. A news item in the same issue describes the praiseworthy, but vain, efforts of a group of charitable ladies in Bradford (a few miles from Gomersal) to alleviate the deprivation and suffering of local people. Their resources had proved quite inadequate to meet the widespread, acute need for blankets and clothing.

It was not until December 1826 that Taylor's arrangements with his creditors were finally settled. He paid them initially 5/- in the pound.[15] The bank was closed but Taylor remained in business at the Hunsworth mill. Creditors, most of them local people, with whom the standing of the family and the firm was high, would prefer to see the debts being paid off rather than foreclose on a viable business. The debts were repaid in full by 1843, soon after Taylor's death.

If the Taylors enjoyed a reputation for dissent and fierce radicalism, they were by no means unique in the Heavy Woollen District. Industrialisation was marked by economic instability and profound social upheaval, with the displacement by the machine of long-standing traditional skills, the exodus of workers, including children, from households into factories, and the influx of new workers from other districts with differing backgrounds and cultures. The wars with France (1793-1815) had a devastating effect on trade. Even though a number of local manufacturers, including the Taylors, were producing army cloth, other profitable markets were lost in Europe and in America, as a result of the Government's Orders in Council which placed heavy restrictions on the export trade.

Frank Peel, whose *Spen Valley: Past and Present*[16] is a classic work of the history of the area, writes:

> The state of this district at the close of the last [i.e. the eighteenth] century was simply deplorable. The home trade was crippled on all sides, and the little foreign trade that still existed was carried on amidst dangers and anxieties which must have entailed upon all who were engaged in it many sleepless nights, and, in spite of the most skilful management, tremendous losses.[17]

These pressures intensified the manufacturers' need to cheapen production, and new machinery was being introduced in industrial areas of the East Midlands, Lancashire and Yorkshire, including the Heavy Woollen District. Here it was the skilled workers, the 'croppers' responsible for the finishing of the cloth, who were being replaced by machines. Around 1812, according to Peel, one half of the population in Spen Valley seem to have been paupers.[18] There was, naturally, resistance to de-skilling and impoverishment. It took the form of secret combinations (combinations of workmen for the improving of wages were illegal) and oath-taking. On the night of April 11th 1812, Rawfolds Mill, owned by a manufacturer called Cartwright, about one mile from where the Taylors lived, and about two miles from their own Hunsworth Mill, was attacked by men determined to break the new machines. The local mill-owners were already prepared for trouble, and troops were stationed at Rawfolds. The attackers were finally repulsed with two of their men killed. Four days later there was an attempt on Cartwright's life. Though that attack failed, a manufacturer, Horsfall of Marsden, near Huddersfield, was ambushed and murdered.

Initially not one of the Rawfolds' attackers was identified – the valley kept its secrets – but some were eventually arrested and tried through an informer connected with the Horsfall case. The attack on Rawfolds Mill, which was fresh in people's memories as Mary was growing up, is one of the central incidents in Charlotte Brontë's *Shirley*.

The Luddite attacks were followed by the Plug Riots in the 1820s when strikers pulled the plugs out of the mill boilers and engaged in pitched battles with those millhands who refused to join them. Unrest and drilling and secret combinations continued with the Chartist movement, mobilising the discontent. The 'physical force' tendency, calling for armed struggle to achieve the aims of the Charter, was strong among Spen Valley Chartists. A mass demonstration of 250,000, addressed by Bronterre O'Brien and Fergus O'Connor took place in Spen Valley at Peep Green, Hartshead, in 1836, by which time Mary Taylor, aged 19, was aware of the activities and demands of the Chartists, and remembered them when she, in her turn, came to write her novel. Well-known figures of the radical movement including William Cobbett, Major Cartwright, Orator Hunt and Samuel Bamford visited the district. When there were strikes against wage reductions in 1842, local workers were again to the forefront.[19] With the collapse of Chartism, and as trade expanded, relative stability was established.

The Spen Valley communities experienced other changes characteristic of the industrial areas, such as the development of local government, the founding of various kinds of schools for children of working people, and the growth of the Mechanics' Institutes (the Gomersal Mechanics' Institute was built in 1850, little more than a stride from Red House). Communications improved rapidly. The arrival of railways brought not only accelerated industrial development but, for better-off people such as the Taylors, enhanced possibilities for travel and social contact outside their immediate neighbourhood.

Though there was conflict between textile workers and their employers, there were also strong patriarchal links. Their communities were small; people knew each other personally. The employers generally worked actively in their businesses, as the Taylors did, visible to their work-force every working day. The labour-force in the mills of the time consisted by modern standards of small numbers of people. Mary's brother had 120 employees in 1861 at Hunsworth. Employers generally lived near their mills, and consequently near their workers. Some members of the Taylor family lived in a house actually in the mill yard at Hunsworth. Workers and employers often attended the same chapels, which were vitally important religious and cultural centres of the communities, often transcending more obvious class divisions, though there were some which combined political radicalism with their religious beliefs and were predominantly working class. Though the textile industry had links with many foreign countries through trade, and while communications were expanding, working people were generally still quite isolated, with a strong local culture reinforced not only by their working relationships in the predominant industry, and by religious dissent, but by their distinctive Yorkshire speech.

The Taylors' radicalism was no barrier to their vigorous application to money-making, but they retained strong religious and cultural links with the local working people. Fluent he may have been in foreign languages, but Mary's father almost certainly spoke in a Yorkshire dialect: without it, he would have been incomprehensible to his employees, and, no doubt, like them he was proud of it![20]

For her part, Mary felt a sense of closeness throughout her life with working people and she especially admired working women. Writing to Mrs. Gaskell[21] in connection with *The Life of Charlotte Brontë*, Mary referred to the comments in the book on the Luddites and expressed her sympathy with the working people of the district of nearly forty years before. While Gaskell describes and sympathises with the sufferings of the men who became Luddites, she nevertheless treats the Reverend Hammond Roberson (1757-1841) as a hero. Roberson was notorious, or famous, in the area, depending on the point of view. He was a Church of England clergyman and aggressively hostile to Dissenters, characterising the West Riding as 'the seat of Dissent'.[22] He was also a magistrate and thought working people needed discipline; he played an active part in investigating the Rawfolds riot and was regarded by some as a ruthless persecutor of the Luddites. Mary wrote:

> I had the impression that Cartwright's mill was burnt in 1820, not in 1812. You give much too favourable an account of the black-coated and Tory savages that kept the people down and provoked excesses in those days. Old Roberson said he would 'wade to the knees in blood rather than that the state of things should be altered,' including Corn law, Test law, and a host of other oppressions.[23]

Mary confused the dates of the Rawfolds attack with later unrest in the district in the 1820s. In her references to the Corn Laws and Test Acts she is reflecting the tensions between the local gentry and the industrialists. The new industrial towns of the early decades of the century, with their growing populations, were under-represented in Parliament, compared with many smaller rural areas where landowners dominated politics. Numbers of manufacturers were disfranchised. Their influence on Government was not commensurate with their expanding economic power and they believed Government represented the interests of landowners and agriculture. The Corn Laws, finally repealed in 1846, kept up the price of bread and affected wage levels. Significant numbers among industrialists were, like the Taylors, Dissenters, and until 1828 when the Test Acts were repealed, they were excluded from positions in either national or local government. They remained, along with all women, excluded from the universities.

These tensions were exacerbated by hostility between the Church of England and the Dissenting sects whose members were required to pay tithes to the Church they had rejected. The Church of England tended to be identified with the gentry, but not with either industrial workers or with the earlier generations of industrial capitalists.

The numerous chapels in the Spen Valley area provided strong community and cultural links. Though representing a range of doctrines, they had much in common. They generally held Sunday schools which offered classes in reading, writing and arithmetic to both children and adults. Chapel brass bands and choirs flourished. Musical rivalry would reach fever pitch at Christmas with performances of oratorios, especially *Messiah*. The chapels organised bazaars, concerts, lectures, Whitsuntide walks, picnics, and (after the coming of cheap rail travel), seaside outings.

When Mary Taylor came to write her novel *Miss Miles*, she depicted a textile town, of the 1830s, Repton, which with its class, religious and cultural characteristics, is strongly reminiscent of the Spen Valley where she had grown up.

This society and her own family, intelligent and cultivated, radical and politicised, constituted the world of her formative years. It shaped her thirst for education and her love of books and music. The tradition of dissent, which she inherited, influenced her determination to live in the light of her principles of committed feminism.

Standing on the heights dividing the Calder from the Spen Valley stands Roe Head, a spacious and airy house commanding magnificent views towards the Pennines. It was here in January 1831 at the girls' school kept by Margaret Wooler (1793-1885) and her three sisters that Charlotte Brontë, aged 14, met Mary Taylor, almost the same age as herself, and her friend Ellen Nussey (1817-97). Charlotte was attending school for the first time since her traumatic experiences at Cowan Bridge. Brought up and educated somewhat idiosyncratically at home in an enclosed tightly-knit family and self-sufficient atmosphere, prospects at Roe Head must have seemed bleak to her. Fortunately she joined a small school whose pupils never numbered more than ten while she was there, and who were in the care of sympathetic teachers. Above all she met Ellen Nussey and Mary Taylor. Ellen, warm-hearted and sentimental, mothered the awkward stranger while Mary, intellectually her equal, vigorous and extrovert, offered stimulus and generous friendship. The two girls had the advantage of Charlotte: the school was not far from their homes, and they were already friends living not much more than a mile apart; in addition Mary had her sister Martha with her

The girls studied English and French grammar, history, geography, Milton and Shakespeare and drawing, but Mary and Charlotte probably owed their education more to their intensive private reading of the books available to them in their homes than to Miss Wooler's old-fashioned curriculum. Among their textbooks they had *Mangnall's Questions*, which was based on an earlier school book of 1773![24]

The school regime provided for plenty of outdoor activity, games and walks and fresh air. Characteristically Mary informed Mrs. Gaskell that Charlotte was hopeless at ball games and that she had expressed surprise to Charlotte that she simply stood on the rocks contemplating the stream at Cowan Bridge when she might have been fishing!

On the surface the girls' friendship would have seemed unlikely. The Taylors were manufacturers, Dissenters and radical while some of the Nusseys had members who were professional men, clergy and apothecaries, though others were small mill-owners. They were Anglicans. The two families were, nevertheless, friends. The Brontës were the social equals of neither the Nusseys nor the Taylors. Though Anglican and Tory they lived nearer the fringes of poverty than the other two families, and they lacked the supportive networks of relatives and other connections available to the Taylors and Nusseys.

Ellen's reminiscences of schooldays written for Mrs. Gaskell include descriptions of the two Taylor girls. She recalls Mary (who was sometimes called 'Pag' or 'Polly') as very pretty, quiet, hard-working, determined, even stubborn, while Martha ('Patty'), her father's favourite child was boisterous, popular and insubordinate. She tells how Mary's strong sense of justice was outraged when Miss Wooler gave Charlotte a low mark for an unreasonably difficult task and in protest withdrew for the rest of the term from lessons and the general life of the school. Even when the teacher retracted she maintained her embargo.[25] The Taylors were a stubborn, stiff-necked lot! This was an incident epitomising concern for justice and courage to challenge authority which lingered in Charlotte's memory and fired her imagination throughout her life.

Ellen, who was very fashion conscious, remembers that Charlotte was badly dressed and that the Taylor girls suffering the effects of the bankruptcy dressed little better, though to Ellen they appeared quite unperturbed by it. According to her:

> They were not dressed as well as other pupils, for economy at that time was the rule of their household. The girls had to stitch all over their new gloves before wearing them, by order of their mother, to make them wear longer. Their dark blue cloth coats were worn when *too short*, and black beaver bonnets quite plainly trimmed, with the ease and contentment of a fashionable costume.[26]

Important as it was to them, the friendship between Charlotte and Mary was not always sweetness and light. There were deeply felt political differences which erupted in furious debate and no doubt loss of temper. In 1832, during the agitation for Parliamentary reform when political tensions were running high especially in the industrial areas, Charlotte defended her hero Wellington while Mary, who despised all politicians of the time, was enthusiastic for reform. There must also have been occasional rivalries for being the top of the class.

Mary's youthful candour could be brutal. In her letter to Mrs. Gaskell she referred to the Brontë children's isolation. 'I told her sometimes they were like growing potatoes in a cellar. She said sadly, "Yes! I know we are!"'[27]

She also informed Charlotte that she was ugly, a remark Charlotte never forgot, though she seems to have forgiven her. Typically Charlotte, with her masochistic tendencies and painful self-suppression, accepted Mary's apology with the comment, 'You did me a great deal of good, Polly, so don't repent of it.'[28]

She may have forgiven but she didn't forget. Eleven years later Mary's cousin, Mary Dixon, proposed making a portrait of Charlotte. It was intended for Mary Taylor who had just left Brussels for Germany but Charlotte wrote:

> I surrender my unfortunate head to you with resignation – the features thereof may yield good practice as they never yet submitted to any line of regularity – but have manifested such a spirit of independence, unedifying to behold – You are mistaken however in your benevolent idea that my portrait will yield pleasure to Mary Taylor – do not give it to her, or if you do – do not expect thanks in return – she likes me well enough – but my face she can dispense with – and would tell you so in her own sincere and truthful language if you asked her.[29]

Charlotte was poetic and dreamy, Ellen sentimental. Mary was passionately, even simplistically, practical, over-confident in her own judgment and tactless. Her abrasiveness may have caused the coolness in the school friendship which Charlotte could not, or perhaps was not willing to explain to Ellen, but which was eventually completely overcome.

Mary's practical common sense led her early to recognise that if they did not marry, all three had to face the problems of earning a living or enduring poverty. From her own reading she was already aware of opportunities opening up for women as writers and sensing Charlotte's potential she showed an interest in the magazines produced by the Brontë children, though Charlotte backed down from her promise to show them to her. Mary urged Charlotte to follow through her dreams and imaginings, to 'make out' and record them. 'She told me early one morning, that she had just been dreaming; . . . I said, but go on! *Make it out!* I know you can . . . '.[30]

For Charlotte 'making out' was an escape from her frustrations and misery. She retreated into a trance-like state, 'seeing' romantic landscapes, imagining characters and situations.[31]

Throughout their friendship it was always Mary urging the other two on. As they grew older she continued to play the gadfly to get them to strike out on a life of independence. She tried to persuade Ellen to break free of convention and of the demands of family and acquaintances for her services as nurse or companion. Though they had discussed earlier the possibilities of both of them going to France to improve their languages, it was Mary's practical help which got Charlotte and Emily to Brussels. It must be said that it was her only success in her campaign to get her friends to strike out for independence, persistent as she was. The correspondence between the three often gives the impression of Charlotte and Ellen huddling together to fend off the cold winds of Mary's energetic challenges. She rarely let up even from New Zealand. To cope with the pressure Charlotte resorted occasionally to irony: 'I had a long letter from Mary Taylor . . . She mentioned you, and seemed impressed with an idea of the lamentable nature of your unoccupied life.'[32]

In spite of political and religious disagreements and Mary's frustrations at Charlotte's passivity, there grew up an enduring friendship. Religious differences narrowed as Mary along with Martha moved away in the mid-1830s from her family's traditional non-conformity and began to attend Church of England services.[33] Mary soon came to regard religious belief as an intensely personal matter; she shared and admired Charlotte's tolerance.

Mary and Charlotte's friendship was based on the mutual recognition of their intellectual equality and an appreciation of the stimulus it provided. It was based on a deep respect and an affection strong enough to survive the vast physical distance between them after 1845 and for Mary to feel its influence even after Charlotte's death ten years later.

> She made poetry and drawing, at least exceedingly interesting to me; and then I got the habit, which I have yet, of referring mentally to her opinion on all matters of that kind, along with many more, resolving to describe such and such things to her, until I start at the recollection that I never shall.[34]

Mary left Roe Head in 1832 and from then until the age of 24 remained at home. In a household consisting of seven adults (her parents, three of her brothers, Martha and herself) and given the economies imposed by the repaying of debts, she was no doubt expected to take her share of domestic tasks and of nursing when her father became seriously ill.

Charlotte left Roe Head at the same time as Mary with both girls pledged to keep up their friendship. Travel between Haworth and Gomersal was slow, depending still on horse-drawn transport, but there was some visiting between Haworth and Gomersal and Birstall and there was always correspondence which was their main means of keeping in regular contact. The three friends were to develop a system of public letters which could be passed on to other people and private letters for more intimate matters. They maintained the system into adult life. Charlotte and Mary often wrote their public letters quite consciously as exercises in literary form, trying out descriptions, dialogue, debate and a heightened vocabulary. Mary's letters from the early years of their correspondence do not survive but they were no doubt characteristic of her later correspondence which always shows a keen critical spirit, an active sense of humour, a relaxed, idiomatic style, and lively imaginary conversations. The two engaged in political debates and took pleasure also in discussing and criticising what they had been reading. Mary had the advantage of Charlotte in this respect. Despite the need for economies there were always plenty of books in the Taylor household, in foreign languages as well as English. Ellen felt left out of this intellectual correspondence and to reassure her Charlotte at least once departing from custom discussed politics with her, and then explained why.

> . . . don't you remember telling me to write such letters to you as I write to Mary Taylor? Here's a specimen; hereafter should follow a long disquisition on books, but I'll spare you that.[35]

The correspondence lapsed occasionally. Charlotte would prod Ellen into reminding Mary to write. Mary in her turn made her complaints of neglect, but directly.

> I received a letter from Poll Taylor yesterday, she was in high dudgeon at my inattention in not promptly answering her last epistle.[36]

Certainly later in her life letters were to provide Charlotte with some consolation in her tragic bereavements and in alleviating the dreadful pressures of her acute loneliness.

Meetings of the friends which now generally included Martha became more frequent when Charlotte moved back to Roe Head as a teacher in 1835. The Taylors would send their carriage to the school to take Charlotte back to Gomersal.[37] Typically, Mary criticised Miss Wooler for offering Charlotte a low salary and blamed Charlotte for being prepared to accept it.

In 1838 when the school moved to Dewsbury Moor visits were even easier. There were calls from the Taylors (Martha often riding there on her pony) and Ellen to see Charlotte at the school while Charlotte (though she agonised about it as a self-indulgent pleasure) could from time to time be persuaded to visit their homes. While telling Ellen that she would probably decline an invitation to visit at Red House, she declares: 'the society of the Taylors is one of the most rousing pleasures I have ever known.'[38]

Visits for Charlotte and Ellen became more practical with the development in the following decade of rail travel linking Bradford with Keighley, the nearest station to Haworth.

Ellen visited Haworth from time to time and was very popular in the Brontë family. Mary, along with Martha, paid her first visit in June 1838 and if Charlotte is to be believed it was brilliantly successful, bringing laughter, music at the piano and characteristic Taylor liveliness, though

Martha would be the noisy one.[39] It brought a strengthening of the friendship which now extended to Charlotte's sisters and brother.

Charlotte reports at this time that Mary was unwell and she feared that her lungs were affected. To help her convalesce the Taylors, whose money problems must have been diminishing, made a tour of Wales, starting in the following August, spending some time at Aberystwyth and returning to Gomersal at the end of September.[40] Charlotte's understandable fears were groundless: Mary was apparently suffering from a 'disordered stomach'. Now 22 years of age with nothing achieved and with no prospects, she was more probably suffering from frustration and boredom, fretting at the loss of opportunity for education, travel and some way of earning her own living, dreaming of independence and an interesting future. To add to her frustrations she was in conflict with her mother who was gloomily pious and repressive in her relations with her high-spirited children. She had little sympathy with Mary's temperament or aspirations. Mary remembered an occasion when they were children when Mrs. Taylor unexpectedly returning to the house found her and Martha dancing in the hall, and sternly rebuked them in Old Testament language. She was impatient and unsympathetic when they complained of being ill. At a later date when someone commiserated with her having been out of England when Mrs. Taylor died, Mary had replied, 'My Mother has never been a mother to me.'[41]

In June 1840 Mary was at the Parsonage again and we get a glimpse in Charlotte's letter to Ellen of an apparently somewhat quieter but enjoyable visit, Mary playing chess against the curate Weightman as Charlotte wrote. The following November, though, there is a letter from Charlotte which is either a coded rebuke to Ellen or a breach of Mary's confidence, or a misunderstanding of Mary's behaviour towards Branwell. Charlotte warns Ellen against ever showing symptoms of love towards a man before marriage and cites an example . . . apparently Mary. She suggests that Mary had been indiscreet, behaving in a manner 'wrought to a pitch of great intensity' and showed some partiality for 'a relative of mine' who, though up to then he had liked her, 'instantly conceived a sort of contempt for her.'[42]

Confined to narrow social circles young women would inevitably speculate that their own marriage prospects might be linked with the male relatives of their close friends and hope that the same friends might become their sisters-in-law. Ellen's brother Henry proposed to Charlotte, and Ellen seemed to have hopes sometimes of John, sometimes of Joe Taylor.

If, indeed, Mary was falling in love with Branwell and revealing her feelings, any criticism called for might have been more appropriately levelled at Branwell. Mary, who enjoyed a genuine friendship with her brothers, especially John and Joe, probably treated Branwell with the same openness and camaraderie which was quite liable to misinterpretation, with Branwell thinking she was 'setting her cap' at him. If she had found herself falling in love with Branwell Mary would certainly never have played the demure young miss. Masculine vanity and unfamiliarity with young women might explain Branwell's reaction. For her part, Charlotte manages to face two ways, criticising Mary while paying tribute to her and simultaneously deriving satisfaction from an attitude of moral superiority and wisdom. Her letter rather sententiously continues:

> ... [but] I have two studies; *you* are my study for the success the credit, and the respectability of a quiet, tranquil character. Mary is my study – for the contempt, the remorse – the misconstruction which follow the development of feelings in themselves noble, warm – generous – devoted and profound – but which being too freely revealed – too frankly bestowed – are not estimated at their real value. God bless her – I never hope to see in this world a character more truly noble – she would die willingly for one she loved – her intellect and her attainments are of the very highest standard . . .[43]

Not without reason Charlotte swore Ellen to secrecy 'never as you value your ears mention the circumstance'; what remains of the letter has been heavily cut. Mary would have regarded the values Charlotte advocates here as hypocritical and if that letter had been leaked by the not very reliable Ellen, that would have been the end of the friendship and Charlotte must have realised this. She herself was torn between conflicting values, and aspirations, self-fulfilment, emotional honesty and ambitions for liberty as represented by Mary, self-suppression, and passivity, pietism and submission to whatever Providence chose to inflict, as represented by Ellen. If Mary did indeed develop an unrequited passion for Branwell she must have looked back with a strong sense of relief at her escape. We know that she was critical of the distinctions Miss Branwell made in her treatment of her nieces and Branwell. She saw that the young man was indulged while the young women were kept at their domestic tasks and at their needles sewing for the charity basket.[44]

Though the Taylors had their financial problems, they were generous, and they had room in their lives for friends. The Taylors were enthusiastic readers and for Mary, certainly, books were among the most vital needs of her being. Her brothers, Joshua and Joe, were lifelong shareholders in the Leeds Library which had been founded in 1768. It was Mary's father who began the Taylor custom of providing Charlotte with French language books and newspapers, gifts which provided her with rare sources of intellectual stimulus and pleasure.

> I have got another bale of French books from Gomersal containing upwards of forty volumes – I have read about half – they are like the rest, clever wicked sophisticated and immoral – the best of it is, they give one a thorough idea of France and

Paris – they are the best substitute for French conversation that I have met with.[45]

In her earliest novel, *The Professor*, written in 1846 but published posthumously, Brontë had drawn on her memories of Mr. Taylor for the character of Hunsden (an echo of Hunsworth!). A passage there may provide us with a clue to what some of the books were, and give us an idea of what was freely available in the Taylor household.

> While he [Hunsden] removed from the centre-table to the sideboard a few pamphlets and periodicals, I ran my eye along the shelves of the book-case nearest me. French and German titles predominated, the old French dramatists, sundry modern authors, Thiers, Villemain, Paul de Kock, George Sand, Eugène Sue; in German – Goethe, Schiller, Zschokke, Jean Paul Richter; in English there were works on Political Economy.[46]

Joe Taylor continued to supply Charlotte all her life with French language newspapers and journals, helping her to overcome the feelings of isolation and monotony which marked her life so frequently at Haworth.

1840 was a watershed in the lives of the Taylors. Joshua, now 74 years old, fell seriously ill, lingering on through the year and dying in December. Mary herself became ill again, probably caused by anxiety on account of her father, to whom she was devoted. The frustrations of being tied to the home and the round of domestic tasks which she detested probably exacerbated her condition. Her father's death not only deprived her of a loving parent but of a dear and respected friend. Added to the grief of bereavement it looked as if she might be faced with the depressing choice between going out as a governess or remaining at home in relative poverty with an unsympathetic mother, tied by domesticity and by dependence on her brothers. Neither possibility held any attractions for her.

> My Dear Ellen,
> I received the news in your last with no surprise, and with the feeling that this removal must be a relief to Mr. Taylor himself and even to his family. The bitterness of death was past a year ago, when it was first discovered that his illness must terminate fatally; all between has been lingering suspense. This is at an end now, and the present certainty, however sad, is better than the former doubt. What will be the consequence of his death is another question; for my own part, I look forward to a dissolution and dispersion of the family, perhaps not immediately, but in the course of a year or two. It is true, causes may arise to keep them together a while longer, but they are restless and active spirits, and will not be restrained always. Mary alone has more energy and power in her nature than any ten men you can pick

out in the united parishes of Birstall and Gomersal. It is vain to limit a character like hers within ordinary boundaries . . . she will overstep them. I am morally certain Mary will establish her own landmarks, so will the rest of them.[47]

The splitting up of the family which Charlotte Brontë had foreseen as inevitable after Mr. Taylor's death came quickly. A few months later there was a re-arrangement of households. Joshua, the eldest son, and his family moved to live at Red House with Mrs. Taylor where they stayed for the next five years. The rest of the family moved down to Hunsworth where there was a small hamlet of dwellings attached to the mill. At last they were free from their mother's oppressive surveillance. Here the three youngest, Mary, Martha and Waring, contemplated their futures.

Joshua III, whose temperament was not an easy one, was now the head of the business which had to provide work for the four sons and maintenance for Mrs. Taylor, Mary and Martha and for his own growing family.[48] Radical the Taylors may have been in some things but there never seems to have been any suggestion that either Mary or Martha might work in the business.

The family's financial and property affairs were complicated. Taylor was still bankrupt when he died; debts remained to be paid. To his widow he left £1,000 to pay his personal debts, and property which was mortgaged to the sum of £4,000. Joshua and John, the two eldest, formally gave up any legal claims on the will. There is no mention of legacies to any of the others. It is to be assumed, therefore, that there was some agreement that once the bankruptcy was cleared and the business at Hunsworth freed from the burden of repaying debt there would be some adjustments which would provide each member of the family with some share of the considerable property in land and buildings and the proceeds of the mill.

John and Joe worked at the Hunsworth mill with Joshua but either there was no room for the youngest, Waring, or he decided along with Mary to make a dramatic breakaway, free from the business and the family.

> Matters are progressing very strangely at Gomersal. Mary Taylor and Waring have come to a singular determination, but I think under the circumstances a defensible one, though it sounds outrageously odd at first. They are going to emigrate – to quit the country altogether. Their destination unless they change is Port Nicholson, in the northern island of New Zealand!!! Mary has made up her mind she can not and will not be a governess, a teacher, a milliner, a bonnet-maker nor housemaid. She sees no means of obtaining employment she would like in England, so she is leaving it.[49]

Brontë's style as she discusses Mary's decisions seems to embody Taylor's own energy, determination and brusque speech.

If, as the New Zealand family believed, the Gomersal family was opposed to Waring's leaving, they would certainly be against Mary going with him.[50] The sea voyage took around five months and conditions on board were frequently primitive and unpleasant. Living conditions for the new settlers in New Zealand were difficult, the territory was virtually unknown, there was a shortage of adequate housing and of the day-to-day necessities of life. For her part, though, Charlotte refused to join in the attempt to dissuade Mary from going with Waring. Even after he had been settled in New Zealand for nearly five years she seemed to think it was necessary for Mary to join him in order to care for him, that he was a 'weak vessel' and needed Mary's strength.[51] The 'weak vessel' established what for a long time appeared to be a successful business, married and fathered twelve children and died aged over 80. His weaknesses were not made evident until 1884 when he was found guilty of embezzlement. He sailed in November, 1841 as an 'intermediate' passenger (i.e. paying part of his fare), along with a number of West Riding people, receiving a form of help which was probably not available to Mary as a woman intending to be neither a servant nor a governess![52]

Radicals were heavily involved in emigration schemes, seeing them as a solution to unemployment in Britain. A John Dixon of Birmingham, probably connected through marriage with the Taylors, was involved in a commercial company which traded with New Zealand so Waring may have started out with some advantages when he established his import-export business.

Though he persisted in emigrating despite family opposition there was no question of his being 'cut off'. He maintained his links with Gomersal, some of his children visited there and one of his daughters subsequently married a Gomersal cousin, a son of Joshua III.

Before Waring set sail Martha had already left Hunsworth. In May 1841 she travelled to Brussels to begin her studies at a finishing school for young ladies, the Château de Koekelberg owned by Mme Goussaert, an Englishwoman married to a Belgian and which received significant numbers of young Englishwomen.

So, with Martha gone and Waring preparing to leave, was Mary to be left behind entirely? Since the age of 19 she had cherished the ambition to earn her own living which would guarantee her independence.[53] She must have asked herself: 'What am I to do?', the anguished question which formed the title thirty years later of the opening chapter of her book *The First Duty of Women*. How, indeed, was she to begin in 1841 to inaugurate the process of her own liberation?

The facts of her eventual career and her articles of the 1860s and 70s bear witness to her determination to refuse the narrow constraints imposed on women like herself and to make a break for freedom. In *The First Duty of Women* she reproduced what had been her first published article, a review of the journal of *Eugénie de Guérin*. Quoting first from the journal, she then deplores the passivity and dependence on a brother.

> 'How I long, how I long to hear of your having a social position! for my future attaches itself to yours; they are brothers'. Women in her position always are a burden to their relations. It is the practical result of denying themselves, and neglecting the care of their own interests.[54]

She also attacked women's acquiescence in poverty as reprehensible and urged that their first duty was to be prepared to go out to earn their own livings instead of spending their time and energy working hard in the home to save paltry amounts of money. This she sees as true especially in families which resembled her own in some respects and which she terms 'the uneasy class', those with an apparently established social position but without the means actually to live up to it. Families, who as she says, entertain 'an ostrich-like belief that no-one knows they are poor, because they are able in some few things to look like richer people'.[55]

> The women's work is, to do without what they cannot pay for; a duty which takes up not more of their time but less. Often to this misery is added the imaginary duty of appearing to have, or not to wish for, the things the privation of which afflicts them so much . . . These 'appearances' it is peculiarly the wife's duty to keep up . . . The constantly narrowing limit to that wealth is a perpetual pain. If few complain of it, there are numbers who know it well; and most truly are they called the uneasy classes that have this skeleton in the house. At every meal, at every family meeting, the thought must come – 'If we were but richer!'[56]

From the earliest days of their friendship Charlotte Brontë was to find intellectual and imaginative stimulus in the personality of Mary Taylor. The incident at the close of their schooldays at Roe Head, when Miss Wooler made unreasonable demands on Charlotte and found herself challenged by Mary, who withdrew from the life of the school, haunted her memory and imagination. It was a situation she re-worked into a number of different fictional incidents.

In 1839 Brontë gave up her job at Miss Wooler's school and returned to Haworth, where she took up and developed the 'Angrian' fictions she and Branwell had created together from childhood. During the period 1839-40, she was writing a novel entitled *Ashworth* which, though she was at work revising it during 1841, she never completed.

The character who seems to be intended as one of the heroines of the novel is called Mary Ashworth with aspects of personality which seem to be shaping up in a way that reminds us of Mary Taylor. Like Taylor, this proto-heroine is a serious student, keen reader of literature, a talented musician and a credit to her school. She is quietly self-sufficient. She unostentatiously protects the weak, intervening on their behalf against teachers and protesting against 'tyranny'.

The first incident of the novel in which she features takes place on Mary's last night at the school. She is now sixteen and taking her final leave. Though privileged and rich herself, she shows interest in the plain, oppressed half-boarder, Ellen Hall, who is treated as a domestic slave and is toiling at the packing of young ladies' trunks. Mary enquires into Ellen's future. Ellen explains that she is intended as a nursery governess and Mary exclaims 'Nursery-governess! You might do better than that!'[57] To Ellen's surprise she receives a parting gift from Mary, a token of friendship . . . the works of Scott and Byron.

The offer of friendship and sympathy for the ill-treated is characteristic of Mary Taylor, but the incident of the gift of the poetry books is, paradoxically, something of a reversal of the actual situation for we know that it was Charlotte who introduced Mary to poetry and encouraged her appreciation of it.

We also meet in this fragment of a novel the familiar situation of incompatible brothers, as well as a middle-aged man who speaks in a strong Yorkshire accent and dialect, forerunners of characters in *The Professor* and *Shirley*.

Over *Emma*, the unfinished piece which Brontë was working on just before her last illness and death, the Roe Head incident and the personality of Mary Taylor once more hover in the character of Diana and her public rebuke to her schoolmistress.

> There was a girl called Diana – the girl alluded to before as having once been Miss Sterling's pupil – a daring, brave girl, much loved and a little feared by her comrades. She had good faculties, both physical and mental – was clever, honest, and dauntless. In the schoolroom she set her young brow like a rock against Miss Fitzgibbon's pretensions; she also found heart and spirit to withstand them in the drawing room.[58]

Diana's performance at the piano (Mary Taylor played the piano well), is interrupted by the schoolmistress's fawning praise of the supposed heiress, Miss Fitzgibbon, whereupon Diana rises from the music stool:

> 'Ma'am,' said she to Miss Wilcox, 'that girl does not deserve so much praise. Her behaviour is not at all exemplary. In the schoolroom she is insolently distant. For my part I denounce her airs; there is not one of us but is as good or better than she, though we may not be as rich.'
>
> And Diana shut up the piano, took her music book under her arm, curtsied, and vanished.[59]

Not only Mary, but the whole Taylor family, with the exception of Waring, deeply interested Charlotte and she drew on aspects of their personalities and relationships in her creation of the Yorke family in *Shirley*.

After the success of *Jane Eyre* (1847) Brontë's publishers with their eye on the current success of the 'condition of England' novel suggested she, too, should write a novel with an industrial setting. *Shirley* was the result, published in 1849 in the year after Mrs. Gaskell's *Mary Barton*. The genre was inappropriate for Brontë and it is the weakest of her three major works. She researched conscientiously in the files of the *Leeds Mercury*, and, in writing the novel, leaned heavily on actual events for some of the situations and for characters on people she knew. She fixed on the Luddite riots of thirty-seven years before, placing her story in a landscape and society closely resembling Spen Valley.

There are dangerous pitfalls in regarding fictions as some form of documentary representations of actual personalities and situations and only an author, possibly, is in a position to say how far actual and imaginary life are intertwined to produce the final work. The fiction has its own, autonomous needs of plot, motivation and circumstances which draw on more than historical fact and which are the product of the author's creative imagination. However, the nineteenth century novel with its sense of moral responsibility, and its claims to 'realism', was particularly prone to interpretations which assumed that fictional characters were really rather simplistic reflections of actual people and the incidents mere records of 'real' life. Readers liked to flatter themselves that they were in the know about the 'originals' of characters.

Mrs. Gaskell, discussing the novel, insists that Brontë took 'the idea of most of her characters from life' but that as the incidents and situations were fictitious thought 'she might draw from the real without detection.'[60]

Brontë had, for example, told Gaskell that Emily inspired the character of Shirley herself, but exactly what 'inspires' means, how far imagination worked on her concept of Emily's personality to create something largely quite distinct, is impossible to say.

A letter to W. S. Williams suggests that Brontë was herself ambivalent, possibly genuinely uncertain, about how far she had been inspired by friends and acquaintances in creating the fictional characters.[61] To Ellen Nussey, however, she says firmly:

> You are not to suppose any of the characters in *Shirley* intended as literal portraits. It would not suit the rules of art, nor of my own feelings, to write in that style. We only suffer reality to *suggest* never to *dictate*. The heroines are abstractions, and the heroes also. Qualities I have seen, loved and admired, are here and there put in as decorative gems. Since you say you could recognise the originals of all except the heroines, pray whom did you suppose the two Moores to represent?[62]

Again Mrs. Gaskell tells us that:

> The whole family of the Yorkes were, I have been assured almost daguerreotypes. Indeed Miss Brontë told me that before publication, she had sent those parts of the novel in which these remarkable persons are introduced, to one of the sons; and his reply, after reading it, was simply that 'she had not drawn them strong enough.'[63]

It was almost certainly Joe Taylor who assured Gaskell that the Yorkes were daguerreotypes of the Taylors. In judging how far they 'were' the Yorkes we must evaluate what we read in *Shirley* against information from other sources.

Topography and historical events apart, there are other 'real' elements in the novel suggested by the Taylors. There is Red House itself, the Taylor home, still standing, light and spacious, though with some structural changes added since the mid nineteenth century, but much as Mary recognised it in the description of Briarmains.

> On Wednesday I began *Shirley* and continued in a curious confusion of mind till now, principally at the handsome foreigner who was nursed in our house when I was a little girl. By the way you've put him in the servant's bedroom . . . I have not seen the matted hall and painted parlour windows so plain these five years.[64]

A chapel near the Yorke's house and the setting of fields with a new road subsequently constructed alongside, describe the actual location of Red House.[65] A feature of the back parlour at Red House, which Mary mentions, the two stained glass windows depicting Shakespeare and Milton, are still preserved in the house.

> Those windows would be seen by daylight to be of a brilliantly stained glass – purple and amber the predominant hues, glittering round a gravely tinted medallion in the centre of each, representing the suave head of William Shakespeare, and the serene one of John Milton.[66]

The gaze of the great men of literature failed apparently to subdue the young Mary and Martha who 'laughed all poetry to scorn' as their father may have done, but perhaps it was only contemporary poetry, the Romantics, they despised or perhaps exceptions were made for the two great men of literature!

In 1886 and 1895, Edward Sigston Taylor (1846-99), Mary's nephew, annotated the margins of two copies of *Shirley*, one an edition of 1875, the other of 1891.[67] These annotations confirm that pictures of Italian views and a painting of 'a night-eruption of Vesuvius' described as hanging in

Briarmains, were in the Taylor parlour as well as the [presumably] 'John Wesley' chair which was always reserved for the head of the family. Yorke, it will be recalled, flouts the norms of common hospitality by turning Robert Moore out of 'an old-fashioned chair by the fireside'; 'That place is mine.'[68]

Though some of the description of Briarmains probably embellishes the actual Red House, the impression of a cultured and extremely comfortable home is most certainly suggested by the house even today.

> The gentlemen were ushered in at the front entrance. They found themselves in a matted hall, lined almost to the ceiling with pictures, through this they were conducted to a large parlour, with a magnificent fire in the grate; the most cheerful of rooms it appeared as a whole, and when you came to examine details, the enlivening effect was not diminished. There was no splendour, but there was taste everywhere, unusual taste, – you would have said, of a travelled man, a scholar and a gentleman. A series of Italian views decked the walls; each of these was a specimen of true art; a connoisseur had selected them: they were genuine and valuable. Even by candlelight, the bright clear skies, the soft distances, with blue air quivering between the eye and the hills, the fresh tints, and well-massed lights and shadows, charmed the view. The subjects were all pastoral, the scenes were all sunny. There was a guitar and some music on a sofa; there were cameos, beautiful miniatures; a set of Grecian-looking vases on the mantelpiece; there were books well arranged in two elegant bookcases.[69]

The Taylor note is struck with full force early in the novel with the set-piece character sketch of Yorke and the visit of Moore and Helstone to Briarmains.[70] Brontë creates a man forthright of speech, implacable in his opposition to the established authority as embodied in monarchy, aristocracy and clergy, dogmatic and intolerant himself, while arguing against suppression of freedom of opinion. 'Revolt was in his blood: he could not bear control; his father, his grandfather before him, could not bear it, and his children after him never could.'[71] And Edward Taylor confirms this as a continuous family characteristic by adding in his note 'nor his grandchildren'![72]

Yorke combines brusqueness and radical views, expressed in a strong West Yorkshire dialect, with a high level of culture and taste, though with no use for imagination, and he is especially contemptuous of poetry. In this set piece of character description, Brontë seems to be remembering the arguments she was drawn into on her visits to the Taylors when she had to defend both her Tory views and her love of poetry against a gale of opposition; her tone suggests she is savouring the sweets of mild revenge.

Though deficient in general benevolence Yorke is a considerate employer, treating working people without condescension.

> [Yorke] would spend an hour any time in talking freely with a shrewd workman of his own, or with some queer sagacious old woman amongst his cottagers, when he would have grudged a moment to a commonplace fine gentleman, or to the most fashionable and elegant, if frivolous lady.[73]

This echoes a comment from Mary about herself in a letter to Brontë who was just beginning work on *Shirley*.

> Did you never notice that the women of the middle-classes are generally too ignorant to talk to? and that you are thrown entirely on the man for conversation? There is no such feminine inferiority in the lower. The women go hand in hand with the men in the degree of cultivation they are able to reach. I can talk very well to a joiner's wife, but seldom to a merchant's.[74]

Edward Taylor expresses no fundamental doubts that the character of Yorke is largely based on Joshua Taylor, though with the reservations, 'well but much overdrawn' (1886 edition) and 'well drawn but caricatured' (1891 edition).[75]

Edward was born after his grandfather's death and must be echoing what came to be the received family view of Joshua II. He reports that his own father, Joshua III, had exclaimed on reading the book, 'Either my brother Joseph wrote that book or someone who knew him very intimately'.[76]

Mary described the Taylor household to Mrs. Gaskell as 'our house of violent Dissent and Radicalism', and while she recognised parallels between the Yorkes and the Taylors, she had her reservations.[77] Most notably she was anxious to dissociate her father from Yorke's cynical advice to the near bankrupt Robert Moore to salvage his business by marrying the heiress Shirley for her money:

> But my father is not like. He [Yorke] hates well enough and perhaps loves too, but he is not honest enough. It was from my father I learnt not to marry for money nor to tolerate any one who did, and he never would advise any one to do so, or fail to speak with contempt of those who did.[78]

While she defends her father Mary is significantly silent about Mrs. Yorke and the character's relation to Mrs. Taylor. Charlotte was probably paying off old scores, not only on her own behalf but Mary's and Martha's.

> In her [Mrs. Yorke's] estimation, to be mirthful was to be profane; to be cheerful was to be frivolous: she drew no distinctions. Yet she was a very good wife, a very careful mother, looked after her

children unceasingly, was sincerely attached to her husband; only the worst of it was, if she could have had her will, she would not have permitted him to have any friend in the world beside herself: all his relations were insupportable to her, and she kept them at arm's length . . . Yorke had a shadowy as well as a sunny side to his character, and . . . his shadowy side found sympathy and affinity in the whole of his wife's uniformly over-cast nature. For the rest, she was a strong-minded woman; never said a weak or a trite thing; took stern democratic views of society, and rather cynical ones of human nature; considered herself perfect and the rest of the world all wrong.[79]

Edward Taylor, who was ten when his grandmother died, regarded Mrs. Yorke as 'A fair but slightly overdrawn description of Mrs. Taylor . . . C.B. could not bear her'.[80]

Certainly Charlotte actively disliked Mrs. Taylor, though she seems always to have felt more warmly towards husbands than to wives. Ellen Nussey must have been in agreement with her about Mrs. Taylor. Gossiping in a letter about a friend of Ellen's, Mrs. Gorham, Charlotte writes:

Mrs. Gorham I always stand a little in awe of; I fancy her somewhat cold and severe, even suspicious. I think I confuse her character with that of our old friend Mrs. Taylor; doubtless I do her a great injustice.[81]

Mary's brother Joshua and his wife lived with Mrs. Taylor at Red House after the death of his father but in 1845 they left. Charlotte attributed the move to Mrs. Taylor's difficult nature: ' . . . her unhappy disposition is preparing her for a most desolate old age'.[82]

Mrs. Taylor reacted sharply to Charlotte's novel, presumably resenting it on behalf of the whole family, not only for herself. 'Mama has written to Waring abusing Miss Brontë for writing *Shirley*.'[83] This prompted Waring to read the book and he loyally backed his mother. Mary reported that he thought all the characters were unfaithful and denied that his father ever talked broad Yorkshire but she added: 'He seems to have forgotten home altogether' and went on to tell how when asked what sort of room he would have liked to have if he had been rich: ' . . . he [once] described our old dining-room in every point and said he didn't know he'd ever seen such a room!'[84]

Mrs. Taylor's reserved and cold personality as Charlotte Brontë saw her is confirmed in Grace Hirst's reminiscences to Susan Taylor. 'Anna Waring [sic] was a hard narrow Calvinistic type, never really loved by M[ary] and Martha'.[85]

So much for the parents. What of the children? As there were in the Taylor family there are six Yorke children in *Shirley*, four boys (one a baby), and two girls. In evaluating possible factual elements of the novel for a view of the Taylor children we need to remember that Charlotte got to know them only in 1832 when they were older than the ages she uses for the Yorkes. Joshua III was already about 20, while the 'baby' of the family, Waring, was about 13. The articulate, argumentative young people Brontë knew and who provided such rousing pleasures had not, as young children, enjoyed the liberties extended to the fictional Yorke children.

> You make us all talk much as I think we should have if we'd ventured to speak at all [as children] . . . There is a strange feeling in reading it of hearing us all talking.[86]

There are acute tensions in the fictional, Briarmains, family. The parents indulge the eldest son's difficult and abrasive temperament. 'Matthew is never to be vexed, never to be opposed'.[87] The younger brothers, Martin especially, deeply resent the eldest's favoured position and are reported as threatening to emigrate to Australia to escape Matthew's tyranny: 'The dragon's teeth are already sown amongst Mr. Yorke's young olive-branches: discord will one day be the harvest.'[88]

Edward Taylor is utterly silent about these fictional conflicts, both those between Matthew and the other children, and between them and their mother. He neither confirms nor denies any parallels with relationships within the Taylor family, responding only to aspects of the characters of Mark, and of Martin, equated respectively with John and Joseph. John is taciturn: 'very phlegmatic as I knew him . . . Very fair description' while 'Joseph – always Joe . . . Joe was a clever practical and theoretical chemist, and practically C.B.'s hero'.[89]

He accepts Matthew as modelled on his father, Joshua III, but makes no comment about Brontë's fictional characterisation of the indulged young heir, arrogant and already developing into a tyrant.

The young Yorkes are, as Robert Moore exclaims, 'vraiment des enfants terribles',[90] overwhelmingly articulate, terribly knowledgeable, sententious and outspoken and, it must be said, barely credible. Mary Taylor responded half humorously and deprecatingly to the 'portrait' of herself and wrote to Charlotte 'What a little lump of perfection you've made me.'[91]

The young Rose Yorke is briefly described in Chapter IX mainly in relation to her young sister Jessy who has 'the power to charm' while she was not destined to have 'the manner to attract'.[92]

Rose reappears more fully later in the novel on the visit to the Hollows where she meets Caroline Helstone. She is an avid reader and we see her here absorbed in reading Mrs. Radcliffe's *The Italian*. This gives rise to their conversation in which Rose tells of her ambitions to travel and her determination to break free from the confines of Briarmains and the stultifying round of trivial domesticity. Her aspirations are roundly condemned by her mother with whom, Rose, like most of her siblings, is in conflict. All these are characteristics which we know from other sources to be true of Mary Taylor; so are the quietness and composure while Jessy, like Martha, is the lively, outspoken one. In the long set piece describing Briarmains and the family, Brontë looks into the future and sees Jessy dying abroad, tended by her sister, and Rose herself, two years later, 'a lonely emigrant in some region of the southern hemisphere. 'Will she ever come back?' asks the novelist and promptly comes the reply in Edward Taylor's marginal notes: 'Yes & now lives at Gomersal' and 'She did and lived at Gomersal for many years'.[93]

Edward Taylor's almost final comment is: 'C.B. was surprised & pained to find the thin cloak she had thrown over her characters had been so transparent'.[94]

Certainly with *Shirley* Currer Bell's gender was becoming clear and 'his' identity gradually emerging. Other local people, in addition to the Taylors, were designated the originals of many of the other characters. Brontë's statements about the relationship between her fictional characters and actually existing people seek to stress the part that imagination played in the creation of the novels, while many of her local readers reductively searched for mirror images of themselves or people they knew. The quality which seems to invite the speculations as to who Caroline Helstone, or any other of the characters, *really* is, is expressed by Leslie Stephen in his article in *The Cornhill Magazine*.

> The most obvious of all remarks about Miss Brontë is the close connection between her life and her writings . . . All the minor characters, with scarcely an exception, are simply portraits, and the more successful in proportion to their fidelity.[95]

This over-emphasises the degree to which Brontë was merely describing people she knew or had heard of, and she would have rejected the suggestion. On one occasion at least, as a persuasive and diplomatic ploy she herself was not above exploiting the 'real' people game. In 1851 she was a guest of the family of George Smith, her publisher, and wished to pass on to them a cushion embroidered for her by Amelia Taylor who had married Joe the previous year. We can sense embarrassment behind the coy and pompous style.

> It is somewhat too bright and pretty for my sitting room at home – I do not need either cushion or chair or stool or any other sitting apparatus to keep you in my recollection – it would look well in a certain apartment wherein I am now writing and would be vastly esteemed as the work of 'young Mrs. Martin Yorke'. May I give it?[96]

Shirley has had more than its share of simplistic and reductive readings. We are justified in drawing only the most tentative conclusions about the Taylor family from the internal evidence of the novel, while it cannot be a reliable source of hard information about them, it can usefully confirm knowledge we may have from other sources

It does provide a clear, factual picture of some aspects of Red House and its elegant furnishings. Joshua Taylor's own family confirm his bluntness, his independence, his republican and dissenting opinions and his culture, such as Brontë depicts in Yorke. I think we can accept Mary's view of his integrity in relation to mercenary marriages and one which Brontë herself would be unlikely to challenge. For the purposes of her novel she needed that aspect of Yorke's character as an element in the development of the plot, creating tension around the possibility of a romance between Shirley and Robert Moore.[97] Edward Taylor's notes give us useful confirmation of aspects of the personalities of his grandparents and his uncles and his aunt which appear in the book. We have the facts from other sources to confirm that Mary's passion for reading, for travel, for her determination not to be confined to lower middle-class domesticity were the inspiration for Rose Yorke and conversely these aspects of her personality come alive for us through the fiction. We know that Martha was attractive and outgoing, Mary quieter and that the two sisters were close and affectionate friends.

Letters between Charlotte, Ellen and Mary provide us with glimpses of Joe at a time when he seemed to be a restless flirt,[98] the prototype for Yorke's prophecy about Martin.[99]

There were family tensions caused essentially by difficulties about property and the business which was bequeathed to Mrs. Taylor but run by the three brothers. Joshua III does appear to have been difficult and was later alienated from his family. The problems of the firm were doubtless exacerbated by the toughness and stubbornness of the Taylor character. They were a difficult lot, quick to take offence, resistant to others' influence: '. . . when Shirley [sic] came out someone said to him [Joe Taylor] that it made the Taylors out a queer lot – he had said "Ah but we're a lot queerer than that."'.[100] Maybe he was right, but Joe was a tease or his response might have been a tactical conversation stopper, blocking off further gossip about either his family or the book.

Chapter 2

Outside the Cage

1841 saw Mary, now 24 years of age, without Martha who was in Brussels, and with Waring preparing to leave for New Zealand. Her other brothers, John and Joe were working at the Hunsworth mill with Joshua. The break-up of the family which Charlotte had foreseen was now under way. Two immediate possibilities seemed to offer themselves to Mary. The most obvious was that she could remain at Hunsworth keeping house for her two brothers but dependent on them. Although both John and Joe were generous to her neither was particularly satisfactory for sharing a home with. John, though often generous to his sisters, was taciturn and moody, while Joe was restless, constantly on the move and rapidly gaining a reputation for himself as an irresponsible flirt. They were, in any case, both eligible bachelors and there seemed to be no reasons why they should not marry and set up their own homes without her. Such uncertainty and dependence had no attractions for her, especially if the final outcome was to be an enforced return to Red House and domestic life with Mrs. Taylor.

She was sufficiently well educated to go out as a teacher or governess and Charlotte, already in employment, passed on to her the possibility of a post as governess in Ireland which she declined. Charlotte was rather piqued at Mary's turning down this opportunity and believed Mary's brothers had discouraged the idea.[101] If they had intervened in this way they were merely confirming Mary's own inclinations. Only a few weeks before, Charlotte herself had reported to Ellen Nussey that Mary had expressed her firm determination never to be a governess. Living in someone else's home, occupying an ambiguous position between servant and social equal, providing the rudiments of education to the very young or a smattering of accomplishments to older girls was not a tempting prospect. It represented neither an intellectual challenge nor an opportunity of earning an adequate living.

Clearly Mary had to make some decisive move if she was to embark on a course for the new, independent life which she yearned for. She knew already that she wanted to win her independence by congenial, adequately paid work. Her hopes centred on the possibility of achieving a first-rate education, and mixing in improving society. Already she aspired to 'the freedom from too early and too confining labour' along with books and travel. These constituted the ingredients of the good life she longed for and as she defined it many years later in *The First Duty of Women*.[102] With the possibility of emigration denied her for the time being, she had to consider how to acquire special skills and find an opportunity of using them.

She made no move until the beginning of the following year. Meanwhile in August 1841 she went with John and Martha for a month's holiday in Belgium and Charlotte wrote to Ellen:

> Martha Taylor it appears, is in the way of enjoying great advantages – so is Mary – for you will be surprised to hear she is returning immediately to the Continent with her brother John – not however to stay there but to take a month's tour and recreation.[103]

It was Martha, not Mary, who was returning to the Continent having been back at Hunsworth during her school's summer break. Escorting the two young women abroad for a holiday was typical of the friendship and generosity of both John and Joe towards their sisters. Apart from the problem of not having the money, Mary's possibilities of travelling independently were, like those of most young middle-class women, considerably circumscribed. The Taylors seem always to have been concerned not to have the two young women travel unescorted. It was not impossible but stressful. Charlotte who in 1843 travelled entirely alone to Brussels encountered no problems but commented: 'I had no accident, but of course some anxiety'.[104] The anxiety found dramatic expression in *Villette* with Lucy Snowe's trials on her lone journey to Bassecour.

Mary wrote to Charlotte from such places as Liège and Spa describing 'pictures the most exquisite – and cathedrals the most venerable' and vivid accounts of their experiences, inducing in her friend a painful yearning for the opportunity of seeing the wider world of beautiful architecture, art and other new sights.[105] The sisters also sent Charlotte generous presents of gloves and a silk scarf which she appreciated but in a characteristically self-repressive reaction, after the first flush of pleasure she comments:

> I should think Mary and Martha have not more than sufficient pocket-money to supply themselves . . . [106]

Mary and John left Martha in Brussels in the early part of September to return home leaving Martha to resume her studies at Château Koekelberg.[107]

Mary's holiday tour had suggested two practical steps which might be taken, one by Charlotte and one by herself. Already they had talked about the possibility of going abroad to improve their languages and with Charlotte's imagination already fired by the letters from Belgium, Mary found her a willing listener. Now speaking from practical experience of foreign travel, Mary began her campaign of encouraging Charlotte to undertake her great adventure. Mary must have quickly realised the inadequacies of the French they had been taught at school (perhaps she had always suspected them); she could now talk about them with authority. With her shrewd and practical business sense she recognised that if Charlotte were to establish a viable boarding school at Haworth she would need to improve her languages and the best way of doing that was by living abroad.

> I think, Nell, I see a chance of getting to Brussels. Mary Taylor advises me on this step. My own mind and feelings urge me.[108]

Charlotte opened negotiations with her aunt, Miss Branwell, softening the alarming novelty of the proposal by referring to Martha Taylor's presence in Brussels as a feasible precedent and a source of practical advice and assistance as well as some guarantee of companionship.[109] If Charlotte was at all hesitant, Mary persisted in her urging.

> Mary Taylor cast oil on the flames – encouraged me and in her own strong, energetic language heartened me on . . . [110]

There was not only Martha's presence in Brussels to provide a sense of security to Charlotte and reassurance to her aunt and her father but a network of British residents, numbering around 2,000 in the city at this time.[111] For the Brontës there was the Church of England connection. The pastor to the English Protestants in the city was the Reverend Evan Jenkins who with his family was a friend of the Nusseys and whose brother was known to Mr. Brontë. In addition to Martha Taylor herself, there were frequent visits by John and Joe on business trips to the city and there was the Dixon family. Abraham Dixon (b.? d.1850) who had married Mary's aunt Laetitia (1780-1842) described himself as an inventor and seems to have been engaged in selling textile machinery in Belgium. As he was frequently in financial difficulties he probably lived in Belgium because it was cheap compared with England. Charlotte thought the cost of living there was about half that at home. Dixon lived in the rue de la Régence and provided hospitality to his Taylor relatives which was extended to their friends Charlotte and Emily Brontë. Mary Dixon, Abraham's daughter, became a lifelong friend of Charlotte. After her father's death she was housekeeper to her brothers, George and Abraham Jnr. in Birmingham. Their home was a stop-over for the Taylors on their travels south and to the Continent.[112]

For the Brontës the autumn of 1841 saw a flurry of correspondence, and changes of plans. As late as January 20th 1842 they were on the point of fixing on Lille with Charlotte regretting not being near Martha, but shortly afterwards, with the help of Mrs. Jenkins, arrangements had been finalised for Charlotte and Emily to become pupil teachers at the Pensionnat Heger in Brussels, a cheaper school than the Château Keokelberg. Charlotte was deeply grateful to Mary for her encouragement and help.

Nothing in this hurried correspondence refers to any plans for Mary but clearly she had decided on an initial step. On February 8th 1842, when Charlotte and Emily set out on their journey to Brussels they were travelling not only with their father and with Joe Taylor as experienced traveller to escort them, but with Mary too, on her way to join Martha at Château Koekelberg! While a young ladies' finishing school was unlikely to provide an opportunity for 'hallacking' around Europe it meant at least the experience of living abroad, offering more promise than housekeeping at Hunsworth.[113] It reunited her with Martha and opened up possibilities for extending her education by developing a thorough proficiency in French and German.

In her third edition of *The Life of Charlotte Brontë*, Mrs. Gaskell incorporated a section of Mary Taylor's description of the three-day stay in London before the travellers set out for the Channel crossing. Joe was their untiring guide whose enthusiasm for showing them everything was apparently matched only by Charlotte's urgent need to see it all. Mary was impressed by Charlotte's determination 'to see all the pictures and statues we could' and by her knowledge of where they were to be found; she herself remembered only a visit to St. Paul's.[114] Nine years later in 1850 Charlotte recalled the visit and the sightseeing as utterly exhausting, for which she blamed Joe, but that was at a moment when she was feeling particularly critical of him!

It was night when the party arrived in Brussels, having spent two nights in Ostend, and the following morning the Brontës and the Taylors went their separate ways 'much pre-occupied, and our prospects gloomy';[115] a comment which suggests that for Mary resuming her education in a finishing school was not what she herself would have freely chosen. Château Koekelberg, which no longer exists, was probably situated about two miles north-west of the city.[116] Mary was to be a student there until October.

Six weeks after her arrival she and Martha were visited by Charlotte and Emily, the four of them freed by the Easter holiday. Their happy reunion would have been perfect if Ellen could have been among them. A letter already written to her by Mary and waiting to be sent was adapted as a serial letter with messages added at various dates from Martha and Charlotte. In her section Mary describes her long daily routine with its concentration on German and drawing and some French composition. She's frustrated because their French teacher has not yet arrived to begin her duties and if this humorous passage is to be believed, the English certainly needed her services as much the French students needed a good teacher of English!

> In the enumeration of my employments I have forgotten the writing of French compositions. This is the plague of Kockleberg [sic] schoolroom. 'Avez-vous fait votre composition?' 'Oui, mais je ne puis pas – *put a beginning to it.*'
> 'Pouvez-vous m'aider?' Silence! 'What's the French for "invite"?' 'It is eight *hours*! *When* shall we have the tea? How many years have you?' This is a French girl talking English.[117]

She extracts humour too from her descriptions of their dancing lessons and also remarks sardonically that the headmistress is 'so outrageously civil that I every now and then suspect her of hypocrisy'.[118]

The reunion for the day was like a breath of home to Charlotte, already somewhat homesick, 'for one's blood requires a little warming, it gets cold with living among strangers' and she reassured Ellen, 'You are not forgotten as you feared you would be'.[119]

Closing the letter a few days later Martha, lively and impertinent as usual, makes fun of Mary's seriousness as she works at her German dictionary and ends irreverently:

> When you see my brother Joe, have the kindness to pull him his hair right well for me and give John a good pinch.[120]

Martha was back at Hunsworth in June for the summer holiday but Mary, keeping aloof from both Hunsworth and from her mother's household, remained behind. Teaching began again in August at Château Koekelberg and Martha returned but Mary for her part was already planning her next steps towards independence. She was preparing a move which would distance her yet further from the constraints of home.

By October 1842, Charlotte and Emily had decided to remain in Brussels, having accepted offers of pupil-teachers' posts at the Pensionnat Heger. In a letter to Ellen written sometime during the latter part of summer or early autumn Mary announces her intention of following their example by staying abroad and at the same time defies anyone to criticise her decision.

> I . . . sincerely hope I have bid adieu to your confounded 'patrie' (my own though it be) for ever and a day. The stones will turn another side towards me when I do come back again and[121] if anything looks at me with its old face I'll knock its teeth down its throat.[122]

Not without cause did Martha compare her to a tiger! There would be criticism of her for staying away from home during the holiday and a view among their friends in Gomersal (which Ellen would not fail to pass on), that as the elder sister her place was really back there either with her mother or keeping house for Joe and John. At this time Ellen seems to have assumed that Mary was again hoping to emigrate to New Zealand but Mary vigorously denied it and hinted at Germany.

> When in the name of the *grand dieu de la foudr*e (a Koeklberg [sic] expression) (it means Jupiter) did you find or steal the description of New Zealand? I never *knew* anything about the country – which however does not prevent my having described it in some overflow of poetic frenzy – if this be the case pray refer me to the volume of my works in which it is to be found – or at least mention the date of the night on which I dreamed it –
>
> What do you think of Germany instead of New Zealand? I have heard they are nice and savage there too . . . [123]

Life at Château Koekelberg was becoming intolerable. The enclosed female society of a young ladies' finishing school was not likely to prove congenial. Mary was, after all, 25 years old and she had not lived in an exclusively female environment since leaving Miss Wooler's school ten years before. With her decided opinions she was not one to take kindly to a discipline based on principles she disapproved of. She was, above all, outspoken and honest, not to say tactless, and placed a high value on truthful relationships. Soon after her arrival she thought she detected hypocrisy, a view which further experience confirmed and it was repugnant to her. She wrote of life at Château Koekelberg: 'An artificial kind of life that prevents you from ever enjoying any simple or natural pleasures'.[124]

Mary was highly intelligent, already well read and eager for education of a high and challenging standard. Koekelberg was intended, partly, as a finishing school committed to teaching middle-class young ladies the conventional feminine accomplishments. This was not what Mary had in mind as necessary either for her personal development or her future career.

Koekelberg had, however, provided the opportunity for loosening the ties of home. By September she was planning a new move. She was preparing to go to Germany, there to earn her living by teaching English, at the same time as improving her German and her music. Frau Schmidt, mother of a *pensionnaire* at Koekelberg offered the young Englishwoman accommodation in her home near Iserlohn for the winter months. After that she would move out and fend for herself.

Mary justified her decision to go to Germany on the grounds that, like the Brontës, she wanted to stay 'outside the cage – though it is somewhat cold.'

> Cold or warm, farewell. I am going to shut my eyes for a cold plunge – when I come up again I [sic] tell you all what it's like.[125]

Mary exulted: ' . . . what's the use of grumbling when I'm going away? Going! Going!' though in the knowledge that she would need to summon up all her courage for that cold plunge into the unknown.[126] Tragically, before she faced that stimulating challenge, her courage was put to a different, unforeseen and devastating test.

While Martha was at home on holiday there was cholera in the North of England. The disease at that period was of pandemic proportions in Europe. William Weightman, Patrick Brontë's curate, died of it in September. Martha, who returned to Brussels a few weeks before, found that the disease was claiming victims there also. At the end of September she too fell ill and died on October 12th. Charlotte was shocked to learn suddenly of her friend's death. She had been unaware that Martha was ill but she reported to Ellen that their friend had suffered the same symptoms over the same period of time as Weightman, information she must have been given by Mary.

Cholera is a water-borne disease, not contagious, and patients suffer appalling pain while generally retaining consciousness. Until the middle of the nineteenth century it was neither thoroughly understood nor always accurately identified. There has nevertheless been speculation that Martha died during pregnancy. Daphne du Maurier in her biography of Branwell Brontë[127] suggests a mystery surrounding Martha's death. Maureen Peters in *An Enigma of the Brontës*[128] discusses it in some detail. Margot Peters raises the subject in a note in her Brontë biography *The Unquiet Soul, A Biography of Charlotte Brontë*.[129]

The evidence in support of this theory rests on the death certificate which was not signed by doctors, and Mary's letters. The death was reported by M. Goussaert but the cause was not specified. Three possible reasons (and no doubt others) could be advanced. There may have been genuine ignorance of the cause, or, if it were cholera and known to be so M. Goussaert wished to avoid publicity about unsatisfactory hygiene at the school and used his influence to suppress the information; or, it could mean that the real cause of Martha's death was something deeply disgraceful and everybody conspired to protect her reputation and that of the school. Mary's letter to Ellen Nussey two weeks after Martha's death holds back on any detailed account. Her lament, 'She is better where she is' seems to suggest either some permanent physical disablement, moral transgression, or some unsupportable social disgrace. She nevertheless promises to let Ellen have a full account of the tragedy. Close as Mary was to Ellen at this time, it is doubtful if she would have given information if it had concerned wrongdoing and she assumes that Ellen might hear from other sources.

> You will wish to hear the history of Martha's illness – I will give you it in a few months if you have not heard it then; till then you must excuse me. A thousand times I have reviewed the minutest circumstances of it, but I cannot without great difficulty give a regular account of them. There is nothing to regret, nothing to recall – not even Martha. She is better where she is. But when I recall the sufferings that have purified her, my heart aches – I can't help it, and every trivial accident, sad or pleasant, reminds me of her and[130] of what she went through.[131]

So soon after the shattering loss of the sister she dearly loved Mary was obviously still deeply shocked and grieving. She had carried the main burden of nursing and anxiety among comparative strangers. She struggled to control her feelings by the exercise of reason and she could well have felt that to write a more detailed account of Martha's death would be to plunge back into despair and anguish. The close of the letter asking Ellen to convey greetings to mutual friends does suggest that Mary feels vulnerable to gossip. On the other hand we know that she disliked display of feelings and was regarded as self-controlled and private.

We get a reference to the tragedy a year later on June 25th 1843. Mary, responding to the news that there is an outbreak of some kind of fever at a school in Birstall suggested that it would harm the school, and tells Ellen:

> Martha's death though not from a contagious disorder has exceedingly affected Mde [sic] Gaussaert's school, which I am very sorry for and would gladly repair if I could.[132]

Mary's feeling of responsibility for the damage to the reputation of the school and her 'the sufferings which purified her', could be understood as meaning that Martha had transgressed. The fact that she was pretty, vivacious and attractive to young men adds weight to the speculation. On the other hand, if she died actually in childbirth, she must have been pregnant when Mary joined her at Château Koekelberg in February or soon after. It would have been difficult for Martha to conceal her pregnancy from her sister. Her own letters, both from Brussels and from Hunsworth during the school holidays give no inkling that she was in any kind of trouble. They are in her usual light-hearted and confident style. If she knew she was pregnant she would have been likely to want to remain in Brussels but away from the school as well as from home and friends. On the contrary she went home, spent some part of the holiday in Ilkley, some in Leeds with her Dixon relatives, organised a house warming for the Hunsworth house and went to some trouble to arrange to spend time with Ellen Nussey at Brookroyd, where Ellen's family was living. Then she went back to Château Koekelberg.

The disgrace of a sister's extra-marital pregnancy would certainly have affected Mary's relationship with the Goussaerts but in December 1843 Abraham Dixon is writing that Mme Goussaert intended to call on Mary while touring in Germany. If Martha did die of cholera or an illness attributable not to lack of moral supervision but to poor hygienic conditions at the school, Mary's comment about the fever at Birstall and the damage to Château Koekelberg is perfectly logical.

There is a letter from New Zealand which seems to confirm the cholera theory.

> There has been a man talking of cholera in England till he has made me melancholy – His 'brother's wife's father' died of it at Bradford.[133]

Charlotte was witness to Mary's stoicism and calm, despite the anguish so evident in her letter to Ellen. The Brontës mourned with her when they joined Mary for the walk to visit Martha's grave. Charlotte re-lived the experience in *The Professor* with its description of the Protestant cemetery and in *Shirley* where she anticipates Jessy's death in a foreign land.[134]

Following Martha's death Mary stayed with the Dixons in Brussels. Torn between the conflicting options of remaining with this kindly and affectionate family in Brussels, or returning to Hunsworth or proceeding with her plans to go to Germany, she decided to take the 'cold plunge', rationally explaining to Ellen that she believed activity would be better 'for my spirits, health, and advantage'. She carried out her resolution and for the next fifteen years devoted her energies to pursuing that advantage which she firmly believed meant improving her education, and gaining an independent livelihood, while if possible, enjoying experiences acquired through travel.

Carrying through her rational decision Mary left for Germany where we find her by the end of December 1842. It is not clear from letters written early in her stay in Germany if she actually took advantage of Frau Schmidt's offer to lodge her through the winter at their home in Iserlohn. Her hospitality would have provided her with some stability while she adjusted to life in a strange country and improved her German; on the other hand Iserlohn was smaller than nearby Hagen which offered greater opportunities for finding pupils wanting to learn English and for enjoying music. There Mary took piano lessons from Frederick Hallé. Hallé, whom she described as 'a genius' was a leading figure in the town's musical life. His son was to be the founder of the Hallé orchestra in Manchester. Whether living in Iserlohn or Hagen she soon settled down to work at both German and her music. She reported to Ellen in a flow of high spirits and exuberant humour that she was in good health, better than at any time since leaving England, and feeling cheerful.

> If you can't understand it all [her comic discourse on musical good taste] – remember I've been learning German – and how is it possible to keep one's brains clear in this land of Swedenborg, philosophy, abstract ideas and *cabbage*? This last word is a literal translation of a German one, always applied to everything very confused – my letter for instance. However, I thrive with it all.[135]

Though she was within a few days of her 26th birthday this was the first time in her life that she had been entirely alone, away from any member of her family. She reacted positively to her new life, beginning to experience that sense of power which independent control of one's own life brings.

Though Mary was enjoying the stimulus of the 'cold plunge' she never ceased to feel a sense of responsibility and care for Charlotte. She encouraged her cousin Mary Dixon to keep contact with her friend. Charlotte had returned to Brussels alone in January 1843 and Mary was worried that without Emily's company her life at the Pensionnat Heger might prove difficult and depressing. How right she was! Each young woman worried about the other. Mary, apparently happy and cheerful, envisaged Charlotte in misery, while Charlotte, naïvely unaware of her own emotional danger, wrote to Ellen only three weeks after Mary's exuberant letter declaring that their friend was not happy!

I have had two letters from Mary. She does not tell me she has been ill, and she does not complain; but her letters are not the letters of a person in the enjoyment of great happiness. She has nobody to be as good to her as M. Heger is to me; to lend her books, to converse with her sometimes, etc.[136]

As winter declined Mary seems to have moved to some new accommodation, almost certainly in Hagen, either because the period of the Schmidt's hospitality was drawing to a close when as had been planned she would have to fend for herself or because she was establishing herself successfully and free to live where she chose. Certainly by early summer of 1843 she had made changes. Her new domestic arrangements were the first of her moves to outrage some of the censorious of Gomersal though Charlotte for her part was cautiously approving.[137] Her 'intrepid proceedings' as Charlotte described them must have been a decision to live alone. Ellen reporting the gossip, as usual, had told Mary that one of the Wooler sisters was outraged and was proposing to cut her in future, an item of information received by Mary with self-assured equanimity. She was not over-respectful of her former teachers!

In June she took time off from her work to enjoy a holiday with Joe in Austria where they met up with friends from Gomersal and with Mary Dixon and her father. Apparently there were friends and relatives not disapproving of her way of life and no doubt Joe encouraged her to go ahead with her new domestic arrangements while making sure she would be comfortable.

On her return from holiday she sent Ellen a long letter which ranged over a number of interesting topics and which in her own lively style is characteristic of her intelligent, vigorous, sometimes ironic view of the world and people, including herself. She was still busy settling into her new living quarters, thanking Ellen for a cushion (a 'brioche'!) and announcing the arrival of a new sofa. She could afford to be indifferent to critical, prudish censure of her lone way of life. Her career was flourishing and she was making money, aware that she let money run through her fingers very easily but unashamedly wanting to earn as much as she could lay her hands on. She had so many pupils that she was considering getting rid of the idle ones; describing these she reveals that her pupils are boys mischievously describing them as 'nice *dull* ones'. She is continuing with her German and music and for the rest visiting friends. Unperturbed by Miss Catherine Wooler's disapproval she launches an energetic attack on narrow-mindedness, specifically as shown by Ellen's sister about books and she urges Ellen:

> Read away Ellen books of all sort and all characters. As you cannot leave home and see something of real life the next best thing is to *read* read read . . . the idea of picking out a few as the

exclusively good ones, and that because they treat of religious subjects is stupid enough to be worthy of the narrowness of Birstal [sic] 'little flock'.[138]

Lest Ellen might think she is favouring Hagen at Birstall's expense she assures her that Hagen also has its 'little flocks'; many of her acquaintances are:

... blessed with the same narrow notions that exist in all small communities when the members of them get no ideas from without – None of them are equal to some old friends I left behind to whom believe me as true as ever.[139]

Mary's passion for reading never left her and was one of the great pleasures, indeed consolations, of her whole life. She continued to read not only English literature but German and French, and she had enormous admiration for George Sand which was shared by Charlotte. Mary's own novel was to be influenced by Sand's epic scale novel *Consuelo* which she writes about to Ellen in the winter of 1843. Ellen had enquired about a French novel and Mary concluded it was Sand's published in serial form during 1842-3. She tells Ellen it is the thing that has interested her most in the past month and:

... you would not have given yourself too much trouble if you had learned French for the express purpose of reading it.[140]

To be an admirer of George Sand in the early 1840s was to declare a breadth of culture and broad-mindedness which represented a bold challenge to conventions. Sand's delineation of female sexual passion, her claim for women's emotional and sexual freedom, her lovers, her male cross-dressing, her cigar-smoking, her radical politics, provoked shock and outrage.[141]

Music came second only to reading as a cultural necessity of Mary's life and much of her experience in travelling in Europe came from her visits with Joe to music festivals. She is also taking an interest in algebra partly because she likes it, but also (her humorously challenging feminism coming now to the fore) because 'it is odd in a woman to learn it, and I like to establish my right to be doing odd things'.[142] Mary's other current enthusiasm, reflecting her pleasure in living alone, was her collection of indoor plants, leading her to decide to have a garden.

Hagen's more intimate social life was based on close-knit family groups, and though Mary was feeling somewhat isolated as a consequence she was still in buoyant spirits. Charlotte on the other hand was plunged in despair, her state of mind fulfilling Mary's worst fears. Generous, supportive and practical as always Mary proposed that Charlotte should join her in Hagen, confident that they could earn their livings together but Charlotte feared she would be abandoning security for an uncertain future.[143] With this possible solution rejected, and still alarmed by Charlotte's utter depression, Mary urged her still to seek a change even if it meant returning home.[144] Finally, Mary's advice prevailed and at the end of the year Charlotte returned to Haworth. It is quite possible that Charlotte had confided in Mary about her feelings for M. Heger and this was one reason for Mary not keeping Charlotte's letters. If Joe and Mary had not been told by Charlotte about her feelings they must have guessed. It was Joe who carried Charlotte's letters to M. Heger and who had to give the disappointing news that he carried no letters in reply.

Naturally Mary did not reveal this reason for Charlotte's unhappiness to Mrs. Gaskell, though Gaskell was later to guess the truth of the situation. Mary believed that there were further reasons for Charlotte's unhappiness and she explained them to Gaskell. She knew that Charlotte thought some of her colleagues, in their fear of remaining unmarried, had lost their sensitivity and integrity and she feared this might happen to her. Mary for her part interpreted Charlotte's worries as essentially fear of poverty and urged her constantly to exert herself to earn her own and a better living.[145]

For her part Charlotte changed her opinion of Mary's way of life in Hagen and particularly she disapproved of her teaching boys. Yet again, Charlotte was raising a familiar criticism of Mary. It was the same which she had made about Mary's behaviour (as she saw it) towards Branwell and which she was to repeat from time to time. She deplored Mary's indiscretion, and her lack of prudence. Charlotte believed Mary left herself open to being misunderstood and incurring suffering as a consequence.

> ... I do not give to the step Mary Taylor has taken the unqualified approbation you do. It is a step proving an energetic and active mind, – proving the possession of courage, independence, talent, but it is not a *prudent* step. Often genius, like Mary's, triumphs over every obstacle without the aid of prudence, – and I hope she may be successful – hitherto she is so, – but opinion and custom run so strongly against what she does, that I see there is danger of her having much uneasiness to suffer. If her pupils had been girls, it would be all well; the fact of their being *boys*, or rather young men, is the stumbling-block. This opinion is for YOU only mind.[146]

Charlotte instructed Ellen to keep these views to herself. This was unlikely to have been motivated by fear of their reaching Mary; their relationship was often marked by plain speaking. It is more likely that Charlotte was reluctant to be identified with the disapproving gossip about Mary in the circle around the Nusseys.

Charlotte abandoned her career in Brussels and left for home at the very end of 1843 but Mary for her part resolutely stayed away from Gomersal.

She was about to be visited by Madame Goussaert at this time and was also expecting a visit from Joe.[147]

Mary worked on in Hagen for fifteen months without returning to England, but in April 1844 returned unexpectedly to Hunsworth where she had a happy and affectionate reunion with Charlotte and Ellen. Later in May she left with one of her brothers for the music festival at Cologne.[148]

She returned to Hagen but she was beginning to feel depressed and restless. By September 1844 Charlotte knew that Mary had decided after all to emigrate, to join Waring in Wellington. A much defaced letter from Mary to Ellen written probably at this time seems to express disillusionment and criticism of other people's lack of honesty and faith. There is no firm evidence to show what or whom Mary was complaining about. The financial affairs of the Taylor family were improving; the debts from the bankruptcy were being discharged. Perhaps Mary had harboured expectations of receiving some share of her money from the business at that time and had been disappointed, receiving either nothing or very little. It was not until she returned home, fourteen years later that she came into a considerable inheritance. Mrs. Gaskell's belief that Mary went off to New Zealand after inheriting her patrimony and that she had a reasonable income at that time is borne out neither by Mary's life in her early years in Wellington nor her letters.[149]

With her mind made up to join Waring her stay in Hagen was drawing to a close. In November she went on a holiday with Joe to Switzerland, called in at Brussels and was back at Hunsworth at the beginning of 1845, in the first few days of January. Almost immediately she went on a visit to Charlotte who in turn stayed at Hunsworth shortly afterwards for a final farewell.

Charlotte, sad to be losing one of her two dearest friends, was also depressed on her own account, unwell and miserable about her own future. Mary decided on a final effort to rouse her to make a radical move to leave home and earn her living. She described the poignant scene to Mrs. Gaskell:

> When I last saw Charlotte [Jan. 1845] she told me she had quite decided to stay at home . . . I told her very warmly, that she ought not to stay at home; that to spend the next five years at home, in solitude and weak health, would ruin her; that she would never recover it. Such a dark shadow came over her face when I said, 'Think of what you'll be five years hence!' that I stopped and said 'Don't cry Charlotte!' She did not cry, but went on walking up and down the room, and said in a little while, 'But I intend to stay, Polly.'[150]

On March 21st 1845, now 28 years old, Mary Taylor set sail for New Zealand where she was to stay for fourteen years. Charlotte declared:

Mary Taylor is going to leave our hemisphere. To me it is something as if a great planet fell out of the sky. Yet unless she marries in New Zealand, she will not stay there long.[151]

Mary was indeed a shining planet in Charlotte Brontë's firmament. The friendship with its roots in their early adolescence survived the differences of temperament and politics and personal situation.[152] It was a friendship that each valued and made efforts to maintain and develop. When Charlotte spent three unhappy years teaching at Miss Wooler's school one of her few sources of relief was a call from the Taylors, or a short visit to their home. The stay in Brussels which Mary had done so much to help bring about, her support to Charlotte in the latter's emotional crisis, their shared intellectual interests, all strengthened a bond which was to endure the coming ten-year separation from 1845, from Mary's emigration to Charlotte's death.

In 1868, thirteen years after Charlotte's death, Mary set out her views of friendship. She believed it should be based on genuine inclination and affection, and that it was likely to be enjoyed with only a few choice spirits. She defines friends as:

... [those] who keep up our faith in mankind by giving proof of their goodness, and rouse the ever returning wish for their welfare, and liking for their company.[153]

This surely epitomised her feelings for Charlotte.

Mary was vigorous of speech and action, bold and outspoken, but sometimes woundingly blunt. Gripped by strong convictions about the need for women to be active in their own interests to the extent of defying the conventions and the claims even of family, she could be over-insistent in her efforts to persuade Charlotte and Ellen to be bolder and more enterprising. When Charlotte felt unable to answer Mary's certainties with convincing arguments she would take refuge in silence or in irony. But Mary's urgency reflected genuine, affectionate concern for their welfare. She knew that they all three faced the possibility of poverty and dependence and she wanted the other two to make the same efforts as herself to earn money and establish some basis for an independent life.

Mary had more *savoir faire* than the other two. When, daringly, Ellen and Charlotte decided to go on holiday together, unchaperoned, they followed Mary's suggestion and went to Bridlington in 1839![154]

From New Zealand she urged Ellen to emigrate and join her, commanded her not to accept a post of unpaid companion, told her to read widely, cheer up, not to sulk and so on. She was the one who encouraged Charlotte to go to Brussels. When Charlotte was in the depths of despair there in 1843 she offered her a home and in effect a teaching partnership in Hagen. Though she described herself as 'terribly wanting in tact' towards her friends, Mary was not dogmatic or insensitive.[155] She knew when to stop the argument. Failing to persuade Charlotte to join her in Hagen she urged her, very sensibly, to go home. In the painful discussion about Charlotte's future during their last, 1845 meeting, she gave up the effort to influence her when she saw her friend's distress.

Mary was impetuous and, though she worked hard for money, regarded herself as careless with it 'me with my headlong self-indulgent habits'.[156] She tried to cultivate her courage through action, while Charlotte was cautious, even timid, reserved and self-repressive to the point of hysteria and masochism. Ellen accepted the rôle of spinster, companion, general domestic support. Charlotte stayed on at Haworth, suppressing her own wishes and ambitions. Mary broke free from home and from her mother for whom she felt little affection. She rejected the view that self-sacrifice was a sort of natural fulfilment for women or that it constituted their sacred duty. 'I don't think myself that women are justified in sacrificing themselves for others'.[157]

Already by 1845 Mary's feminism was rooted in a consciousness that women's unequal access to material wealth, not their inherent natures, was the root cause of their subordinate status and she set out to work to achieve financial independence. Charlotte, equally conscious of the insecurity of her lot was, in practice, unable to bear either physically or emotionally the pressures and tensions of being a governess or a teacher, the only career which seemed possible for her. She also feared that insistence on the need for money would result in worldliness. Mary's feminist principles were systematically developed and tested as she consciously acted to apply them in her personal life. Charlotte's feminism was ambivalent.[158] Yearning for freedom she was emotionally incapable of rejecting elements of the very ideology which justified keeping women in their subordinate place. For Charlotte the principle of self-sacrifice, for example, had the force of a religious belief which in her young womanhood, conflicting as it did with her ambitions, led her to feel a neurotic sense of sinfulness.

Charlotte certainly found Mary more stimulating than Ellen, but Ellen offered an undemanding refuge, though she shared, even encouraged, Charlotte's tendency to religious morbidity. It was, however, to Mary that she could confide her more rebellious views and aspirations, without feeling the need to confess to a feeling of sinfulness as she did with Ellen. Perhaps she could even confide in Mary about her feelings for M. Heger knowing that with her breadth of understanding and tolerance Mary would understand and that, moreover, her utter discretion and her honour could be relied on.

Mary had inherited none of her forebears' religious extremism. She was reticent about parading her beliefs and she shared Charlotte's tolerance of other people's religious views and commitment. Describing Charlotte's religion she comments:

She had a larger religious toleration than a person would have who had never questioned, and the manner of recommending religion was always that of offering comfort, not fiercely enforcing a duty. One time I mentioned that someone had asked me what religion I was of (with the view of getting me for a partizan) and that I had said that was between God and me; – Emily (who was lying on the hearth-rug) exclaimed, 'That's right'.[159]

The affection between Mary and Charlotte was strengthened by deep respect and admiration for each other's abilities and by shared intellectual interests. Both were highly intelligent, and intellectually active constantly expanding their knowledge and experience through reading. Both had hopes of establishing careers as writers. At school Mary urged Charlotte 'to make it out' [her imaginings] and she went on encouraging her:

Look out then for success in your writing. You ought to care as much for that as you do for going to Heaven.[160]

After literature Mary's other main cultural interest was music; Charlotte's was fine art. Mary recognised that she had benefited from her friend's knowledge and critical gifts.

She made poetry and drawing, at least exceedingly interesting to me; and then I got the habit, which I have yet, of referring mentally to her opinion on all matters of that kind, along with many more, resolving to describe such and such things to her, until I start at the recollection that I never shall.[161]

Mary was generous and supportive. She had more advantages than either Charlotte or Ellen. The Taylors were relatively much better off than the Brontës and in spite of family tensions they shared a lively intellectual life in the home until their father's death. John and Joe were generous friends to Mary, sharing holidays, enthusiasm for music, helping with money.

The Nusseys were better off than the Brontës but their fortunes were declining. Some of the men of the family were clergymen or in medicine but they don't appear to have shared intellectual interests with their womenfolk.

Both Mary and Ellen provided Charlotte with some social contacts, however narrow, outside her own home. She visited the Nusseys. The Taylors were also hospitable to her and generous. In Joe Taylor she had a lifelong friend. Critical of him she may have been from time to time but it was to him she turned when she needed a reliable support and someone to confide in. Joe was the trustee for her marriage settlement.

When they were young Charlotte and Ellen exchanged confidences about Ellen's romances, real or imagined. All three women had brothers and perhaps hoped that marriage might bring them even closer together. Charlotte thought Mary was in love with Branwell, Ellen from time to time considered that Joe or John Taylor might propose, Henry Nussey actually did ask Charlotte to marry him but she refused. Fond as she was of them Mary came to regard John and Joe as rather aimless and hypochondriacal and she gossiped about them with the other two.

Though Charlotte was sometimes critical of Mary, deploring her imprudence because she believed it caused her difficulties and pain, she deeply appreciated her loyalty and generosity. Writing about Mary's help in getting to Brussels she said:

> . . . Mary has been indefatiguably kind in providing me with information . . . she has grudged no labour and scarcely any expenses to that end . . . Mary's price is above rubies . . . I have in fact two friends you and her staunch and true . . . in whose faith and sincerity I have as strong a belief as I have in the bible [sic] . . . [162]

A year and a half after Mary had emigrated Charlotte was consoling herself and Ellen with the thought that Mary was not intending to settle in New Zealand unless she married and that she would stay 'as long as she can find serious work to do – but no longer'.[163]

Much as she regretted Mary's leaving she thought the decision to go was correct; it seemed to correspond to Mary's ambitions and abilities.

> Mary Taylor finds herself free – and on that path for adventure and exertion to which she has so long been seeking admission – Sickness – Hardship – Danger – are her fellow-travellers – her inseparable companions.[164]

Chapter 3

New Zealand

Frustrated in 1841 in her hopes of emigrating, Mary was sufficiently persistent eventually to carry out the long-cherished project which was to be the next and decisive step in her search for a livelihood which would guarantee her financial independence.

Important as her relationships were with Brontë and Nussey, with her two brothers John and Joe and with the Dixon family she was prepared to separate herself from them. The Taylor family's discouragement in 1841, probably very prudent at the time, lost some of its rationale when there was a home to go to with Waring whose business was now established. Emigration still, however, often implied flight from some kind of disgrace at home, but that would not deter Mary, given her general indifference to public opinion even her desire to be seen to be defying convention.

Despite the relative domestic stability that was waiting for her in Wellington the settlement itself was still struggling. There were acute shortages of ordinary consumer goods such as clothes, furniture, cooking utensils, familiar foods. Travel beyond a few miles outside Wellington was difficult. The weather was often stormy, there were volcanic eruptions, sometimes prolonged and frequent, wooden houses presented the danger of serious fires, and there were mosquitoes and fever.[165] She was exchanging not only comfort and the proximity of family and friends, but opportunities for European travel, easily accessible books and music, for a life among strangers, in a raw new society where she would experience not only physical separation but acute cultural isolation. The distance from England and slow communications meant that she received news from home some four to five or even six months after the events. Letters were often lost. *Jane Eyre*, published in October 1847, reached Mary in June 1848; she had to wait six months before getting *Shirley* (though she had earlier read an extract from it in a periodical). In March 1851 Mary was reading one of the numbers of *David Copperfield* which was actually serialised in 1849-50. When Charlotte and Ellen pass on news to one another from Mary's letters it is already virtually out of date; the Wellington earthquake of October 1848 is mentioned by Charlotte in May 1849; news of Waring's marriage which took place in February 1848 reached her in June.

But before Mary adjusted to the problems of settling down in a new society she faced a daunting long sea voyage to the other side of the world. In the 1840s the journey to New Zealand was expected to take at least four months. Conditions on board ship were cramped and primitive even for the few privileged cabin passengers. Food was monotonous, water was in short supply: there was, for example, insufficient for clothes to be washed on the voyage. Steerage passengers who paid the lowest fare were crowded together and exposed to dangers from disease. Medical facilities were often rudimentary.

The better-off emigrants took great quantities of supplies with them, horses, cattle and other livestock, furniture, clothing, tools of all kinds, even pre-fabricated houses.[166] There were natural anxieties about Mary's well-being on the voyage which took her round Cape Horn and with a landing at Santiago, but she represented herself as enjoying the adventure in cheerful, reassuring letters about the state of her health and her capacity to withstand the hardships of the journey. No doubt she provided shrewd and not over-respectful accounts of fellow passengers. She would have had little time for the pretensions and snobberies of the cabin class and once again she provoked Charlotte's disapproval of her 'flightiness'.

> I have just read Mary's letters; they are very interesting, and show the vigorous and original cast of her mind. There is but one thing I could wish otherwise in them, that is a certain tendency to flightiness – it is not safe, it is not wise, and will often cause her to be misconstrued.[167]

Perhaps Charlotte was offering an indirect reproof hoping that Ellen might pass her remarks on to Mary.

After a voyage of a little over four months Mary disembarked on July 24th 1845 at Wellington from the *Louisa Campbell*. Waring was now running his own trading business in Herbert Street where he also had a cottage.

Wellington had been founded only five years before Mary's arrival and it must often have been unstable and turbulent. Inhabitants totalled under three thousand, about one third were children, and it constituted a large proportion of the total settler population of the North Island. The population more than doubled between 1840 and 1852. Settlers arrived not only from Britain, but from Australia, many of them originally from Ireland; small groups of convicts were shipped out and some soldiers from military garrisons stayed on after their service was completed.

Though the British Government annexed the territory in 1840 there was considerable confusion in the development of the administration and the application of British law; was it to apply, for example, to the Maori population who had their own distinctive social and political structures? There were problems relating to the finances of the colony, taxation, customs duties, even the currency itself. Just as there was no well-established policy defining the settlers' relations with the Government back in Britain, there was confusion about relations with the Maori peoples from whom they were buying land and with whom they were developing trade. Some of the Maori chiefs became uneasy about land sales and its alienation from their people and launched armed resistance to European encroachments which was not put down until 1847 when fighting ended for a period. There were also tensions between the settlers and the missionaries who were concerned not with trade but with converting Maoris to Christianity and reluctant to see an influx of Europeans.

These political problems as well as difficulties arising from lack of roads and adequate maps meant that travelling, especially for women, was difficult and the virtual confinement to small areas of settlement very frustrating for the more adventurous like Mary. One of her ambitions was to have enough money to keep a horse and see more of the country.

There is no discussion in the extant correspondence between Mary and her two friends about the politics of the settlement, no suggestion that they held any but the conventional colonialist, European-centred views on the 'rights' of Europeans to settle in other people's territory and take over. Though Mary was acutely sensitive to so many aspects of women's oppression, her feminism never seems to have led her to question the colonisation processes or its consequences for the Maori population.

There were many different motives for emigration but for most settlers the aim was either to escape actual poverty or to make more money than they would be able to get at home. For some that meant a temporary stay, for others permanent settlement.

Mary had no permanent commitment to New Zealand. She had no intention of becoming a New Zealander. Her aim was to make money in a way that she found congenial. Short of marriage (and she was not the sort of woman deliberately to be seeking a husband), she always intended to return home. In this she was by no means unique. While New Zealand offered no guarantee of prosperity and some settlers were very poor, some, especially those who started out with some resources, did thrive. Samuel Butler is a famous example. His initial capital of £4,400 invested in sheep-farming almost doubled in the four years from 1860 to £8,000.[168]

> The pioneers of New Zealand were not from the highest, nor were they usually from the most down-trodden, sections of British society. They were people, who, while poor, while usually from the upper working class or the lower middle class – the 'anxious classes', Wakefield called them – had lost neither enterprise nor ambition.[169]

Mary has a perhaps unconscious echo of Wakefield's description in *The First Duty*[170] when she is describing those families who feel they have an appearance to keep up but lack the actual means to do it. She writes: 'most truly are they known as the uneasy classes'.

Enterprise and ambition were not the only socially binding aspects of settler ideology. They seem to have put up fierce resistance to snobbery and any attempts to impose marked class distinctions, a characteristic which pleased Mary.

> We see some company – not much, but I think much better than we should in the same circumstances in England [presumably

as shop-keepers]. Classes are forced to mix more here, or there would be no society at all. This circumstance is much to our advantage for there are not many educated people of our standing.[171]

This observation was to be echoed a decade later by Butler. He, like Mary, admired the democratic spirit but felt culturally starved.

... there is much nonsense in the old country from which people here are free ... but it does not do to speak about Johann Sebastian Bach's fugues or Pre-Raphaelite pictures.[172]

Mary felt the same reticence in speaking of *Jane Eyre*.

I mention the book to no one and hear no opinions. I lend it a good deal because it's a novel, and *it's as good as another!* They say 'it makes them cry.' They are not literary enough to give an opinion. If ever I hear one I'll embalm it for you.[173]

Though class snobbery was resisted there is no evidence to suggest much resistance to sex discrimination or that women enjoyed greater equality in New Zealand society than at home. Such advantages as they might have enjoyed derived from their scarcity. Their opportunities for marriage were certainly greater than in England but they seem to have lived by the stereotypical values which conditioned them in Britain. In their characters and attainments Mary thought they were like women at home in England, no better, no worse, though she considered her New Zealand associates were more energetic.

The women are the same every where [sic] never educated and so far as female friends go, I think our present set have as much principle and kindness as most of those we left while they have certainly more energy.[174]

She missed educated conversation and cultural exchange and was acutely aware of how the middle-class women were excluded, or excluded themselves, from interesting conversation.

I have just made acquaintance with Dr. and Mrs. Logan. He is a retired navy doctor, and has more general knowledge than anyone I have talked to here. For instance, he had heard of Philippe Égalité; of a camera obscura; of the resemblance the English language has to the German, etc., etc. Mrs. Taylor, Miss Knox, and Mrs. Logan sat in mute admiration while he mentioned these things, being employed in the meantime in making a patchwork quilt. Did you never notice that the women of the middle classes are generally too ignorant to talk to? [sic] and that you are thrown entirely on the man for conversation?

W. S. Hatton. Ridgway and Guyton's Wharf.
Courtesy Alexander Turnbull Library, Wellington, New Zealand.

There is no such feminine inferiority in the lower. The women go hand in hand with the men in the degree of cultivation they are able to reach. I can talk very well to a joiner's wife, but seldom to a merchant's.[175]

New Zealand women were, however, to win the vote before their sisters in Britain.

On her arrival Mary lived in Herbert Street with Waring. Wellington was above all a commercial and trading town and he had set up in business as a general dealer and import agent. He was also dealing in land. A considerable amount of trade was carried on with Australia and when Waring was travelling there Mary was left in charge, in effect, serving her apprenticeship for the business she was later to establish on her own account. As well as learning about business she was earning some money from teaching piano.

While Mary represented herself as on the whole busy and cheerful, Charlotte tended to concentrate on her friend's difficulties, suspecting she was homesick: ' . . . she finds it [New Zealand] too barren. I believe she is more homesick than she will confess'.[176]

Charlotte envisaged Mary enduring Spartan conditions, describing her as living in a log house, sitting on a wooden stool without a back, and with no carpet on the floor. Mary was later at pains to explain to her that the houses were constructed of worked planks with wooden roof shingles, though it's doubtful if Charlotte appreciated these fine distinctions.

A year later Charlotte is yet again thinking of Mary as lonely and homesick, but if that was so Mary was not likely to admit it, or give in and return home. Charlotte, faced with emotional problems, isolation and homesickness in Brussels had lapsed into a state of virtual nervous breakdown; Mary was more resilient.

Though towards the end of 1847 she was claiming that her health was better than it had been in Europe[177] she had nevertheless been suffering from 'constant low fever'.[178] She may have been suffering from the effects of insect bites or from the influenza which swept through the settlement from time to time. She felt much better the following year. 'She [Mary] spoke of her own health as being excellent'.[179]

Even into her 30s Mary says she experienced a feeling of never being really well. It's difficult to reconcile this with the dominant impression of an energetic, high-spirited and forceful personality and she perhaps exaggerated the significance and tedium of those phases when she felt less energetic, less able to cope with life.

I am most afraid of my health. Not that I should die, but perhaps sink into a state of betweenity [sic], neither well nor ill, in which I should observe nothing, and be very miserable besides.[180]

Rousing and lively most of the Taylors may have been but they had their dark and gloomy moods which Mary to some extent shared, and which she often noted in her letters with comments about Joe and John, their restlessness and depressions.

As she began to experience success in her New Zealand business so her health and spirits seemed to improve. Mary's account of her health written shortly before her return to England acknowledges her dispiritedness when she was younger and its effects on her general health.

> I wish I knew how to give you some account of my ways and doings here and the effect of my position on me. First of all, it agrees with me. I am in better health than at any time since I left school. This difference won't seem much to other people, since I never was *ill* since then; but it is very great to me, for it is just the difference between everything being a burden and everything being more or less a pleasure. Half from physical weakness and half from depression of spirits my judgment in former days was always at war with my will.[181]

There may have been a more objective physical cause of her feelings of lassitude when she was younger. The chest weakness of her youth was to recur in her fifties and leave her with a somewhat weak heart (probably exacerbated later by middle-age overweight and the heavy smoke pollution around Gomersal), but at this stage of her life when she was nearly 40 years old and experiencing the effect of her success she was in good spirits and enjoying improved health.

After three years of living with Waring, Mary was faced with the familiar unmarried sister problem. On a voyage returning from Australia, Waring made the acquaintance of a fellow settler, Dr. Frederick Knox, and subsequently of his family. In February 1848 he married one of the doctor's daughters, also called Mary.

Mary Taylor took a gloomy view of their prospects of happiness; she thought Waring was 'constitutionally hypochondriacal' and she entertained no great opinion of Miss Knox.[182] She enjoyed teasing her conventional sister-in-law, 'The lady is a Methodist and very religious',[183] shocking her by slangily calling her favourite parson a '*spoon*' meaning that he was foolishly sentimental.[184] She had a low opinion of the Knox family, generally, but especially of Dr. Knox.[185]

Charlotte uncritically echoed Mary's views of the Knox family. She also looked on Waring as 'a weak vessel' and thought that Mary had been sent out to New Zealand to keep him from straying.[186] In fact he ran a successful business for twenty years and raised a large family though financial difficulties and public disgrace were to overtake him in the 1880s.

When the young bride moved into the Herbert Street cottage Mary changed places with her, taking up lodgings with Mrs. Knox. She was not dependent financially on Waring but houses were in short supply. She was in business already on her own account, and beginning to calculate the possibilities of accumulating enough money to travel around New Zealand and then return home via India. Her estimated time-scale, which seemed to be something like three or four years, was grossly over-optimistic. She was doing quite well nevertheless, buying land and cattle with money lent her by John and Joe at a low rate of interest. She bought a cow, probably with five pounds sent her by Charlotte who, for some reason, thought she was hard-up and to whom she reported its progress.[187] As an investment she owned a five-roomed house which she rented off for 12/- a week.

Despite her earlier determination never to be a governess she earned money by teaching the daughter of a rich widower, William Couper. Mary knew her own worth and she drove a hard bargain, demanding £70 a year in addition to board and lodgings. Couper had a farm on the coast at Porirua six miles north of Wellington where Mary stayed from July 1848 to February of the following year. Life there must have been very uncomfortable. According to Thomas Arnold, brother of Matthew, writing in June 1848:

> . . . untidiness and squalor [which] prevailed everywhere, – no garden, no orchard, an ugly house, and a filthy homestead – everything else sacrificed to the one end of making money.[188]

Arnold's evident distaste for Couper was echoed by Mary as her work for him was drawing to an end: 'Mr. Couper himself is coarse, ugly, selfish, ignorant, cunning and dishonest and all this in the highest degree'.[189]

When she first announced her agreement to teach Miss Couper she had humorously commented that the community thought she had her eye on him for a husband. He for his part was on the look-out for a wife and appears to have paid her some attentions, 'interested civilities' which she disliked.[190]

Mary had no desire to marry him but she was indignant when in September 1848 he married one of the Knox girls, Margaret, because the bride was so very much younger than he, and scarcely older than his daughter.[191] She expressed similar outrage about the projected marriage of another Knox daughter to a man called Rhodes, whom she considered something of a rogue.[192]

Though getting money by trading, teaching and renting her house, she had not given up her ambitions to earn money by writing. Mary was not meeting with success as a writer herself but with characteristic generosity she welcomed Charlotte's success with the publication of *Jane Eyre*. While Charlotte had been secretly hard at work Mary had been lamenting her friend's 'dull, uneventful and unoccupied existence' and was amazed to learn about the book.[193] In the long and informative letter of (postmark) July 24th 1848 she praises the novel as 'so perfect as a work of art' and laments her own slow progress with only around 150 pages of 'my own affair' completed.[194] This 'affair' is presumably her novel published in 1890 as

Miss Miles. She sent articles to Joe for placing with *Tait's Magazine* and one for *Chambers* reporting the great earthquake of 1848 but they were not published.

In 1849, having left the Coupers, Mary went once more to lodge with Mrs. Knox. The uncertainty of her accommodation, her incompatibility with the Knox family and her loneliness stimulated her to write to Ellen Nussey, seriously trying to persuade her to join her in Wellington, provocatively arguing:

> There are no means for women to live in England but by teaching, sewing or washing. The last is best. The best paid the least unhealthy and the most free.[195]

As Mary was writing this letter and looking forward confidently to the future, Charlotte was wracked by the anguish of Anne's decline into death.

Dr. Knox returned to his family, making Mary's lodgings even less congenial and she made preparations to leave. Her decision represented another step in her advance to independence. She made arrangements for repairs to be made to Waring's old cottage which had been damaged in the earthquake and by the beginning of April she was preparing to move into it.[196] It must have been a great relief for her to contemplate the possibility of a home of her own for the first time since Hagen days.

Mary was now 32, and making progress only rather slowly. Her loneliness, at least, was soon to be ended and her career prospects were about to improve. She was expecting the arrival of her cousin Ellen Taylor and anticipating joining with her in a partnership either in establishing a school or a shop. Mary's preference was for shop-keeping 'decidedly the most healthy but the most difficult of accomplishment'.[197]

Ellen and Henry Taylor were the children of Margaret Mossman and her husband William Taylor (1777-1837), the youngest brother of Mary's father. Ellen (1826-51), was 10 or 11 years old when her own father died and the extended Taylor-Dixon clan accepted some responsibility for her and Henry (1823-99). Abraham Dixon took the 15-year-old Henry as an apprentice in Brussels. Ellen seems to have spent some time at Hunsworth but in the summer of 1848, when she was 21, Dixon was attempting to arrange for her to study at the Pensionnat Heger.[198] It was in connection with this project that in early June of 1848 Joe Taylor took Henry and his cousin Miss Mossman, to visit Charlotte Brontë to get information and advice about the school.[199] Charlotte was very bad-tempered about her visitors: 'it was all rattle, rattle'; they in their turn were offended at her reception of them. No doubt their enquiries stirred painful memories, neither was it a propitious moment for the Brontës to be receiving visits, especially if they included relative strangers. Branwell, incurably ill and needing constant attendance, was keeping the household in turmoil. He died on September 24th that year.

We don't know what advice Charlotte actually gave but in the event Abraham Dixon's promised financial support was not forthcoming because of one of his many, frequently recurring, business disappointments.[200] Early in 1849 the two young cousins decided to join Waring and Mary.[201] They arrived in Wellington in August.[202]

Rejecting the idea of setting up a school, the two young women decided, as Mary had hoped, on the alternative project of becoming shopkeepers. With money borrowed from their brothers they commissioned the building of a two-storey house and shop on the corner of Cuba Street, now one of the most important in Wellington.[203]

For Mary the days of a close, affectionate intimacy with a kindred spirit, lost to her with Martha's death seven years before, had now returned. Ellen was lively, intelligent and hard-working, eager for success and excited by this great adventure.

> Ellen has come out with just the same wish to earn her living as I have and just the same objection to sedentary empl[oy]ment.[204]

The two young women were simultaneously optimistic and anxious. They expected to make profits of around £300-400 but they were trading in a male-dominated society, were inexperienced and afraid of seeming foolish in their business dealings and risking a lot of capital. The journey to the warehouses took Mary into parts of the town she had never before visited in all her five years of living in Wellington, small as the settlement was. Neither cousin had ever worked in a business before, and had certainly never engaged in dealing with the public in a store. According to his cousin Ellen, Waring was very sceptical about their enterprise but helped them. Mary cheered herself with the thought of the benefit of Waring's experience and her own knowledge of the people of the town, her potential customers, but confessed a little later

> We were frightened, shy, and anxious [about the business.]. Neither the shyness nor the anxiety are at an end, as we very well know, but *we know* what we have to contend with and can never feel so thick a mist round us as there was when we first began.[205]

Nevertheless, Mary, who according to Ellen got as fierce as a dragon, penetrated the trading district, costing goods and placing orders and found herself being treated civilly! It was when she was ordering goods that she saw an advertisement for *Shirley* in material lying on the counter.

The recognition that self-reliance and the chances of success come not through contemplation and worry but by active engagement with the new and unknown, was to be the foundation-stone of Mary's views about women's capacities to achieve independence and influence the course of their own lives. At the same time it has to be acknowledged that Mary and

Te Avo House, corner of Dixon Street and Cuba Street. Windows arranged for the closing down sale in 1866.

Photograph courtesy Alexander Turnbull Library, Wellington, New Zealand.

Ellen benefited from the generosity and solidarity of male relatives. Though the men may have been somewhat sceptical about the success of the venture, Henry and Waring provided important support with loans, advice and, no doubt, useful contacts. The very fact of their presence in the community, especially Waring's, offered a kind of protection. Mary was also consistently helped by Joe and John who contributed to the gathering together of the capital of the shop, around £600-800 'as large a capital as any in Wellington'. Loans were often turned eventually into outright gifts. They were assisted too, by Ellen Nussey and Charlotte and by Amelia. They despatched boxes of scarce goods which would attract the women customers.

The pioneering spirit and determination of the two women and their good fortune in having sympathetic male relatives can be appreciated when we consider the situation back in England. Bessie Rayner Parkes, a women's rights activist, discussing, a decade later, the problems for middle-class women in finding gainful occupations, deplored the 'want of courage to face social opinion' by engaging in trade:

> ... the idea that a young lady cannot engage in business without losing caste must be conquered if any real way is to be made.[206]

Sharing the business and building it up was important to Mary but equally significant for her happiness at this time was the friendship of a kindred spirit. Ellen was sympathetic to her political ideas and shared Mary's cultural interests and pleasures.

> Besides nonsense we talk over other things that I never could talk about before she [Ellen] came. Some of them had got to look so strange I used to think sometimes I had dreamt them. Charlotte's books were of this kind. Politics were another thing where I had all the interest to myself, and a number of opinions of my own I had got so used to keep to myself that at last I thought one side of my head filled with crazy stuff.[207]

They joined in the setting up of a Mechanics' Institute, helping to organise dances, one of the 'non-objects' of the Institute as Mary put it. Together they were able to go into the nearby surrounding country on sketching expeditions, though they were somewhat amused at their own lack of skill. Ellen was a true Taylor, happily ignoring the niceties of convention. When a ship brought supplies of goods, the two women laboured at opening packing-cases and stacking away their stock. In a marvellously vivid passage Mary writes:

> How we work! and lift, and carry, and knock boxes open as if we were carpenters by trade; and sit down in the midst of the mess when we are quite tired, and ask what time it is, and find it is the middle of the afternoon and we've forgotten our dinner! And then we settle to have some tea and eggs, and go on reading letters all the time we're eating, and don't give over working till bedtime, and take a new number of 'David Copperfield' to bed with us and drop asleep at the second page.[208]

Housework, which in truth normally occupied very little of their time, was cheerfully abandoned when the letters and new books for which they thirsted actually arrived.[209]

> Letters have been recently received from Mary and Ellen Taylor in New Zealand – I wished I could have shewn one of these to you – it gives such a thoroughly characteristic notion of their way of life. According to the description it contained of their sitting room – neither of them were [sic] in the way of meriting the Roe Head Neatness Prize: they deserve on the contrary loss of tickets and an early adjournment to bed. More shame to them.[210]

Mary's social life expanded after her cousin arrived. Ellen was young and attractive and there were plenty of bachelors happy to seek out their company and enjoy the dancing at the Mechanics' Institute.

> I cannot tell you with what zeal I labour to spite the 'uneasy virtues' that are always saying something against 'promiscuous

dancing' – what a phrase. With many of them the objection is not to the character of their company but to their station. Of course *we* think our character much above our station. I don't approve of being so slighted.[211]

This enrichment of her life and expansion of her activities got in the way of her writing, not for want of time but because she was unable to give it the concentration it required. She nevertheless still held on to her hopes of going on with it.[212]

Within four months of Ellen's arrival the two women were hard at work in the business which was to become a well-established store in Wellington and survive Mary's eventual departure from New Zealand until 1866. Their happiness in their enterprise and partnership is reflected in Charlotte's letters to Ellen Nussey where she regularly notes how well Mary is getting on, how she is thriving.[213]

Ellen continued to be an enthusiastic partner and congenial housemate and Mary hoped that the business would yield enough money for Ellen to make the fullest possible use of her independence while she was young. Ellen, however, had been very ill on the journey out to New Zealand and must already have been consumptive. She died on December 27th 1851. Mary lost an irreplaceable friend. Once more she faced a life without an intimate companion, of relative loneliness and cultural isolation, once more a challenge to her strength of character, her stoicism and determination to make her own way.

Mary gradually bought Ellen's share of the business from Henry Taylor and settled to running the shop and living alone. Her letter of 1852 to Charlotte is subdued, sorrowful but stoical. She signs it 'Pag', the name they used in her youth.

> I am sitting all alone in my own house, or rather what is to be mine when I've paid for it . . . I have begun to keep the house very tidy; it makes it less desolate. – But the best part of my life is the excitement of arrivals from England. Reading all the news, written and printed, is like living another life quite separate from this one. The old letters are strange, very, when I begin to read them, but quite familiar notwithstanding. . . . I am just now in a state of famine. No books and no news from England for this two months. I am thinking of visiting a circulating library from sheer dulness. If I had more time I should get melancholy . . . Fortunately the more I work, the better I like it. I shall take to scrubbing the floor before it's dirty and polishing pans on the outside in my old age. . . . Oh, for one hour's talk! You are getting too far off and beginning to look strange to me.[214]

She felt her bereavement and its consequent loneliness represented a moral crisis. Deprived of a companion for whom she felt deep affection and who shared her interests and tastes, she recognised that she would have to steel herself to continue with her work. She feared her isolation might lead her to grow hard and selfish. Abandoning the shop and returning to England was not a solution she could contemplate. It would be to admit the failure of her whole enterprise; it would mean returning as the dependent, unmarried sister, the maiden aunt, the unmarried daughter. Mrs. Taylor was still at Red House alone. Mary had escaped the cage once; she was unlikely to want to walk back into it. Charlotte was saddened at Mary's obviously low spirits but she, too, saw no way in which Mary could get on if she returned to England.

> The news of Ellen's death came to me last week in a letter from Mary; a long letter which wrung my heart so, in its simple, strong, truthful emotion, I have only ventured to read it once. It ripped up half-scarred wounds with terrible force. The death-bed was just the same, – breath failing, &c. She fears she shall now, in her dreary solitude, become a 'stern, harsh, selfish woman'. This fear struck home; again and again I have I felt it for myself, and what is *my* position to Mary's? May God help her, as God only can help.[215]

Stoically Mary worked on at the business and keeping the house. She was learning her trade quickly and gaining confidence. The shop prospered so that in 1854 she was able to extend the premises. She is credited with importing the first sewing machine into New Zealand, not impossible since we know how heartily she herself detested hand-sewing. She regarded much of it as one of the forms of women's oppression, an outdated, time-wasting occupation. Through hard work she overcame her sadness and adjusted to living alone in the house, facing occasional alarms. One night, hearing something moving in her room and screwing up her courage to confront whatever it was, she found herself being lovingly licked on the face . . . by Henry Taylor's dog![216]

She cultivated the friendship of a few families whom she would visit in the evenings after the shop was closed, to enjoy good talk though she was later to describe them as:

> not many and no geniuses. A book is worth any of them all put together, Mamas included.[217]

Sometimes she attended local dances though she laughed at the bashful young men who were too lacking in self-confidence to carry off the occasion in style. Reading the books, periodicals and letters which arrived from England was one of her greatest consolations. In later years she told her friend Grace Hirst that when they arrived she would pace up and down the garden completely absorbed in her reading while her customers would come into the shop, take what they needed and leave the money without disturbing her. This absorption in reading never left her. Much later when she was at home in Gomersal her constant pacing of the floor as she read wore out a clear path on the carpet.[218] This great consolation in reading, indeed its necessity to her, explains the depth of feeling in her comment about women being discouraged from spending their time with books.

> Reading may be the amusement they prefer to all other; if they are not rich, it may be the only one within their reach, and tears rise to one's eyes at the idea that they may be deprived of it because 'I,' or 'we,'or 'they,' or all the world do not want them to have it.
>
> Let them undertake, then, the duty of providing for their own mental progress, as they must bear the consequences of neglecting it.[219]

By 1853 she had sufficiently recovered her spirits and sense of humour to send a long, mock letter to Ellen Nussey who had been been offered a position as companion to a clergyman and his wife in return, not for wages but for her keep and clothes, and some nebulous promise that they would remember her in their wills! This was just the sort of situation to elicit all Mary's indignation and her satirical spirit, and to outrage her shrewd business sense. The 'letter' was addressed to 'My Dear Mr. Clergyman and Mrs. Clergyman' analysing all the patent disadvantages of the offer.

> Your letter is as indefinite about the services you require as about the wages you offer. As to the companionship, affection, etc., I have very little to offer to a stranger, and it strikes me I should never have much for you. Your coarseness of feeling that allows you to pay me the greater part of my wages only after your death, your evident dishonesty in leaving the engagement so indefinite that I might do two women's work for twenty years to come and then have no legal claim on you or your heirs, your evident notion that an expensive dress and diet is to compensate for the absence of money wages, all make me think that your feelings, principles, and pleasures are very different to mine, and there could be no companionship in the case. As to my services, I would not give them without certain money paid quarterly, and certain time to be at my own disposal. These are what every servant gets! and I should want something more.[220]

In the event Ellen did not take up Mr. and Mrs. Clergyman's offer. Neither distance nor time served to weaken the bonds of friendship between Mary and Ellen. It was, paradoxically and sadly, to be proximity which divided them after Mary's return home. In the meantime they gossiped in their letters about their respective families and their friends, often referring to Joe Taylor as an irresponsible, flirtatious bachelor and later, after his marriage to Amelia Ringrose and the birth of their daughter, as husband and obsessive father. Joe became chronically ill, depressed and lethargic and, in addition, he and his wife appear to have been constantly worried by the health of their little girl. He died of a disease of the liver, probably the consequence of his work as industrial chemist in the dyeworks.

In the December of 1852 Arthur Nicholls, who for eight years had been Mr. Brontë's curate, proposed marriage to Charlotte. Yielding to her father's opposition she declined the offer but the relationship with Nicholls developed nevertheless and, eventually, they married in June 1854. Despite the fact that Ellen Nussey considered Nicholls not a good enough match for her friend Charlotte, she was confided in to some extent and in turn discussed the situation in letters to Mary. Ellen was content to leave the outcome to 'providence' who would, hopefully, have already decided that Charlotte had been born to live and die a spinster. Mary on the other hand had not struggled for her own happiness and material success to advocate submission to a pre-determined but unknown 'lot'. Women, she believed, had the right and duty to exert themselves for their personal happiness. She was provoked into sending a stinging rebuke to Ellen.

> You talk wonderful nonsense about Charlotte Brontë in your letter. What do you mean about 'bearing her position so long, and enduring to the end'? and still better 'bearing our lot, whatever it is'. If it's Charlotte's lot to be married, shouldn't she bear that too? or does your strange morality mean that she should refuse to ameliorate her lot when it is in her power. How would she be inconsistent with herself in marrying? Because she considers her own pleasure? If this is so new for her to do, it is high time she began to make it more common. It is an outrageous exaction to expect her to give up her choice in a matter so important, and I think her to blame in having been hitherto so yielding that her friends can think of making such an impudent demand.[221]

Perhaps Mary hoped the letter or the gist of it would be passed on to Charlotte and encourage her to strike out for her own happiness. Charlotte, however, had independently come to a somewhat similar conclusion as Mary. By April 1854, while Mary's letter was still on its way, she had become engaged to Nicholls and the marriage took place on June 29th. Miss Wooler, the former schoolmistress, 'gave away' the bride. Mr. Brontë at the last moment was unable to bring himself to do it.

Charlotte's marriage re-ordered the priorities in her affections and Ellen Nussey probably realised that their friendship would be different. She came to dislike Nicholls and in later years she certainly bore him a strong grudge arising from their disagreements connected with Mrs. Gaskell's *Life* and the fate of Charlotte's letters to Ellen. We know from her comments on

Shirley that Mary approved of honest marriages based on genuine affection free from mercenariness. She felt no threat from Charlotte's marrying and was no doubt delighted when Charlotte asserted her right to married happiness.

In this same letter of 1854 rebuking Ellen, we hear the first mention of Mary's prospects for returning home. She reports on the growth of the business, which became one of the largest in the town and on her expectation of having to work on for a further two or three years before she could actually prepare to return. She felt confident the business would continue to develop because of the expansion of immigration and the growth of New Zealand's trade. She was drawing additional income from rents from the house and from grazing land. Her hopes for the future were based on returning to England though she was somewhat over-optimistic in her time-scale: her two to three years eventually extended to five.

Charlotte Brontë died on March 31st 1855. For Mary the blow would fall when letters arrived around August or September. The tragic news was to be followed soon after by a request for information from Mrs. Gaskell who was on Mary's trail by July, asking George Smith, the publisher of the Brontë novels and subsequently of *The Life*, to trace Joe Taylor's address and Mary's whereabouts.[222]

Almost every statement in Gaskell's letter to Smith about Mary is wrong. She had Mary emigrating to Australia and living in Melbourne, setting out specifically to set up a shop, utilising her so-called 'patrimony'. Did Charlotte never speak about Mary to Gaskell or did Gaskell simply fail to register the information?

1856 saw Mary compiling her memories of Charlotte. Her response to Gaskell's request for information was characteristically generous. What she wrote was to prove very valuable and Gaskell resorted to using considerable parts of it *verbatim* to replace the material from the first edition withdrawn under the threats of libel actions.

Mary's search into the details of the past led her to regret her destruction of all but one of Charlotte's letters, that describing the visit with Anne to the office of Smith, Elder. Like Ellen she provided an account of her first meeting with Charlotte, described some incidents of their schooldays and the encounters between Charlotte and the ebullient Taylor family. Unlike Ellen she had no desire to represent Charlotte as some kind of unworldly saint. While she paid tribute to her friend's intellectual and moral strengths and acknowledged the personal debt she owed her, Mary faced up to describing Charlotte's problems of temperament; her tendency to acute depressions, her difficulties of social intercourse, her misery as a teacher at Miss Wooler's, the days in Brussels and Charlotte's despair towards the end of her stay there. But she understood the objective, social reasons for Charlotte's personal tragedy. The more she contemplated the frustrated and repressed life that Brontë had led, the sacrifice of her inclinations, the ever-present threat of poverty, the ill-health, the social isolation, Mary veered between anger and despair and declared to Gaskell:

> She thought much of her duty, and had loftier and clearer notions of it than most people, and held fast to them with more success. It was done, it seems to me, with much more difficulty than people have of stronger nerves, and better fortunes. All her life was but labour and pain; and she never threw down the burden for the sake of present pleasure. I don't know what use you can make of all I have said. I have written it with the strong desire to obtain appreciation for her. Yet, what does it matter? She herself appealed to the world's judgment for her use of some of the faculties she had, – not the best, but still the only ones she could turn to strangers' benefit. They heartily, greedily enjoyed the fruits of her labours, and then found out she was much to be blamed for possessing such faculties. Why ask for judgment on her from such a world?[223]

The complacency with which reviewers of the biography were able to contemplate Charlotte's sacrifices and loss of opportunity for a fuller life aroused Taylor's contempt. Though recognising Brontë's superior talents perhaps she saw her friend's life as a kind of paradigm of the lives and condition of so many more women of her day. Mary's motivation for continuing to work at her 'other book', developing the ideas which were to appear subsequently in the *Victoria Magazine* articles could only have been clarified and strengthened by her contemplation of her friend's fate though she was too scrupulous and reticent to exploit it explicitly in her own later work.

In 1856, Mrs. Taylor died and in March the following year, Joe died too. Mary's feelings of isolation, of losing touch with home, her sense of leading a culturally divided life, were intensifying, yet her longed-for return was being postponed. She was not accumulating money at the rate she had anticipated but again she fought her way through depression and at the beginning of 1857, now nearly 40 years old, she is attributing her health and energy to a sense of wholeness of purpose, to an ability to force her will to achieve what she would like to do. In the following year friends were discussing her return as a real possibility. Miss Wooler mused on what Mary would see:

> Many changes have occurred since Mary left England, and if a year must elapse before she again treads its shores, there may be many others.[224]

By the middle of June 1858 Mary's plans were clear. She had stopped ordering goods and expected to be in England during the following year. On leaving she invested £400 in the purchase of New Zealand land.[225] She was now mature enough to have developed an idea of some of the ways of being happy; a recipe she passed on to Ellen as she prepared for their reunion.

> Keep yourself well, dear Ellen, and gather round you as much happiness and interest as you can, and let me find you cheery and thriving when I come.[226]

Mary Taylor left Wellington on May 20th 1859 calling off *en route* at Wanganui on the coast, north of Wellington where Waring had property and where his brother-in-law managed estates. She was about seven months on the return journey, arriving back in Yorkshire at the turn of the year. Now almost 43 years old she was in good health, and enjoying the confidence which comes from personal success and a sense of achievement in the face of considerable obstacles. She had enough money from her business and from the inheritance waiting for her to live independently for the rest of her long life. At last she could establish herself comfortably, indulge her passion for books, for music, for travel and continue to work more systematically on her novel and on her 'other book'.

Chapter 4

The Emigrant Returns

Mary Taylor was one of those rare emigrants who actually return to their roots after many years absence abroad. Her own life up to 1860 had progressed more or less according to plan, albeit somewhat more slowly than she had anticipated. She had taken risks, left home, learned a trade, worked at it and accumulated property and money enough to return home to an independent way of life.

It was with increasing impatience that she herself had begun to look forward to returning but neither Joshua nor John was likely to indulge in any kind of rapturously demonstrative welcome. Mary's return would be acknowledged quietly, even dourly, which would be neither more nor less than she would expect. They had made preparations to receive her nevertheless, even though there were delays in her being able to establish herself in her own home.

John Taylor was still a bachelor despite Charlotte Brontë's speculations that he would emulate Joe and find a wife and he remained unmarried.[227] By the time of Mary's return he was living in a substantial house called West Villa not far from the Hunsworth mill. It was here Mary came, joining John and her sister-in-law Amelia who, now bereaved of husband and child, had vacated the house at the Hunsworth mill and was living there too. This was a merely temporary arrangement while Mary was waiting to move into her own home. As Margaret Wooler had gossiped to Ellen, it seemed that Amelia was not inconsolable, she remarried and as Mrs. Helsing, lived once more in East Yorkshire, in Beverley. Sometime after 1867 John, in his turn, emigrated to New Zealand, dying there in 1901.[228] Mary had doubts about his ability to prosper there and took the precaution in her will of leaving money in trust for him in case of bankruptcy.

Living with John and Amelia gave Mary time to arrange her affairs and adjust to relationships and surroundings which, though familiar in many ways from the past had, inevitably, undergone changes.

Mary's mother had died in 1856, having lived alone at Red House for eleven years. She died intestate, characteristically leaving problems with the family property which was put into Chancery. Joshua, as the eldest was the heir. After his mother's death he had moved back to the family home, bringing it alive again after Mrs. Taylor's lonely occupation of it. He had six children, three of whom had been born before Mary emigrated. In 1860 she found those three older sons grown-up and already working in the textile industry. A year later the eldest, Joshua IV, was listed as a manufacturer employing ten 'hands', though still only 21 years of age.

Joe, always a generous friend to Mary, had died in March 1857. Now Mary was to get to know the sister-in-law with whom she had so far only corresponded. In the early days of Joe's courtship she had speculated that Amelia might be German. Her family was English though she had in fact been born in Holland. Joe, 'cloth merchant and farmer, employer of labour' and Amelia, lived near the mill at Hunsworth.[229] Seventeen months after his death his little daughter, Emily Martha (1851-58) had succumbed to dysentery, so that Mary was never to see the child she had heard so much about from the anxious parents, and discussed with Charlotte. She scarcely had time to establish a relationship with Emily born 1849 or 1850, Joshua's youngest and last child, who died in 1862.

In 1854 Mary had been estimating that she would be able to sell the shop and return home by 1856 or at the latest 1857 and the family needed to make preparations for her to come into the money her father intended for her. The debts from the failed bank were by now almost all repaid, and the Taylor mill had prospered during the Crimean War with the demand for army cloth. The Taylors also owned considerable areas of land between Gomersal and Hunsworth. With coal-mining developments, other land they owned in the neighbourhood increased in value throughout the rest of the century. They were also extending their ownership of local houses. Despite this apparent prosperity Joshua, even in 1856, seems to have had difficulties in providing Mary's legacy. He had, it is clear, many demands on his resources. His sons at this time were still either serving apprenticeships or at school. It was John and Joe who had always helped Mary financially while she was away, who seem to have co-operated with him to make it possible for her to have what was due to her. In 1856, Joshua negotiated a mortgage from the two brothers of £3,000, the amount he was to hand over to Mary when she arrived home four years later.[230]

Mary came back to enjoy ample resources, interest from investments and the money she had earned in New Zealand as well as her inheritance. She became Joshua's tenant in his house, High Royd, on a site on Taylor land high above Spen Valley, among fields and woodlands with an outlook stretching in the distance to those same hills which she, Charlotte and Ellen saw from their Roe Head school.

She now had to make manifest her status as an independent, self-reliant woman to people who had previously known her only in relation to the rest of the family, as the elder daughter of Joshua Taylor, or the sister of the Taylor brothers. She had to learn to adjust to family and friends who did not share her radical ideas about women's rights and how women might live.[231]

Living alone as she did, carefully conducting her own affairs, regularly travelling abroad, seeing some friends but not much given to sharing social life with people she did not care for, the Taylor aura of a family of distinctive and interesting individuals hovered around the returned emigrant. As well as being identified as Rose Yorke in *Shirley* she was credited with having made money keeping a store in the Australian goldfields and (presumably employing the skills she had acquired there), guarding High Royd by shooting a round or two of pistols each night before retiring. She also became, in reality, that unusual woman, a published writer, with moreover, advanced ideas about women's rights.

Employing a living-in maid, keeping a coach and employing a coachman, she maintained her own independent household in the solid, characteristically middle-class, High Royd. She went her own way in religion. Joshua's family, continuing the Dissenting tradition of the Taylors, were members of the local Moravian Church which had been established in the village for over a hundred years.[232] Mary, who had attended Church of England services in Birstall before she emigrated, now worshipped at the local parish church, in Gomersal itself, near to her home.

Members of early generations of the Taylor family had attracted interest and curiosity notably because of their militant religious dissent or their political radicalism. Later generations were conscious of their unusual and interesting heritage which included the picture of the Yorke family and Briarmains in *Shirley*. This consciousness is reflected in the marginal comments in the two copies of the novel by Mary's nephew Edward noting similarities between the characters in the fiction and the relatives he remembered. In the interview that his daughter, Susan Taylor, conducted with Grace Hirst for the latter's memories of Mary, Susan briefly recorded her own impressions when she was taken as a child, aged about 5, to visit her great-aunt.

Hirst talked to Susan Taylor in 1931. Though Hirst was by this time 86 or 87 she seems to have been still reasonably fit, travelling alone to meet Susan Taylor and promising to visit her in the following summer. Susan Taylor was impressed by Grace Hirst's reliability, commenting that she 'Had [an] excellent memory for Swiss places and names – & names of people. Very sure of her facts, and you felt she was right in them'.[233]

Grace Hirst provided an affectionate, though not uncritical, account of Mary. She knew about Mary's alienation from her mother and Mrs. Taylor's unsympathetic personality.[234] She was also sensitive to her friend's reluctance to talk about the Brontës and was consequently circumspect in mentioning them but Mary, eventually, of her own volition, discussed them with her. It is our loss that Hirst left no record of what she was told.

Grace found in Mary Taylor a generous friend and mentor. Taylor paid for their holidays in Switzerland together and brought intellectual stimulus into Hirst's life. Grace emphasises Mary's generosity and kindness belied by her brusque manner of speaking and forthrightness. She also mentions, surprisingly enough, Mary's tact, a quality the elder woman felt she lacked. Grace describes how once, worried and unhappy, she had visited Mary at High Royd. Mary talked to her about everything but the actual problem, tucked her up to have a rest in the afternoon and only afterwards invited Grace to open up with: 'Now tell me all about it!'[235]

Mary's determination to do what she pleased and live as she liked probably did little to counter Ellen Nussey's view of her as eccentric; Grace simply says she was sometimes 'a bit cranky'. This may refer indirectly to her views on women's rights, which must have been well-known to her friends as she no doubt became embroiled in debates with them about her convictions, withdrawing from further discussion once she had failed to win their agreement.

Grace thought that Mary was deeply religious, though not conventionally so, but more notably, from all the information she passed on to Susan Taylor there is a complete absence of any reference to Mary's writing, either to the women's rights journalism or to the novel, not even a passing mention of Mary's opinions. Perhaps Grace Hirst and Susan Taylor, both women of independent means, both now enfranchised, felt that Mary's ideas had been rendered obsolete in the passage of time since her death. Certainly neither Grace nor the members of the Taylor family could have been ignorant of Mary's ideas or of her writing. In this respect she seems to have been as isolated as she was in Wellington.

As well as adjusting to relationships within the family Mary had to adjust to Ellen Nussey. Though the Taylor-Brontë-Nussey correspondence of the New Zealand period remaining to us is intermittent, there is enough to suggest that it is characteristic of a regularly maintained correspondence. During the fifteen years while Mary remained abroad, the friendship with Charlotte and Ellen had survived strong, affectionate and apparently unwavering, resting on a framework of shared memories and experiences. Stimulating, shared cultural and intellectual interests died with Charlotte, but feeling for Ellen certainly remained. Mary's last letters to her written before she started on her homeward journey breathe warm affection and eagerness to be back enjoying their lifelong intimacy once again.

Letters from afar were one thing, however; day-to-day encounters turned out to be more of a problem. The threads of their youthful friendship were not to be so easily picked up and rewoven into a new tapestry of middle years. In 1845, the two women, in their mid twenties, had parted to be reunited fifteen years later as mature 42-year-olds, shaped by lives which had run quite different courses and were to diverge yet further. Mary's career had been a challenging physical and psychological test of her character and principles; she had come through, successful and self-confident. Ellen had remained essentially within the family and the same local circles, living out the more conventional life of the unmarried daughter and sister, providing companionship and nursing, fulfilling her duties as she saw them conscientiously and devotedly, sustained by her religion and her faithful adherence to the Church of England, but often feeling uncertain and dependent on others for advice and assistance.

Mary's experiences in New Zealand outstripped anything Ellen had come across or could imagine, while her attitudes, as they had in the past, transgressed Ellen's sense of propriety. Ellen's own principles and values seemed to be characteristic of all the constraints on women's lives that Mary deplored. They were both stubborn and determined. We have no reason to think that Mary had lost her youthful habit of patronising Ellen and assuming that she knew what was good for Ellen better than Ellen herself. She had a forceful character, an independent spirit, and she now had the money to live as she pleased. This must have been irksome to Ellen, the dependent spinster who had given up a lot to others, willingly assuming onerous family duties and, as she grew older, feeling increasingly financially insecure.

Their early political differences probably hardened. Ellen was 'not only a good Churchwoman, but a sound Tory to boot', while Mary's more democratic views, derived initially from her upbringing, had been reinforced by living in New Zealand's less class-divided, colonial society.[236] She had retained her sympathy for working-class people and her attachment to such past causes as Chartism, Free Trade, even Luddism, while her concern for women's rights led her to be irreverent about male politicians and sceptical about their political parties. The two women seem to have had debates about politics. When Ellen was on holiday, probably in 1863, Mary suggested two books to her, Mendelssohn's *Letters from Italy and Switzerland*, published in translation the previous year, an innocuous enough recommendation which reflected her own continuing enthusiasms for music and travel, but her additional suggestion must have been offered as a challenge to Ellen as a continuation of an attempt to change her views. There was intense debate in Britain about the American Civil War and slavery. Taylor recommended *A Journey in the Seaboard Slave States with Remarks on the Economy* (1856) by an active critic of American slavery, F. L. Olmstead.

> If there is a library at Hornsea get Mendelssohn's letters from Italy [sic], also Olmstead's American Slave States [sic] and some others of his.[237]

Taylor's interest in slavery and her opposition to it was characteristic of many of the women who were developing the women's rights movement in Britain where women had formed an active section of the anti-slavery campaign as they had in America.[238] Her liberal attitude is reflected in her comments on the possibilities of freed slaves exercising full political rights in 'Liberal Tyranny' in the *Victoria Magazine*, of September 1874, though strangely Taylor seems never to have discussed the rights or culture of Maoris in New Zealand. While in her accounts of travel in Switzerland and Italy she comments on what she perceives as shortcomings, she is never chauvinist, never patronising and she seems to take for granted the enthusiasm among Italians for their independence and unification.

In addition to politics there were sufficient personal reasons to cause division between the two women. Among Mary's closest friends were the Richardson family. Isabel Richardson (c.1821-99), born Nussey, was Ellen's half-cousin. She had inherited considerable wealth and, much against the wishes of the Nussey family, had married her tutor, the Reverend George Richardson, for two years the Vicar of Gomersal, who was considerably older than she.[239] Though the Richardsons moved to the Church living of Kilburn in North Yorkshire their links with West Yorkshire were kept up as was their friendship with Mary which became closer as the years passed. Ellen who seems not to have felt warmly towards Isabel Richardson and shared unfriendly gossip with Charlotte about her, would have resented this continuing association.[240] There were five Richardson daughters some of whom from time to time accompanied Mary to Switzerland. Kate became a well-known Alpinist, Fanny was on the trip recorded in *Swiss Notes by Five Ladies*. A brother of Grace Hirst married the eldest daughter, also Isabel. In 1879 Mary Taylor was at Pontresina with Kate Richardson and the following year with other members of the Richardson family, including Mrs. Richardson.[241]

There was, however, a more fundamental reason for the rift between Taylor and Nussey which related to their feelings for, and memories of, Charlotte Brontë and to Mary's feminism. Charlotte, alive, might have provided the link to keep Mary and Ellen together. Sadly, it was Charlotte's posthumous reputation which was to be the main cause of their separation.

In her interview with Susan Taylor, Grace Hirst touched on the reasons for the quarrel which developed:

> [She] said that after she came back to High Royd there was quite a breach between her and E.N. – due she thought to the way E. courted publicity, while M. made short work of anyone who wanted to interview her or discuss C.B. and was very rude to them. G.H. said she knew of this and never mentioned C.B. but after a bit M.T. began to talk of her own accord.[242]

If Mary had strong principles and a mission, so had Ellen and she clung tenaciously to them throughout her long life. She dedicated herself to the rescue, as she saw it, of Charlotte Brontë's reputation, motivated by reasons and principles which clashed head-on with Mary's own cause, which included the rejection of demands on women for self-sacrifice and self-suppression. The seeds of conflict, dormant in their youth, when Ellen was more accommodating, now germinated, destroying their friendship and generating bitterness and intransigence. Though living only a short distance apart they were never reconciled. Even after Mary's death in 1893, Ellen was still expressing her resentment.

Though neither Mary nor Ellen provided any account of the quarrel about Charlotte there is enough evidence for us to appreciate why it developed and persisted. In the 1860s Ellen began to cast around to stimulate more publications about Charlotte and even began to express dissatisfaction with Gaskell's *Life*. Given the part she had played in getting the biography written she was, no doubt, justified in feeling a certain sense of responsibility for it, but either her objections had developed after the publication of the book or she had concealed her dissatisfactions from Gaskell while it was being written. Inhibited at the time by reservations about her own personal privacy she had demanded virtual anonymity from Gaskell, but, nevertheless, came to resent her exclusion from some share of the credit for the work. She read the manuscript and had apparently unreservedly approved it, but much later claimed that she had been sent it too late to read it thoroughly and make suggestions for changes.

> Mrs. Gaskell was under a promise that every sheet of the MS of the *Life* should be submitted for Miss Nussey's perusal before being sent to the publishers. 'This', said Miss Nussey, 'was certainly done but in a fashion. The sheets were sent to me hurriedly with such urgent requests to forward them at once to London that I had barely time to glance through them'.[243]

This does not appear to be an entirely accurate account, though Ellen was drawing on her memory of events almost thirty years before. According to a letter from Catherine Winkworth to her sister (both close friends of Gaskell), Ellen was staying with the Gaskells early in January 1857 shortly before the completion of the manuscript on February 7th. She must have had the opportunity either of reading virtually the whole work or of hearing it read. Nicholls had tried to place an embargo on Ellen having access to the manuscript and Mrs. Gaskell had sought to evade her promise to him by reading her manuscript aloud to Ellen, a subterfuge, which it appears, broke down.

> Saturday morning I went over to Lily [Mrs. Gaskell] who was unwell all last week, but was hoping to be well to write again this week [at the biography]. Miss Nussey was there all last week reading through the 'Life', and says it is excessively interesting and seems to approve it altogether. I saw her and wished I could have seen more of her.[244]

Ellen claimed that Gaskell had given too sad an account of Charlotte's life.[245] She also felt that it associated the Brontë family with the coarseness of the natives of the West Riding and the sisters with 'the sordid and shameful story of Branwell Brontë'.[246]

For her part, Mrs. Gaskell seems to have been unaware of any reservations Ellen might have had and remained in touch with her after the publication of the book. Their relationship was sufficiently close in 1859 for Gaskell to give Nussey the details of the breaking off of the engagement of one of her daughters. Clement Shorter, presumably repeating Ellen's information, assures us that the friendship 'was closed only by death'. [247]

It is unlikely that Mary would approve of another biography. She had expressed her opinion of *The Life* to Mrs. Gaskell herself and while applauding the achievement asserted that the whole truth could not be told. She would feel that Ellen, in complaining about the book, had been less than open with Gaskell. Given her shrewd business sense, she would also have recognised the commercial difficulty of launching a second biography after Gaskell's success.

In 1863 only six years after Gaskell's biography of Charlotte had appeared, Ellen was considering new initiatives. Apparently unaware of the nature of Charlotte's feelings for Constantin Heger, she thought it would be a good idea if the letters to him were to be published and she wrote suggesting this to him. Heger declined, not revealing anything about the contents of Charlotte's letters but quite legitimately urging the delicate problem of making private letters available to the public, an argument which seems not to have carried much weight with Ellen.[248]

At this time Ellen and Mary were still friends and Mary would certainly have known about the proposal made to Heger, and opposed it. Her rigorous sense of honour and concern for personal privacy which had led her to destroy Charlotte's letters would have prevented her from giving Ellen the real reason, adding to the tensions between the two women. Ellen would have found it difficult to believe that Mary knew something of an intimate nature about Charlotte which was unknown to her. Mary's resistance to further biographical publications she probably attributed partly to jealousy and partly to that eccentricity she had always detected in her, and which she later came to emphasise.

In 1869 Ellen approached George Smith of Smith, Elder proposing the publication of Charlotte's letters. She seems never quite to have accepted the distinction between owning the letters and owning the copyright. Smith explained to her that contrary to what she assumed the copyright belonged not to her but to Arthur Nicholls, Charlotte's husband, who was her literary executor.

The boycott which Mary imposed on interviews or any other participation in the 'Brontë industry' failed to stem the tide of Brontëana which in the early 1870s rose ever higher, much of it as concerned with the details of the Brontë family's private lives as with their literary achievements.

In 1870 Ellen opened negotiations with Scribner which failed because much of the material in the letters she offered had already been published by Gaskell in *The Life*. The firm did, however, publish some which had not been used, as *Unpublished Letters of Charlotte Brontë*[249] and the following year she contributed to the development of the persona of Charlotte with a long article in *Scribner's Monthly* in May 1871, 'Reminiscences of Charlotte Brontë'.[250] There is a detailed description of Charlotte's schooldays with a passing reference to 'Jessie [sic] Yorke' (Martha Taylor), but no reference by name to Mary. The main purpose of the article, however, was to counter accusations of irreligion in Currer Bell's work and in Brontë herself. The Preface is in the form of a letter to the Editor which ends:

> ... daily she was a Christian heroine, who bore her cross with the firmness of a martyr-saint.[251]

– a conclusion which Mary would have deplored.

Chapter 5

Travel in Switzerland

But Mary's life was overshadowed neither by memories of Charlotte nor quarrels with Ellen. She had worked hard for economic independence to fulfil her long-held ambitions to live more fully than most middle-class women of her day found possible. Charlotte Brontë was probably referring to Mary's love of travel when she depicted the young Rose Yorke in *Shirley* reading Mrs. Radcliffe's *The Italian* and declaring her determination to travel when she grows up. In the 1840s Mary had travelled already in Belgium, Germany and Switzerland but escorted by her brothers, now, back in Europe, she organised her own journeys, 'hallacking about', unaided even by Mr. Thomas Cook now organising Swiss package tours!

It was her love of travel and her ability to go independently that led to her friendship with Grace Hirst. It must have been soon after she had settled at High Royd that she was preparing to go abroad and was asked by the Hirsts, a local family, to escort their daughter, Grace, to the Moravian school at Neuwied on the Rhine between Bonn and Koblenz. This was a school with a reputation for offering a very good education to girls as well as boys. Her earliest, most vivid impression of Mary was of their wait for a connection on their journey when Mary sat, quiet and unperturbed, darning her gloves 'so practical and philosophical'.

Soon after this Mary had been disappointed in her two nieces from New Zealand when they were on a visit. They were brought by their uncle John to High Royd and invited by Mary to stay with her. John officiously intervened and possessively insisted that they were to stay with him. They shyly acquiesced and Mary, clearly irritated by John's interference, somewhat unimaginatively and over-impetuously, simply wrote the girls off as feeble and uninteresting. In Grace Hirst, on the contrary, she detected a spirited young woman after her own heart. When Grace's schooldays were over and she took up the invitation to visit High Royd, Mary 'half adopted' her instead. Grace was the daughter she would never have and for whom she acted in many ways as a rôle model. Though, as she reminded Susan Taylor, Grace Hirst had been to good schools, she declared that she had always felt that her real education had been given her by Mary. Part of that education was the opportunity to experience further travel.

Mary invited Grace to holiday abroad with her, and paid her expenses, on no fewer than seven occasions and probably more. One of these holidays in 1874 is recorded in the ironically titled *Swiss Notes by Five Ladies*. In addition to Mary and Grace there were three young women, Fanny Richardson, whose sisters had already been in Switzerland with Mary, along with Minnie Nielson and her cousin Marion Ross, both from Scotland. The *Notes* consist of diary entries from each of the five in turn, recording events and impressions of Switzerland and the Italian Lakes. It was not intended for commercial publication and Grace Hirst said they simply pressed their friends and relatives to buy it. It provides valuable impressions of Mary Taylor in middle age as seen by younger companions and also as she saw herself. The four young women obviously admired her and they were excited and grateful for the opportunity of a holiday she had made possible.

It is Mary, now aged 57, who opens the *Swiss Notes*, by introducing her younger companions, approving of them for their independence of spirit. Her relaxed views of her duties as chaperone and her confidence in their ability to take care of themselves reflect significant aspects of her own personality and opinions, particularly her view that women gained self-confidence by accepting challenges and embarking on action. Her robust and ironic reaction to petty conventions denotes precisely those characteristics which the socially timid Charlotte Brontë had deplored twenty years before as regrettably unfeminine boldness and indiscretion. Characteristically provocative, Taylor from the beginning refuses to shoulder the normally assumed responsibilities of the Victorian chaperone of young ladies and writes, 'As I take no care of them, it is fortunate they are able to take care of themselves' and adds that the one fear she had for them was they might suffer 'the weariness of doing nothing'.[252] The weariness of having nothing meaningful to do was, in her view, one of the major afflictions in the lives of middle-class women. She took pleasure in seeing her younger companions active, energetic and self-reliant.

It is left to Grace to introduce Mary. How to address her was probably a problem for the young women: however informal their relationship it would hardly have been felt possible in 1874, for them to address her by her first name while 'Miss Taylor' was too distant. They came up with 'Frau Mutter', not a solution to modern taste, rather coy and whimsical, but whatever the problem of naming there is no doubt about the warmth of their regard for her and affectionate amusement at her idiosyncrasies:

> ... [she] is always ready half an hour before the time; gets into panics about small matters, but takes the loss of her watch, purse, or head, with the calmness of a stoic.[253]

The journey progressed by rail, lake steamer and carriages. Mary's experience, shrewdness and command of languages equipped her to bargain successfully with carriage drivers, hire guides and arrange accommodation which, given local conditions, was not always very comfortable.

From London via Paris and Geneva, their itinerary took them on to Chamonix where they spent a week resting from the long journey and making excursions to nearby places. Though now 'a stout personage', as she described herself elsewhere, Mary was still responsive to the physical challenge of the mountains. Grace told Susan Taylor:

> M.T. must always get to the top of everything when it was possible
> – (but she had rather a weak heart, so could not do much real
> climbing). She always liked to stay as high as she could . . . [254]

The great achievement of the first stage of their holiday was the ascent of
Mont Blanc by three of the younger women, Grace, Fanny, and Minnie.
They were actively encouraged by Mary to take on the challenge of this
and other climbs which were physically testing. Mountain-climbing
certainly challenged those concepts of middle-class womanliness which
emphasised passivity, propensity to illness and timidity, but ascents were
being successfully made by women and attitudes were changing, albeit
slowly. The periodical, *The Athenæum*, had already commented in November
1869, 'As respects female I think the term "weaker sex" must now be
abandoned.'

The group went on to Martigny and from there made the virtually
obligatory visit to the Hospice of St. Bernard, where their Protestant
susceptibilities were somewhat ruffled. Minnie, the Scottish Presbyterian
who describes their stay, felt oppressed by the cold, the austerity of the hospice
and the harshness of the environment. On the morning of their departure,
out of courtesy to their hosts, the group attended morning service. Minnie
was disturbed by the richly elaborate and colourful Catholic ritual. While
appreciating the sacrifices made by the monks in living in that bleak place
and providing hospitality for travellers she and the rest felt the monastic
system was a waste of the men's lives. In her postscript to this account Mary
referred not very gratefully to the 'guest-master', the monk who received the
visitors and attended to their needs, neither did she intend a compliment
when she wrote, 'We all admired him for being so *lady-like*'. 'Woman-like'
would have been complimentary from Mary, 'ladylike' never![255]

The five women, though one was an elderly chaperone, attracted comment
and mild censure. Not all travellers were as prepared as *The Athenæum*
commentator to concede women's ability to climb mountains, neither did
they approve of women travelling 'without a gentleman'. Mary, not a very
representative chaperone, was rather satirical at the expense of a
conventional fellow-guest she nicknamed 'the waistcoat'. When questioned
by Mary about the condition of the poor in his part of the world,
Gloucestershire, he conceded that farm labourers didn't eat meat but insisted
they were nevertheless 'very well off':

> How could a Yorkshirewoman fraternise with such a man? We
> had scarcely even a language in common.[256]

They were no more fortunate in the next topic of conversation. He
'demurred to [sic] the propriety of ladies making ascents, or even travelling
without a gentleman: ". . . I should not like my sisters –"'; Mary's response
was that it depended on the girl:

... whether she was fit to go alone or not. Some girls perhaps – A slight glimmer of discretion came into my brain, when it was of no use, and there was nothing left for it but to go on with my dinner.[257]

'I should not like my sisters . . .' became a catch-phrase in the group, a joke at the expense of unnecessarily protective males. It was not only Mary who could cope with patronising male attitudes. Fanny tartly informed an American who thought they were 'very plucky to go about without gentlemen', that guides were much more useful on glaciers than gentlemen.[258] A 'talkative bystander' who 'thought he should not like . . . ', provoked the rather timid Minnie into deciding to risk the climb of Mont Blanc.[259]

What probably worried critics was the inevitable physical contact of women climbers with their Swiss, male guides. They stayed in the same mountain inns and shelters, the young women were often bodily supported, hauled and pushed and carefully helped along as they went along difficult

House at Evolena.

Evolena.

Swiss Notes by Five ladies.

slopes. Mary's view that girls had to be 'fit to go alone' was surely referring to this; for their part the four young women developed admiration for the men's skill, efficiency and tact.

A stage on their journey was Evolena, 'another of these little brown villages, with a white church'.[260] Still an exceptionally pretty village, still brown, it offers a gentler, more reassuring landscape than the St. Bernard's Pass. Tucked away down a narrow valley with its rushing river, the village provided only a simple, not to say primitive, rustic life for its inhabitants. Mary was not the sort of tourist who affects blindness to the life of those around her. Her sympathy for the poor was not selective, confined to her own country and discarded as she set out for foreign places. In Switzerland she observed the people closely and responded sympathetically to the plight of those for whom life meant unremitting toil and poverty.

> As a rule, faith seems to dwell with poverty and misery. 'Of course it would have been better for me to have died when I was little,' said a girl to me, 'but you see we must live till God wills it.' She raised her melancholy eyes to my face, as if she would willingly have heard a more hopeful view of things. But, so far as I could see, she was doomed to hard work and scanty fare, until she died of misery before her time.[261]

On the Sunday morning of their stay they watched the worshippers coming in from the surrounding homesteads dressed in their best clothes and then joined them in church. Mary was later to speculate on the significance of the division of the sexes that she witnessed there, with religion regarded as the concern mainly of the women, who remained in church for the next service, while the men stayed away: 'Oh, they think they have done enough'. If the men were believers why didn't they remain too, and if they were not believers why didn't they influence their wives to set their religious beliefs aside, and she asks: 'Was there always such a wide mental and moral separation between men and women?'

She noted how hard the women worked:

> It was at Evolena, that I followed a woman out of the village to the field. She carried a baby, a basket, and a scythe, and two little ones clung to her gown. She would spend the day in mowing.[262]

From Evolena Grace and Fanny, accompanied by guides, embarked on a two-day expedition towards the Matterhorn and a descent of the Zmutt glacier. Grace writes:

> It [the Matterhorn] seems to stand so alone, so proud in its conscious strength, towering up from a sea of glacier, unaided, unsupported by anything.[263]

Saint Nicholas.
Swiss Notes by Five Ladies.

Meanwhile the rest drove on to Zermatt, making a stop at another brown village, St. Nicholas. There Mary discussed with the villagers their attitude to Italian parish priests; they did not welcome them.

Reunited at Zermatt and after a few days further up the valley at Riffelberg the party descended via the Simplon Pass to the lush landscape of the Italian plain and the Italian Lakes, Maggiore, Como and Lugano. They stayed in very comfortable hotels, enjoyed sailing on the lake steamers, visited the gardens on the island of Borromeo, heard music in the evenings. But their main and final destination was Pontresina in the Ober-Engadin where Mary had frequently stayed with Grace. Their enthusiasm for the place fired the others with high expectations. They arrived towards the end of the season, in mid-September, to be warmly received for Mary's sake at the hotel Krone by the proprietor and his family.

> The Frau Mutter is quite an institution, a season hardly being considered complete till she has made her appearance. The usually pre-occupied countenance of Herr Gredig, our worthy host of the Krone, relaxes into a beaming smile at sight of her, and he is never too busy to give her a cheery good morning.[264]

Walter, the head of a family of guides, too, had great regard for Mary and for Grace 'who had made many excursion with him, and Fanny, whose sisters he had known'.[265]

The Krone is today one of the finest hotels in Pontresina – a grand, luxurious palace hotel, which only recently has passed out of the Gredig family's ownership. In Mary's day it was already catering for foreign guests and was popular with British families: the sons of the family were sent to England to prepare them for work in the business.

The high expectations of the young women visiting Pontresina for the first time were certainly fulfilled. As well as walks, climbs and sketching expeditions in a beautiful landscape, they enjoyed a ball given in the hotel for the guests and local people. Not the least of their pleasures was the sense of friendship with hotel staff and villagers and guides. The respect of the villagers for Mary was a passport to genuine friendships for the younger women. They, in turn, had great respect for the skills and independent spirit of the local people. Grace writes:

> We like and respect them all; their uprightness and independence of character being far more agreeable to us than the cringing servility we sometimes meet with. They all consider

Tailor's House at Pontresina.

Main Street, Pontresina.

Swiss Notes by Five Ladies.

themselves quite our equals, yet have nothing whatever of self-assertion in their manners. So it is with the Engadiners generally. We have always found them honest and trustworthy. If you give them respect and consideration, they will do any and everything you want, cheerfully and pleasantly, but if you treat them *de haut en bas* they are apt to become surly, and offend by their independence.[266]

In stating this Grace was consciously differentiating her group from some British tourists whose arrogant behaviour to the Swiss guides and servants they describe and deplore in their narrative.

For the young women the holiday provided an opportunity for vigorous physical activity, for the excitement of meeting severe physical challenges, and for freedom from everyday routines at home.

People ask, 'What pleasure can you find in tiring yourselves to death all for the sake of saying you have been up such and such a height?' That is just the least part of it. There is something delightful in the mere fact of possessing strength and power and endurance which enables one to encounter and surmount difficulties calling for considerable physical force. Then there is a buoyancy, a sense of freedom, an exhilaration in the atmosphere at those heights, which alone makes one glad to be alive.[267]

After three weeks the five 'ladies' reluctantly turned for home. They stayed in Paris for two weeks and then returned to their respective homes in Yorkshire and Scotland.

Mary's recipe for touring successfully in a group was, as we might expect, that they must each be self-reliant. 'They must each be able to go alone', and be able to walk, rest, eat as and when they would each unconstrained by the rest.[268] It could be said that this was, in general, her recipe for living.

The five 'ladies' returned to Britain still friends, despite the view that women were incapable of getting on well together. Mary's very first paragraph of the *Notes* implicitly and ironically glances at the debate, then going on in the periodical press, as to whether women were capable of disinterested friendship.

It must have been a reckless spirit that induced me to set forth for a two month's tour with four more people of the feminine gender . . . How could five women agree for eight or ten weeks together – especially when, to the every-day excuses for ill-humour, were added heat, cold and fatigue, much greater than what we have been accustomed to?[269]

The diary in fact is a celebration of women's capacity for friendship, the satisfaction in shared pleasures. It stands, too, as a tribute to Mary Taylor's generosity, the warmth of her nature and her large sympathies.

One consequence of Mary's admiration and sympathy for Swiss people was the assistance she gave to the Imsengs, the family of a guide.[270] Grace Hirst thought that Mary had first found work for the father in England and then she took a daughter, Clementine, as a maid. Clementine, though not very competent in the house, was apparently a pleasant person. She left and was succeeded in the household by her sister Euphrosyne, who was rude and careless about keeping the house clean. She was really quite young to be working in a foreign country, in the industrial North and unacquainted with middle-class domestic customs in England. It was a generous initiative on Mary's part which was to threaten relations with friends at home in Gomersal.

Mary always had a maid in the house. In one of her short stories, *A Servant Girl's History*, she depicts the plight of a frightened, destitute girl who, with no knowledge of household skills, has gone out to service. The narrator, needing a maid, takes the girl off her friend's hands, discovers her utter incompetence but pities her and protects her from her brutal father who comes trying to seize her wages. Though the story was unlikely to have had any immediate relation to any maid in her employment it reflects Mary's knowledge and sympathetic understanding of the fragile situation of young women who, without training and without friends, were thrown onto the world to make their own way in it as best they could.

> I have often thought what would have become of the girl if my necessity had not disposed me to make the best of her. She would have died of hardship; she might probably have spent two or three years in dying; but if her one hope had failed her, as it was on the point of doing, where could she have turned to get a living by her labour?[271]

As she wrote her story was she recalling the girl at Evolena who thought it would be better to have died young?

One of the chapters of *Swiss Notes* consists of a detailed description by Mary of her attempts on an earlier visit to walk up a glacier near Pontresina. She became disoriented and for a while gripped with terror unable to advance or retreat. Her account is an expanded and more detailed version of part of an article referring to 1870 and published in the *Victoria Magazine* of August 1871 as 'Notes of a Swiss Tour'. It gives us a rare glimpse of how Mary, by now 53 years of age, saw herself.

Waiting for a diligence to take her from Auronzo to Cortina, she was approached by a young Italian who was taking the same route. Her account of this meeting, ironic at her own expense, shows her without illusions about her own personal appearance, even careless of it. She self-critically expresses regret for her apparent rudeness to the young man, a thoughtless reaction to his disinterested kindness. Quickly recovering herself she shows a complete lack of chauvinism and genuine friendliness willingly extended to him.

> In the passage [of the inn] a young man raised his hat with very eager politeness, and asked if I was not going on by the diligence I said yes [sic] 'So am I' with a fresh salutation. With my English habit of isolation full upon me I was just on the point of asking – 'Well, what then?' but the French equivalent to this polite speech not being at hand at the moment I said nothing. He shut his mouth, raised his chin, and put his hat on. Suddenly recollecting myself, I said I hoped we should have a pleasant journey. Never was recollection more opportune or useful. He talked Italian for me whenever it was needed, changed my money, ordered my dinner, got my ticket, besides entertaining me in French the whole way. I puzzled myself to know why he spent so much trouble about a stout personage with few words, grey hair, and decidedly well-worn garments, and came to the conclusion that he liked to be of service where no possible motive but kindness could be suspected. And this motive, thank heaven, is common to all mankind.[272]

The magazine often printed accounts of travels from women reflecting the expanding possibilities for independent activity for those who could afford it. The sheer pleasure and stimulus Taylor derived from her Swiss travels are expressed at the close of her article.

> It is strange that the Swiss, who are perhaps, next to the Jews, the most cosmopolitan people in the world, should be thought peculiarly liable to nostalgia. I believe half the people thought to be dying of it are actually dying of something else, haunted all the while by the recollection of the bodily and mental health that they enjoyed on the mountains. High spirits and vitality float in the air above the limit of the pine trees. There is an attraction among the rocks like that of the supernatural, and those who have once felt it live ever after in the hope of once more standing among the desolate mountain tops before they die.[273]

Mary did return, of course, and not only in the year of the *Swiss Notes*. She was a guest at the Krone in 1879 and the following year, along with members of the Richardson family.[274]

Much as she enjoyed travel and popular as women's travel writing was, it was not typical of Mary's work for the *Victoria Magazine*. Her major aim in writing was to play a part in the debates about women's rights and to offer her views about the causes and forms of women's oppression and how it might be overcome.

Chapter 6

The First Duty of Women

' . . . this first duty, this great necessity . . . ' [275]

In her letter to Ellen Nussey, anticipating Mary's homecoming, Margaret Wooler had mused on the changes which her former pupil would meet. Apart from changes in the Taylor family, the Spen Valley itself was undergoing economic changes with the development of the manufacture of textile machinery and expanding communications.

Though the events of her novel were actually situated in an earlier period, Charlotte Brontë had noted the environmental impact of the changes in her own time in the closing lines of *Shirley* with its description of Robert Moore's new mill.

> The other day I passed up the Hollow, which tradition says was once green, and lone, and wild; and there I saw the manufacturer's day-dreams embodied in substantial stone and brick and ashes – the cinder-black highway, the cottages, and the cottage gardens; there I saw a mighty mill, and a chimney, ambitious as the tower of Babel.[276]

The hated Corn Laws to which Mary had referred in her letter to Mrs. Gaskell had been repealed, the Chartist Movement had passed away to give place to the Trade Unions of skilled workers, and 1847 saw the Act restricting the daily hours of work of women and children in the textile industry to ten hours. Legislation controlling women's working hours was to become a cause of disagreement in the 1870s within the movement for women's rights, generating debate in which Mary Taylor herself took part.

Through correspondence and the eager reading of contemporary periodicals and literature, Taylor had kept up to date with events in Britain. Her consuming interest was in the position of women in British society. She had emigrated and become a tradeswoman to escape the problems faced by many middle-class women which resulted from their exclusion from active economic and political life. Her emigration had in itself constituted a personal challenge to women's subordination and she had returned, successful. She had learnt to be economically and psychologically independent. As a well-educated woman, loving music and literature, with a command of fluent French and German, she experienced cultural isolation in New Zealand but she had proved capable of being self-sufficient and facing loneliness. Though feeling unable to discuss her feminist views openly she had worked on in private, developing the feminist theories she was to publish on her return.

Once back home she found the situation for middle-class women virtually unchanged but the women's rights movement was making its first tentative efforts at articulating its demands and establishing its organisations. It was beginning to identify the specific causes of women's subordinate position in society and the nature of the reforms that might change it. As women emerged into public political life they inevitably generated controversy. It was to these debates around 'the Woman Question' that Mary Taylor contributed in articles published in the *Victoria Magazine* which was founded in 1863 to provide a platform for the movement.

> ... I write at my novel a little and think of my other book. What this will turn out, God only knows. It is not and never can be forgotten. It is my child, my baby, and *I assure you* such a wonder as never was. I intend him when full grown to revolutionise society and *faire epoque* in history.[277]

The 'other book' seems to have formed the groundwork for some of her articles collected and published in 1870 as *The First Duty of Women*.

The editor of the *Victoria Magazine*, Emily Faithfull (1835-95), was associated with the Langham Place group of women who pioneered the campaigns of the 1850s and 60s for changes in women's status and opportunities.[278]

The magazine published a varied range of material. As well as features relating to the women's rights campaigns and related extracts from the contemporary press, it included travel articles and fiction, as well as poetry, reviews of books and exhibitions. It carried a valuable regular feature, 'Miscellanea', which reported the activities of women's organisations. Many of the articles were unsigned but authors named in the first volume include Nassau Senior, Frances Power Cobbe, Thomas Hare and F. D. Maurice. It carried poems by Christina Rossetti and Thomas Hood and fiction by Frances Trollope and Margaret Oliphant.

Mary Taylor's first article of December 1866 was provoked, paradoxically, by the *Victoria Magazine* itself. She challenged a review which had appeared in February of that year of the work of Eugénie de Guérin. In giving hers the title 'A Philistine's Opinion of "Eugénie de Guérin"' she was incidentally mocking Matthew Arnold who had reviewed Eugénie de Guérin's *Journal and Letters* in June 1863 in the *Cornhill* and was well-known for his attack on the middle classes for their 'Philistinism'.[279]

Eugénie de Guérin (1805-48) was the sister of Maurice, who died in 1839 aged 29. Enthusiasm for his poetic prose was stimulated shortly after his death when *La Revue des Deux Mondes* published his *Le Centaure* with an article about him by George Sand. Eugénie's journal, posthumously published, was also warmly received and awarded a prize from the Académie Française. The journal and her letters ran into numerous editions being first published in 1862 as *Diary and Letters* and in 1865 as *Diary and Fragments*.[280]

They record the daily life and religious devotions of a young Roman

Catholic woman, living for the most part in her father's isolated château. Hers is a life of self-denial, quietism, introspection and dependence. The consequent *ennui* from which she suffers she attributes to sinfulness and seeks consolation in prayer and religious devotions. De Guérin's worldly hopes centre on her brother for whom she is willing to make any sacrifice. Only through him does she contemplate the possibility of finding happiness.

Some similarities in the temperaments of de Guérin and Charlotte Brontë, cannot have escaped Mary Taylor. There are similarities, too, in the references to women's self-sacrifice and self-suppression, in the reviews of de Guérin and of Gaskell's *Life of Charlotte Brontë*.

In his review Matthew Arnold, anxious to distance de Guérin from certain aspects of Roman Catholicism which he believes Protestants find repugnant, veers uneasily between sympathy for the young woman's 'profound melancholy' while praising her spiritual quest for salvation. While regarding her self-sacrificing adoration of her brother as perhaps excessive he seems, nevertheless, to admire it, Maurice being, in his opinion, the superior genius of the two. He believed that de Guérin being a woman could not, in her struggles to save her soul, escape her sense of 'nothingness', whereas a man (like Pascal to whom de Guérin refers), could.

The opinions in the *Victoria Magazine* review were not characteristic of the magazine's general stance. The praise for the resignation and self-sacrifice of de Guérin provoked Taylor into submitting her own criticism. After describing the various mortifications de Guérin inflicted on herself such as deciding to write no more poetry because 'God did not ask it of me', and 'alternately sinning or wishing to sin, and thanking God she is kept out of temptation'[281] and how her hopes were centred wholly on her brother, Taylor, characteristically forthright, demands:

> Is it true that we are so placed on this earth that our life arranges itself without us? That we may wisely remain passive, assured that a superior power directs events? So far from it that there is no one so weak and incapable that their own exertions will not modify their condition.[282]

From there she develops a theme she was constantly to reiterate, in a variety of ways with a wide range of supporting arguments, that women should reject passivity, take independent action and work for what they aspire to. This is what constitutes their 'first duty'. She sees de Guérin's problems not as a Roman Catholic's problems but as those of any woman who lives by ideas which advocate women's self-sacrifice and suppression.

Taylor's pungency, liveliness and forthright assertion of women's necessity to work and reject the false values, which lead to idleness and dependence as their inevitable lot, were courageous and refreshing, departing from the often sententious and defensively tentative tones of much of women's rights journalism.[283]

'A Philistine's Opinion' signalled Mary Taylor's breakthrough into journalism. She was on the verge of achieving her long-cherished ambition to contribute through her writing to the women's rights cause. Her radicalism, debating and expositional abilities, range of knowledge and lively journalistic talent established her as a regular contributor to the magazine. Between December 1866 to September 1873 there were twenty-five articles or features with a further three from 1874 to 1877.[284]

The major debates around 'The Woman Question' were concerned with married women's legal status and their rights to own property and the proceeds of their own work, women's access to trades and professions, educational reform with entry to higher education for women, female suffrage and the discrimination against women embodied in the Contagious Diseases Act. Debates around these individual questions involved not only the merits of any particular demand but, almost always, gave rise to assertions that there are innate female characteristics which constitute an *essential* woman's nature, that her social function and status are naturally determined. There were debates about women's capacity for disinterested friendship and for self-sacrifice, their unsuitability for hard intellectual labour, their need for protection.

Mary did not accept the determinist theories of women's essential nature. As early as 1842 she had admonished Ellen Nussey for regarding the male sex as superior in judgment.

> There are two mistakes in the opinion you express as to the superiority of one sex over the other. 1st [sic] superiority does not consist in book learning and for proof I would take your opinion on almost any subject in preference to your brother Joshua's though he no doubt has read as much as you or I put together, and a little bit of Charlotte included.[285]

Mary Taylor contributed comprehensively to these debates. While not directly referring to the Contagious Diseases Act she did write about the pressures forcing women into prostitution in 'Our Feminine Respectability' and almost certainly when she refers to male immorality and the encouragement of women's ignorance of it, in 'Once More the Woman Question', she is expressing support for the campaign for repeal led by Josephine Butler.

The First Duty of Women published in 1870 collects fourteen of her nineteen contributions published up to that point in the *Victoria Magazine*.[286] Each chapter reproduces an individual article though not in the order of their appearance in the magazine. The Preface states the aim of the book as the inculcation of women's duty to earn money and suggests that, addressed as it is to women themselves, it will 'startle and anger the reader'.

Two of the most outstanding articles in the collection are 'What Am I To Do?' and 'Redundant Women'. 'What Am I To Do?' though constituting the first chapter of the book appeared only in July 1870 when the compilation must have been almost complete. It is one of her best. Its reference to an article 'The Cry of the Women' by Professor J. B. Mayor, in the *Contemporary Review* of June 1869, suggests that either it had never been part of the 'other book' or had been adapted to current debates. In the form of a direct address to the reader, it adopts the persona of an inexperienced, young, middle-class woman who, deeply perplexed, questions the conventions which condemn her to ignorance, inaction and possibly to poverty.

The youngest of three daughters, she sees herself as 'the fourth part of a housekeeper' sharing duties with her mother, her sisters and servants. She is told to engage in charity-teaching and visiting or in practising her music. She practises regularly but only parlour pieces or music admired by fathers and brothers seem to be acceptable. Her attempts at serious study have come to nothing because they increase her sense of social isolation; nobody is interested in discussing the ideas she has learnt. She queries Mayor's view in his article that the study of science is unfeminine because there is an established feminine type which is 'universally recognised' and should be preserved and is found in Shakespeare and Homer, typified in Portia and Miranda, Helen and Nausicaa. Taylor's own sardonic wit breaks through in the comment:

> A type that includes Mrs. Menelaus is a curious one to guard at all hazards. I should have thought that in the right type her existence was impossible.[287]

Taylor challenges the proposition that there is a feminine type which Mayor defines as including a merry heart, refined taste, common sense, generous sentiments and a strong sense of duty. As these qualities are to be found in many men and do not seem to exist in every woman, they cannot, she suggests, be essentially and uniquely feminine. Woman's rôle according to Mayor is to teach men 'sweetness and moral height', answered by the comment:

> ... These [male] writers seem to rejoice in the belief, that woman is a very superior being, while forced to admit that generally she does not act like one.[288]

Women, the young speaker declares, are prescribed for, never consulted about their own definitions of their natures or for their ideas as to what their social function might be or even what education they would like. The selflessness recommended to women is not much acted upon by others in their real and daily lives.

There follows a description of the family situation. They are not as well off as before and if the father dies the women will be left without means. A series of rhetorical questions articulates the very substance of what, in

Taylor's system, women's first duty should be; to reject passivity and seek to take action to avoid impoverishment.

Society, however, generally feels that women's first duty is not to safeguard themselves but to serve their families. Consequently within the home women often work laboriously at all kinds of domestic tasks to save insignificant amounts of money, when they might earn much more outside, use some of these wages to buy-in a variety of domestic services, help with the family income and still be better off. Wives of prosperous men buy domestic help with their husband's income and why should not women do this from their own earnings?

While women in the middle-classes and above actually command no money women of the poorer classes, even though they are worse educated, earn it. Why then, asks the young woman cannot better educated women find suitable and well paid employment. They could even engage in running businesses and in trade, though, of course their earnings and profits would if they were married belong to their husbands. 'Commercially speaking she could have no credit or character'. The conclusions she draws are that the scales are deliberately weighted against women, condemning them to dependence and probable poverty if they fail to marry and that 'these arrangements may be mended, and they greatly need it'.[289]

This chapter which is dramatic, clear and tightly organised discusses some of the most important and recurring issues that Taylor deals with throughout the whole range of her work. A letter in expressing appreciation of the magazine selected Taylor's contribution for particular praise.

> I also read a very good (as I thought) essay styled 'What Am I To Do?', that is read the article to a friend who was *against* women's cause.[290]

1870 was a wonderful year for Taylor's writing. 'Redundant Women' published only a month before 'What Am I To Do?' was the lead article in the June issue. It was one of Taylor's boldest in which she engaged with W. R. Greg's provocative 'Why Are Women Redundant?' Greg's article remained for a number of years as the classic statement of the anti-feminist case in regard to women's work and women's 'natural' rôle. First published in 1862 it appeared as a pamphlet in 1869 and was re-published in a collection of his articles under the title *Literary and Social Judgments*. The pamphlet provided the opportunity for Taylor to reply.[291]

In replying to Greg, Taylor draws on her extensive reading and reflects a deep understanding of the inter-connectedness of the many facets of women's underprivilege. With a series of questions she plunges immediately into the controversy and by the third question she has implicitly identified the injustice of Greg's case.

> It gives a curious feeling to a person of the wrong sex to hear for the first time the question – why are women redundant? It

conveys the idea – though not quite distinctly – that there are, in Malthusian phrase, no places for them at Nature's table. But why none for them exclusively? Why should not the redundancy consist of both sexes or of both in proportion to their numbers?[292]

By 'redundant women' Greg means women without husbands. He believes a woman's unmarried state to be unnatural because she cannot fulfil her proper function and is, therefore, 'redundant' except for domestic servants who, by proxy as it were, fulfil the feminine rôle of waiting on and caring for men. Those unmarried women who, for whatever reason, were not fulfilling their natural function were to be encouraged to emigrate to the colonies where they would find husbands and assume their natural rôle.

Taylor undercuts this basic point of Greg's by shrewdly suggesting that the problem is not that numbers of middle-class women are *unmarried* and therefore living unnatural lives, but that a significant number of those unmarried middle-class women are *impoverished*.

> ... the phrase redundant women really means starving women very often, and almost always women whose means have fallen so much below their position that they are miserably poor.[293]

By identifying the problem as one of economics and not one relating to 'naturalness' Taylor can advocate a solution for women's impoverishment, namely employment and adequate wages. The opportunity to work for themselves would free women from constraints and injustice and the dubious morality which underlies Greg's attitude to sexual relations and marriage. In this way she seizes the moral initiative from Greg, rejecting his insistence on marriage as a natural and social 'duty' and counterposing the view of the immorality of dependence and idleness, the morality of work, self-reliance and personal initiative. Marriage, she insists is no cure for poverty, on the contrary, many people wisely remain celibate precisely because marriage would merely exacerbate their impoverishment.

Taylor is angered by Greg's insulting concept of female redundancy and the cruelty of his attitudes and solutions. She notes that because their labour is cheap Greg is not actually opposed to women being employed in certain trades, indeed he is disturbed not so much by single women working as by women not marrying. He is adamant that, once married, women must not be allowed to work outside the home. He is also opposed to any measures, even charitable work, which would make celibate life tolerable for single women, especially employment, which would render them independent. Poverty is to remain unchallenged in order to force women into marriage.

> In plain terms, he wishes to keep single women poor. He wants their life not to be so easy and attractive as that of the married ... If the prescription is intended to force women into matrimony

who prefer a single life, it is offensively unjust; if women in general prefer matrimony, as he says they do, it is wantonly cruel.[294]

Taylor suspects that unmarried women have always been poor, that the problem has always existed and is not, as some women's rights activists believed, the result of some new transitional stage of social development.[295] What is new is women's vociferous complaints drawing attention to their situation.

As for Greg's approval of employing women as domestic servants because they serve men and 'fulfil the essential conditions of a woman's being':

> A housemaid is not supported by her master in any different sense to what a factory girl is . . . If a woman could be an attorney or a banker she would minister as truly as a servant now does.[296]

Here she glances not at those 'caring' professions generally advocated for women such as teaching, nursing and, by extension, medicine, or supervising other women in prisons, workhouses, and in charitable welfare activities but provocatively refers to prestigious professions in finance and the law.

There were disagreements among women's rights activists about employment for married women. Taylor believed that work for married women offered a sensible alternative to married poverty and that it should be a right, not merely a regrettable temporary expediency when times were hard.[297] She is close to the position of Barbara Bodichon (1827-91) one of the most influential leaders of the women's movement, in advocating this right and in insisting on the moral duty to work.

She refutes Greg's suggestions that umarried women should be encouraged to emigrate in order to find husbands, logically explaining that men in the colonies are no more able to marry without means and prospects than men at home. They too have to work and save in order to provide for wives and children. She also had reservations about the work of the Female Middle Class Emigration Society founded in 1861 to assist women to find posts and settle in the colonies.

Her sensible, down-to-earth objection to emigration as a panacea is certainly the result of her practical knowledge of New Zealand but she never refers to her own time as an emigrant in this article or elsewhere. Her silence reflects what we know of her concern for personal privacy and, probably, her unwillingness to relive her experiences. She could have said much about the problems if she had chosen to parade her own personal history.

While she never overtly obtrudes facts of her personal life into her polemics, the experiences and confidence derived from an unusual and successful working life, combined with her vigorous intelligence, good education and high level of culture, made available to her a wide range of knowledge and imaginative sympathy which she brought to the advocacy of her cherished principles, expressed in her lively, pungent and varied prose.

At this stage she was optimistic about the possibilities of progress for women. She believed that opinion was moving generally to the view that they should be allowed to compete in the labour market and that once this was conceded readjustments of opinions about women's rôle and duties would follow.

Other articles reproduced in *The First Duty* discuss not only the need for changes in women's material conditions, but the less tangible problems of the quality of women's lives. Taylor protests at the narrowness, monotony and triviality of much of women's occupations and duties, and suggests that the problems of women's physical and psychological health are intimately linked with these conditions and the moral principles and conventions invoked to justify their subordinate social situation.

Though fierce in defence of women's rights she is neither sentimental nor determinist. She sees that many women collaborate in their own subordination and refuses simplistically to transfer all blame elsewhere. While it is true that women are educated to accept inferior status they must, she believes, strive to break free or take the consequences of their own acquiescence and their acceptance of idleness.

She is concerned about the general perception of women as helpless and attributes it to the training of girls as only future wives and mothers. They grow up learning that men disapprove of women earning money, that they do not admire ability and that it is better for them to conceal it if they want to be attractive to the opposite sex. The result is they don't develop 'nerve and knowledge'; their helplessness may attract:

> Yet exactly in proportion to the attention and service that a man gives to helplessness when he wants it, is the severity with which he condemns it when it happens to be in his way.[298]

The commitment to 'self-sacrifice' which is said to be women's essential rôle, the perpetual giving up their own inclinations and desires leaves them eventually without strength of will or a sense of their own identity. Self-denial arising from powerful affections is a different quality, Taylor argues, a form of self-expression and the gratification of strongly held feelings.

Well-off women were often expected to work for charities and religious institutions and Taylor believes that those who exert themselves for the less fortunate are at least occupied and gaining a variety of experiences they would otherwise never have. But, she asks, if they can be permitted to work for others why not for themselves? and if they are encouraged to intervene in other people's affairs why are they not encouraged to manage their own? She actually doubts if many of them are capable of providing meaningful help for those in need because they are untrained and have no experience of life. She suspects that the main beneficiaries of charitable activity are not the recipients but the donors.

In 'Feminine Earnings' Taylor contrasts the situation of middle-class with working-class women. The employment in textiles of married, as well as single women, was familiar to her and she considered that working women's ability to earn money gave many of them a self-confidence and boldness that the house-bound, middle-class woman under continuous family tutelage, often lacked.

Taylor defends married women's employment on moral and practical grounds. She sees those married, working-class women who work to augment their family income not as neglecting their families but as responding to the most fundamental of their affections by seeking to secure their children from need.

> They are earning money that, the more affectionate they are, the more anxious they are to get. The work of earning it is most certainly their first duty. It is done in order to enable them to gratify their natural tastes. Can anyone blame them for doing it when bread would be wanting without it? Does anyone suppose they do it without such necessity? Are they doing right or wrong?[299]

Challenges to Taylor's rhetorical questions were already being voiced by the skilled male Trade Unions and many others urging that a man's wage should be enough to keep a family and enable his wife to fulfil her natural function in the home, to carry on her 'peculiar duties'.

Movingly she describes the hopes of women for their children's physical and moral welfare and for a loving and trusting relationship with them throughout their lives, a relationship Taylor herself never enjoyed with her own mother. Her observations on the effects of poverty seem to draw very directly from her own experience and aspirations. Not only does she describe aspects of what we know to have been the Taylors' financial position when she was a girl, but her style becomes more eloquent as if under the pressure of strong feeling. Poverty means women have to learn to do without, they see the impossibility of getting for their children what she characterises as some important features of a satisfying life such as:

> . . . the first-rate education, the improving society, the freedom from too early and too confining labour, the books and travels – all the means of mental cultivation and happy pastimes – . . .[300]

Compared with most women of her time, Taylor was well read but she had never had an opportunity of a 'first-rate' education, of systematic training. We might recall Ellen Nussey's comment to Mrs. Gaskell about Mary and Martha wearing clothes they were growing out of, or which were carefully darned against wear. Nussey seems to think they didn't care, but Taylor writes here:

> The constantly narrowing limit to that wealth [the family's wealth.] is a perpetual pain. If few complain of it, there are numbers who know it well; and most truly are they called the uneasy classes that have this skeleton in the house.[301]

Speaking, again no doubt from her own experience, she urges women to be bold and describes the respect they will earn by their success in spite of defying public opinion.

> . . . the most moderate success will convert all her opponents, and the mere fact of taking a decided course will gain her friends. She can be trusted when she has declared herself. She will be astonished to find that the dreadful self-assertion that was to exclude her from society is very respectfully spoken of by those who disapproved of it most completely . . . when it has been justified by success.[302]

While frequently reiterating the principle of women's need to work and earn money she also turns her attention to the psychological, physical, moral and cultural effects of women's economic subordination, providing an important corrective to the view one might otherwise have of her as over-reductive and obsessively concerned with the material factors of poverty, dependence and access to work.

'Feminine Idleness' discusses the problem of the psychological effects of what Taylor calls 'the oppression of the social law', which imposes on women, solitariness, inactivity, a feeble grasp on reality and whose consequences are depression, ineffectualness and a sort of 'half-idiocy'.

In 1858, while Taylor was still in New Zealand, Isa Craig (1831-1903), Assistant Secretary of the Association for the Promotion of Social Science, read a paper at the October Congress, 'Insanity: its Cause and Cure'.[303]

She explains that the numbers of lunatics appears to be rising with the proportion of women disproportionate to their numbers in the total population. She devotes a major part of the paper to alcoholism and extreme pauperism (literally starvation) as two major causes of insanity. She then turns to the problem of mental disturbance among upper and middle-class women, specifically hysteria and depression. These she attributes to defective education which concentrates on accomplishments even for girls who have no inclination or talent for them and which over-emphasises women's affective natures functioning at the expense of reason and balanced judgment. As a preventative she proposes a better female education with the development of a sense of social responsibility.

Taylor also discusses depression and the general social disabling of otherwise potentially normal and balanced women. We know, that while never 'socially disabled' herself she had suffered from mild depression. In a letter to Ellen Nussey of 1857, while discussing the improvement in her health, she refers to former feelings of low vitality and spirits, that state of 'betweenity' she had once described to Charlotte Brontë.

Rejecting the view of emotional and pyschological instability as a basic feminine characteristic, she asserts the primacy of nurture and activity in the formation of women's characters, abilities and mental states.

The themes of confinement, madness, delusion and masochistic self-suppression recur in nineteenth-century women's fiction. Mary Wollstonecraft's *Maria, or The Wrongs of Women* has a heroine imprisoned, treated as mad, driven to desperate flight. Jane Austen's Jane Bennett, Fanny Price and Anne Elliot all struggle with low spirits, Brontë's Lucy Snowe with hysteria and depression, Caroline Helstone's depression is depicted in an image of appalling physical pain ('You held out your hand for an egg, and fate put into it a scorpion'), while George Eliot's Maggie Tulliver seeks escape in religious pietism verging on hysteria.

Taylor believes the way of life prescribed for middle-class women is the main cause of mental and psychological problems. Excluded from the world of work, responsibility and social stimulus, sheltered from decision-making, they are required to develop a form of moral perfection 'easily practised in a convent, but best of all in a desert'.[304]

Life denied action and goals leads to obsessive pre-occupation with small concerns: this 'sheer vacuity leads a woman to fill her mind with imaginary things'.[305] This she regards as approaching the 'borders of insanity'.

She sees signs of improvement, however; women are at least developing the ability to move around unaccompanied and young women's apparent desire for change and travel and crowds seems to suggest that the shelter of their families is not attractive to them. But older women remain a prey to 'ill-health and the fear of giving offence to those on whom they depend'.

Women's lack of medical knowledge and the apparently widespread incidence of female ill health, were publicised by a number of women's rights supporters who were also campaigning for women's right to be educated as doctors.[306]

In 'Feminine Knowledge' Taylor suggests that women are reluctant to consult doctors because of the expense and because, ignorant of their own bodies and the causes of women's illnesses, they cannot judge whether they are seriously ill or not. Francis Power Cobbe in her article of 1862, 'What Shall We Do With Our Old Maids?'[307] argued that sick people turn for help to women who have their own medical skills, and that this justifies the admission of women to the medical profession as doctors. For Taylor, who mistrusts medical folklore, this justifies the need for better scientific and medical education for all women. Lacking it, they do not know how to improve their health, and their reliance on other women for advice explains why they so often talk about their health to one another.[308]

Though we don't know why, Taylor herself seems to have taken advantage of female medical folklore when she wrote to Ellen Nussey asking for medical advice.

> I thank you for your information in medical matters. It is so difficult for women to get that it is a particular favour to come by any at less expense, than an illness of one's own.[309]

More generally, women's exclusion from knowledge creates a sense of helplessness and depression, cuts them off from the power which men enjoy through education and their 'intercourse with knowledge' which is 'the next best thing to having possession of it'.[310]

> Therefore to have the intellect so trained as readily to take interest in matters foreign to its own immediate concerns, is almost as great a blessing as earth has to give.[311]

There is a surge of emotion in her reference to women's exclusion from good education.

> Those who have learnt enough to wish to learn more will feel their hearts flooded with envy at the luck of the favoured sex destined to be educated; who, from ten years old to twenty or twenty-five, are expected and encouraged to spend their days in acquiring knowledge, with all the advantages of first-class teaching arranged and provided expressly for their benefit.[312]

In all social classes women will be the intellectual inferiors; in those societies which despise learning they will be even more ignorant than the men. Her description of the nullity of such women, ignorant, powerless, unregarded, is brutal.

> People no more think of listening to them than digging up a corpse . . . and their joining in the discussion would call forth as violent a repulsion, if not as great a terror, as would a corpse walking about in grave-clothes.[313]

By contrast there follows an eloquent tribute to the power, influence and importance for women of books, her own intellectual life-line in New Zealand. Books will not snub them. In them they will find new self-confidence as they encounter ideas they themselves hold but which find no response in the immediate society around them.

> They no longer doubt their own sanity on those points on which they cannot but differ from their neighbours.[314]

Taylor expresses the intense delight to be gained from reading, which both provides knowledge and expands the emotions and human sympathies, bringing the reader into contact with other minds, expanding mental horizons and developing a sense of the infinite possibilities of human achievement and life. She quickly disposes of the prevailing opinion that men don't like clever or well-informed women. If men fear competition from competent women, Taylor thinks it is probably because they are not very competent themselves; 'her superiors, and even equals will not object to her advancing.'

Once a woman breaks with conventional constraints, takes charge of her own acquisition of knowledge, she will find that in fact most people generally, men as well as women, will forget their disapproval and even admire her for her newly acquired abilities.

In 'Feminine Character' Taylor deplores the moral effect on women from men's emphasis on their physical beauty, and regards women who seek only to please men in this regard as morally lost. Depending only on their personal appearance to win economic support they neglect the true means of ensuring their maintenance which is work. They are perpetually at risk of sinking into poverty and neglect and resorting to all-too-familiar petty dishonesties and subterfuges to survive or obtain what they want.

The consequences of women's search for husbands to maintain them leads often to marriages which yoke together conflicting interests with the wife pressing for more money and the husband resisting.

Her observations of some of her women customers in her Wellington shop provided instances of this kind of morality and its consequences. In a letter to Ellen Nussey she sketches a comedy of manners played out before her in the shop.

> Then the tricks they play on their husbands' head or heart [sic] or purse, to get money! And then the coolness with [which] they'll say they don't care a bit about it [some commodity on display] only they thought they might as well have it! There are some silk mantles coming about which more lies will be told than would make a lawyer's fortune; to me, their husbands, friends and neighbours. Don't think all my customers answer to this description. Yet it's wonderful how many do.[315]

Taylor's ideal of a truly moral woman is one who aspires continuously to live better who, seeing beyond her own subjective needs, develops moral sense in the course of action.

> Justice, truth and kindness are not innate, though they are sometimes thought to be so. They grow by practice, when room for such practice is given, and where there is resolution to cultivate them.[316]

The only justification Taylor can find for women's reliance on men's moral guidance is acquiescence in the rule succinctly expressed in Milton's *Paradise Lost*: 'He for God only, she for God in him'. Rejecting this tutelage

Taylor's advice, equally succinct, is, 'Let her not seek for "God in Him" for he is not there to be found'.[317]

Taylor's resistance to this guidance of women derives from her *laissez faire* philosophy of leaving people free to find themselves and to be themselves.

> The farther our mental cultivation goes, the less we trust the direction of our conduct to others, and the more cautious we become in assuming the responsibility of directing them.[318]

The debate in the periodicals about women's characters and morality continued for a number of years. Three months after Taylor's article, in March 1868, the *Saturday Review* published 'The Girl of the Period', an anonymous attack on women, accusing them of immorality and neglect of their duties. The author was Eliza Lynn Linton. Her article caused a sensation and provoked much debate and many replies in other periodicals. Taylor was to attack Linton's views in 'Revolt and the Revolters'.[319]

In her preface to *The First Duty of Women* Mary Taylor predicts that her message will anger the reader. Every chapter poses a challenge but with 'Our Feminine Respectability' in May 1868 she steps into a minefield of controversy, traditionally an ideological no-woman's land, which women were, nevertheless, beginning to invade. A public controversy was opening up as respectable women, in the face of wounding opprobrium, engaged with the hitherto secret world of the trade in sex.

State intervention into matters of sexual behaviour was marked by the passing of the Contagious Diseases Act of 1864 which reflected concern at the incidence of venereal disease among members of the armed forces. Campaigns of protest against the Acts were being developed because of the harassment of women alleged to be prostitutes (prostitution was not illegal), and the double standard of morality. The Acts focused on the forcible medical examination of women but not men. Repeal was achieved in 1886.

Taylor dealt not so much with the Acts as with the causes of prostitution. In 'Our Feminine Respectability' she reacted to a report in the *Pall Mall Gazette* of January 4th 1867 which aimed to arouse awareness of the prevalence of prostitution in London. As Josephine Butler and her associates discovered, it needed great courage for women to take part in public debates about prostitution, their opponents equated them with prostitutes, and occasionally the women were physically attacked. By including the article, which was originally signed only 'T', in *The First Duty of Women*, Taylor publicly acknowledged her authorship and demonstrated her willingness to risk the vilification which women faced if they discussed these matters publicly.

The *Pall Mall Gazette* reported an inquest on the death, through starvation, of the 7-year-old son of Rosa Easthorpe, a woman who, abandoned by her husband, had become a prostitute.

The linking of prostitution with the 'feminine respectability' of Taylor's title appears paradoxical; she had seized on the claim of the bereaved mother (whom she never names) that, once deserted, 'having been brought up respectable' and having no trade or calling, she had to resort to prostitution. The article creates a vivid, though speculative, account of Easthorpe's upbringing, which equated 'respectability' with bringing her up without any means of self-support, though her own family, a publican's, was hardly well off. With needs and desires of her own, marriage was her only way of satisfying them. 'And to marry, she must above all things keep herself respectable.'

There follows a bleak description of what Taylor imagines as a dreary marriage of convenience and its consequences; she getting whom she can, he settling for whom he can afford. Their struggle to maintain respectable appearances, which precludes her earning money, collapses; the man deserts her and she has to fend for herself first by selling matches.

> If once she forsook her principles and took to selling matches in the street the sin must be forgiven her. It was a very little one. Small profit or reward would she derive from her dereliction of duty; and the feeling of disgrace would probably overpower her when she looked on her pitiful earnings, and she would feel constrained to forsake the forbidden path, and turn to some authorised feminine means of getting a livelihood . . . And so she did.[320]

With a savage logic Taylor concludes that prostitution is the inevitable outcome of the principle of respectability the woman had been taught to live by.

> She was brought up respectable! She might have added – 'I have done honour to my training'.[321]

Taylor leaves for a while the contemplation of the tragic case history and more generally castigates the morality which recklessly, in the name of protecting them, actually denies women the means of earning a living and cruelly exposes them to 'the dangers of hopeless poverty'.

She then looks at some of the current arguments against women earning money. There are notions of women's 'proper place' as being in the home, that the fight for a living in the world outside the home hardens them, there they encounter evil. These ideas are the product of what Taylor calls evolving 'the idea of a woman out of [their] moral consciousness', instead of facing the fact that in real life hardness is as much a feminine trait as tenderness. Those few women who are self-supporting do not seem to deteriorate in character as a result but on the contrary the women who remain passive, waiting for someone to come along to take care of them 'are maimed for life'.

Reverting to her case study she suggests that if the woman had not been raised with false, 'respectable' values she might have acquired a decent trade but it is too late to learn one when poverty has struck and she closes with an impassioned denunciation of the prevailing concept of respectability and its possible consequences.

> A better morality, a different direction given to her own aspirations would have fitted her for an upper servant, an hospital nurse, a prison matron, for many a hardworking place that would have been paradise compared with the one she got into. And they had been within her reach. God forgive those who turned her steps aside! God forgive the cruel selfishness that advocates in any form that idea of feminine respectability that has weighed many women down to their lowest doom, that degrades and injures every one whose conduct it influences at all.[322]

Though the campaigns for a wide range of women's rights provoked public debate reflecting the strenuous efforts and devoted commitment of the reformers, there were, with the exception of advances in women's and girls' education, few successes to record. What was impeding progress in raising women from their low social status?

Taylor's article 'Crystallised Morality' looks at a possible reason in prevailing ideology which locks women into customs which are outmoded, out of tune with the contemporary material reality created by technological innovation. In its consideration of the implications for women of technological change and for its defence of industrial working-class women this is one of the most interesting of all the articles reproduced in *The First Duty*. Morality and rules are 'crystallised' in the principles and practices of the past which, ignoring changes and new possibilities, prevent women from breaking free

Once woman remained in the home, rocked the cradle and worked at her spinning-wheel but, argues Taylor, time-honoured rules for conduct are overtaken by new developments, hand-spinning and weaving are obsolete and women should seek other ways of earning and saving money rather than continuing to use out-of-date methods in the home.

Hand-sewing was also obsolete but some sense of its appropriateness as a woman's peculiarly praiseworthy activity still persisted.

> True, there are many in these degenerate days that get on without such a taste [for sewing] and the 'unco gude', who spend their days at it cannot point to any serious injury arising from their neglect.[323]

Perhaps Charlotte's aunt Miss Branwell figured in her memory as one of Taylor's 'unco gude'. The young Mary, on one of her visits to Haworth, challenged Miss Branwell on the utility of charity-basket sewing and was answered with a firm, conventional rebuke:

She made her nieces sew, with purpose or without, and as far as possible discouraged any other culture. She used to keep the girls sewing charity clothing, and maintained to me that it was not for the good of the recipients, but of the sewers. 'It was proper for them to do it,' she said.[324]

Taylor shows that the 'crystallised rules' which keep women poor and ineffectually occupied have been broken by working-class women in the industrial areas. She challenges other advocates of women's rights (though without naming them) who lament the moral dangers of factory employment for women and deplore married working-class women's employment outside the home on the grounds that their household tasks are neglected, and their husbands driven to spend their time and money in drinking-houses. She, on the contrary, applauds industrial women workers for 'neglecting their needle' and getting a much better living.

She sees the connection between women contributing significantly to the family's maintenance through their earnings and the egalitarianism between the sexes which recognises that women have a *right* to control money. She refers specifically to the Rochdale Co-operative Society, founded in 1844, 'and we believe some others', which ruled that women who bought shares should hold them as their own and that they should not be the property of the husbands.[325]

> Thus setting the law aside as coolly as the German Emperor declared himself above grammar. Is this regulation a sign that man will acknowledge that the fruits of a woman's labour ought to belong to her when they appear in the shape of money, or is it a proof that in the working classes she holds a higher position than in those above them? Certain it is that her labour, capacity, and personal character are of more importance to the welfare of the household. [326]

Taylor then looks to the future and suggests that domestic service will become an obsolete trade for women, a bold prediction when domestic service was the second largest category of employment after manufacturing!

Is middle-class liberation to be achieved at the expense of badly paid working women? On the contrary; she deplores the poor pay of servants and claims that employers as a result get inefficient and often dishonest service but confesses she can not envisage the new employer-servant relationships that might develop in the future.

> . . . some new relationship needs to be found between the buyers and sellers of household work. What this will be no one can prophesy. We can no more guess how our posterity will be served than the master and mistress of former days who eat [sic] and worked with their servants, would foresee the present separation

between them. The only wisdom we can teach is not to crystallise our morality round a set of circumstances in constant change.[327]

The occupation of governess she sees also as one of the disappearing trades and believes that is all to the good. The governess, though expected to teach nearly everything, can not possibly be skilled enough to do so; to get the best teaching girls need to be in schools in sufficient numbers to meet the cost of skilled teachers:

> ... each eminent in his or her own branch, and receiving each as large an emolument as a lady at the head of a school does now.[328]

Women do not yet value education sufficiently, says Taylor, though she detects some progress. The 'thick-headed' opposition which abuses women who seek an education by such terms as 'blue-stocking' or 'strong-minded woman' in fact seem to reflect a welcome movement for change even though they express a negative reaction.

She exhorts women not to waste time learning useless skills but to develop activities that engage both their minds and their bodies. She concedes that there are problems in finding employment for women but she believes perseverance will find it.

> It [employment] won't be in her proper sphere, most probably, since in that sphere there is no work but what is ill-paid. And this being the acknowledged fact a woman's first business is to get out of it. All her sisters will threaten to send her to Coventry for doing so, and may intend it, but let her not doubt the virtue there is in success.[329]

This is perhaps an echo of the declared intention of one of the Miss Woolers to cut Mary, because of her independent initiatives in Germany.

The final chapter of *The First Duty* is a review of February 1870 of the three-volume biography of Michael Faraday and though it gave the opportunity to advocate the teaching of science for women it comes as an anti-climax to the collection as a whole which covered a wide spectrum of problems relating to women's situation and rights. The work attracted some attention in the women's movement. *The Englishwoman's Review* declared:

> We wish the book to be as extensively read as it would be extensively very useful, if read.[330]

The *Victoria Magazine* for its part, quite properly, simply called the attention of readers to the publication.

> As we are sure that our readers will welcome this collection of Miss Taylor's valuable contributions to the *Victoria* [sic] we need only announce the fact of their separate publication.[331]

There was more to come from her, and perhaps she saw this publication as but the very first step on the road to more ambitious and influential work and as the gateway to becoming a professional journalist. Certainly for some women who broke into the profession there was financial success. Frances Power Cobbe estimated that she had earned £5,000 from her work on newspapers and periodicals, more than her inheritance from her father. For a further seven years Taylor was to maintain her contributions to the *Victoria Magazine*, continuing to engage in wide areas of debate, challenging well-known commentators and journalists and, in a modest way demonstrating also, the rôle fiction could play in the service of the cause. She extended her range with 'Notes of A Swiss Tour' and two short stories, 'A Tale', and 'A Servant Girl's History'.

'Feminine Profitable Labour' expresses her optimism. Unlike many she welcomed continuous social change, confident it would benefit women.

> ... we are in the presence of a multitude of innovations. Changes so many and so serious as to frighten the majority.[332]

Others, however, were inspired by the changes. Taylor was encouraged by the growth of an independent spirit among middle-class women, some of whom were inheriting more wealth than before.

> These independent women are, of course, less under the necessity of pleasing the world of possible husbands than their mothers were. They may be fast, or horsey, or charitable, or absurd in any way they like. They do not appear to satisfy the old-fashioned idea of what a women ought to be or do ... Let us hope at least they will not be vicious.[333]

A comment which Charlotte Brontë would have deplored as characteristically flippant.

Two of Taylor's most outstanding articles came at virtually the close of her association with the *Victoria Magazine*. When 'The Shah on English Laws' appeared, a new Parliamentary Bill to restrict women's hours of labour in industry was being introduced. The proposed legislation precipitated splits in the women's movement. There are clear indications of disagreement between Taylor and her editor. Labelled 'Contributed', the article carries an end-note which distances Faithfull from Taylor, who accuses the male-dominated trade unions of pursuing their own selfish interests under cover of concern for working women.

> We are always glad to place before our readers any article coming from Miss Taylor's pen, but in the present instance we feel bound to protest against the opinion she shares with Mrs. Fawcett, viz. that the men who are foremost in advocating the Nine Hours'

Bill, in the apparent interests of women, have a selfish end in view. – EDITOR[334]

Unlike Emily Faithfull, many of the women's rights supporters were hostile to the Trade Unions, sometimes on class grounds, or because some male Trade Unionists demanded the exclusion of women from their trades on the grounds that women's low wages threatened their own. Some women believed that male trade unionists hypocritically supported shorter hours for women merely as a precedent for advancing their own claims for shorter hours. Others opposed the Bill because it excluded non-industrial women workers in badly paid occupations who worked long hours.

Some women were for protection on philanthropic grounds; appeals for legal protection for women and children had already had their effect earlier, resulting in the Ten Hours Act of 1847. Among those favouring the bill was the small minority of Socialist feminists who wanted to see restrictions on employers' unlimited freedom to exploit their employees' labour. For them legislation for women workers was only the first step for protection for both sexes and for inroads into the power of the employers.

Those who had for so long campaigned for the *abolition* of legal constraints on women were suspicious of laws relating exclusively to them, passed by male legislators, elected by male voters and the result of political processes from which all women were excluded. There was, too, a strong adherence to dominant *laissez faire* views of ideas of economic individualism which held that freedom consisted in workers and employers being left free of legal constraints to struggle for changes which suited them.

In 1876, after the Bill had become law, the *Victoria Magazine* referred to a letter in the Report of the Ladies' Sanitary Association:

> [which] shows that while the Factory Acts interfere with the liberty of one class of women, others may slave with impunity . . . We do not point to this extract as indicating a necessity for the extension of the Factory Acts. Far from it: we hold these Acts to be in principle unjust, and in operation mischievous; but have not factory workers double right to complain when their labour is restricted, while their sisters serving behind the counter or in the bar, can with equal ease be reached by law, are left free, and can make their own contracts? . . . Government may interfere for the protection of life, and limb, and health. It has no right to place any impediments to the free action of adults.[335]

The difference between Taylor and Faithfull seems, therefore, to have been not so much about the Nine Hours Bill itself, as about the tone of Taylor's bitter attack on supporters of the Bill, with its accusations of selfishness and indifference to women's problems.[336]

The opening section of 'The Shah on English Laws' is an imaginary interview between the Shah and the British Ambassador to his court. The Shah had recently paid a state visit to Britain. Taylor takes it for granted that most readers would perceive him as practising extreme forms of the oppression of women, hardly an advocate of women's rights. Taylor satirically represents him as observing English society with an innocent eye and amazed at the economic disadvantages inflicted on English women and inconsistent arguments employed to justify them. Into his mouth Taylor puts a range of ingenuous yet logical questions about the Nine Hours legislation and its effects on women. The Ambassador's answers appear as fallacious, riddled with illogicalities, even hypocritical.

The Shah is amazed to learn that the proposed legislation will apply only to women in large enterprises, that it is designed to protect women from being forced by their husbands to work excessive hours, though the Ambassador concedes that only a minority of working women are in any such danger, and that these same oppressive husbands even after the new legislation is passed will still be allowed legally to take possession of their wives' property.[337]

> Then the Shah being much provoked, would look round for his executioner, and scowl fiercely at Sir H. Rowlinson, till suddenly recollecting the inconveniences that might arise from being angry with the wrong man he would turn round to his courtiers and ask who told him that these Englishmen worshipped their women and publicly required of all men to treat them as superior beings? And the attendants, trembling at the sound of his voice would all answer at once: Let not, my lord, believe the words of these abominable infidels. We know that their women have many griefs; that they are wholly in the power of their husbands, even of the most wicked.[338]

Further to the Shah's surprise he learns that it is regarded as unbecoming in the women to protest against the injustices they suffer and the dialogue section of the article ends by his concluding that he would prefer not to be under the protection of such people as support the Bill.

One of Taylor's reasons for doubting the sincerity of advocates of the Bill rested on the inconsistencies in the proposed legislation, its application to some women only while leaving the rest outside its scope. If women's hours of work were restricted their earnings would be lower, driving them back into impoverishment after a decade of some improvements in women's industrial earnings.

> Can it be in a spirit of kindness that it is proposed to fetter their hands?[339]

She launches a bitter attack on men's selfishness, for refusing to give up their powers over their wives' property and extends this to male trade unionists who spend much effort in improving their own wages but want women to leave better paid work in industry and get back into their homes. The reduction of women's working hours would endanger their very employment; what master would keep them on when men can work longer? When they are driven back into the traditional women's underpaid trades the increased numbers will depress wages further. It leads Taylor to conclude that the demand for the new legislation in the name of improving women's situation was for many of its advocates a subterfuge for ridding themselves of women's competition. She believes they are in fact quite indifferent to women's interests.

> If any woman, driven back to poverty by their interference, watches the fight for and against the nine hours' bill, she will see good reason to say, as she works through her eighteen hours' day, or sits at her tea and dry bread – they do not know, they do not think, they do not care.[340]

As earlier articles had shown Taylor was never overawed by well-known personalities. By the time her next outstanding article, 'Liberal Tyranny', appeared, she had already confronted such well-known critics and writers as Matthew Arnold, Professor J. B. Mayor and Eliza Lynn Linton.

She had already in 'Feminine Suffrage and the Pall Mall Gazette' presented the case for women's suffrage. In 'Liberal Tyranny' she took up the debate again in reply to Professor Goldwin Smith (1823-1910), formerly Regius Professor of History at Oxford, a well-known supporter of the Liberal Party and, though not a Member of Parliament, considered politically influential. He was a frequent contributor to *Macmillan's Magazine*, whose owner, Alexander Macmillan believed that 'Hardly any English writer swings his keen blade so powerfully and well'.[341]

Smith had been regarded as sympathetic to a number of progressive causes, signing the petition for women's suffrage in 1867, and reading a paper to the 1868 Belfast Congress of the Society for the Promotion of Social Science, *On the Adaptation of the Old Universities to the Requirements of the Present Day*. There he advocated the lifting of religious tests against nonconformity. His article in *Macmillan's*, 'Female Suffrage', in May 1874, shocked advocates of women's rights. The *Victoria Magazine* printed two replies in September, one the anonymous 'Fair Play v. Goldwin Smith'; Taylor's article was the other.[342]

Macmillan's itself also published a reply from Professor J.E. Cairnes who had been a founding member of the Committee for the Enfranchisement of Unmarried Women and Widows and was surprised by Smith's apostasy, writing:

> It seemed strange and almost portentous that the voice which had been so often, so boldly, and so eloquently raised on behalf

of liberal principles, should suddenly be heard issuing from the Conservative camp, in opposition to a measure which many Liberals regard as amongst the most important of impending reforms.[343]

The issue of the enfranchisement of women was once more pursuing its long and disheartening trek through the political landscape towards defeat. In 1869 single women householders had gained the municipal vote but, contrary to expectations, it was not to be the prelude to further suffrage successes. In 1870 Gladstone's opposition had contributed to the defeat of a Bill to enfranchise women and now in 1874 another attempt was being made, again unsuccessfully. Decades were to pass before the Parliamentary suffrage was won.

Goldwin Smith's article was a protest against the very idea of any female suffrage. He rested his case partly on reiterating the stereotypes of women which, by definition, rendered them inherently unfit to vote or exert political influence and partly on warnings of the dire consequences which would inevitably follow if they were enfranchised. Despite the reference to 'the best and most sensible women' of his acquaintance (who oppose the vote for women), the article is imbued with a deep contempt for women and fierce hostility to the ideas of J. S. Mill.

Smith examines women's suffrage in relation to the family and religion, its possible effects on domestic and foreign politics, and the danger of civil strife, if women were admitted to political power. He warns that the proposal for enfranchising single women was merely 'the crowbar by which the next barrier [to married women's enfranchisement] will be speedily forced'.[344]

The enfranchisement of married women would bring about the collapse of the very foundations of society and the disappearance of the family as a political unit; women would be able to act publicly against their husbands. Once enfranchised they would demand the right to be elected to Parliament and, as most women are engaged in the home, the political field would be occupied by 'adventuresses'.

These were familiar reasons for opposition to women's suffrage but Smith finds more. He fears for foreign policy influenced by women and claims also that as they are particularly susceptible to clerical influence, being 'priest-ridden', they will create the conditions for a tyrannical clerical regime. He appeals to the authority of St. Paul that women should be governed and urges that as women lack self-control their warmth and generosity would be dangerous in politics. Smith also stereotypes men; they are by nature able to wield power responsibly.

> [But] the love of liberty and the desire of being governed by law alone, appears to be characteristically male.[345]

If women are enfranchised Smith prophesies that men will resist laws made possible by a majority of women voters and the consequence will be civil strife and anarchy.

He also opposes the demand for access for women to the professions; the attractions of a pretty woman lawyer would undermine the administration of justice. If women were educated for the professions, even the race would be endangered; if the brains of both parents were taxed, children would be unhealthy. He holds up America's developments of women's rights as an awful warning. He concedes that in current circumstances when there are more marriageable women than men, and the cost of living high 'an abnormal and possibly transient state of things', justice demands that women should be able to work but they will drive down the standard of living yet further. Essentially, women need the protection of men.

Taylor answers Smith's article in considerable detail. Referring to his Liberal reputation she states that his arguments have been used by 'the most Tory of Tories against any progress whatever.' In prophesying civil strife because men will refuse to obey laws passed as a result of women being enfranchised, Smith had turned for a political parallel to the contemporary American post-Civil War situation and forecast that when Federal military force was withdrawn from the Southern states the white minority would defy decisions taken by a black majority. He seems in the interests of his anti-woman stance to take some satisfaction in this. Taylor, reflecting her optimistic, democratic views rather than a depressingly realistic political judgment, responded:

> The *majorities* must be the strongest; and even supposing them to be Negro, cannot be set at defiance.[346]

Taylor acknowledges Smith's concession of the claim by women for access to the professions even though he regards the demand as a passing phenomenon and spurns the view that women need the protection men can provide. What they really need, she says, is the protection that the law can provide which does not in any way preclude such protection as men might offer.

Smith bases some of his gloomy prophecies of civil conflict on the assumption that women will have one concerted view of politics, to which Taylor sensibly suggests that they will mingle into the general political life of the country, divided in their views along the same lines as men; an accurate forecast.

> The class excluded from legislation may look united, compact, and formidable, but once admitted, it is mingled with the rest of the electors. It gets a hearing sometimes – perhaps attention and redress, but even the largest does not become all-powerful, for *as a class it is never united.*[347]

Taylor's last article, 'Once More the Woman Question' came in July 1877. It is a farewell to feminist journalism. She looks back over the previous eleven years to draw up a balance sheet of gains and losses. Age – she was now 60 years old – and poor health may account for her deep pessimism. She sees some faint possibility of progress in the field of manners and morality which might eventually bring about emancipation but little in the material and political sphere. Her verdict is:

> While we are creeping forward in one direction we appear to be losing ground in others.[348]

The restrictions on women's working hours are in her view one of the backward steps.

In morals she believes the changes are marked by politer manners being extended to women: 'Even the *Pall Mall Gazette* has almost left off sneering against "woman"', and there is some civility shown even to those who believe there is still need for reform, even some support for specific, individual reforms, but generally the debate about the situation of women and the need to extend their rights has disappeared from view, the press is silent and in some respects women are losing out – even the changes in manners, which are merely a fashion, may well disappear.

> They have not got the suffrage. They have not got the power to own property if they marry. They have not even got the freedom to help themselves, to educate themselves, and work for their bread against the strong trades-union whose interests are involved. Have they got anything? or are they just where they were, when indecency and ridicule were the weapons used against their first uprising.[349]

While women have won the right to study medicine, in other areas their rights are narrowing. She continues to insist that married women have no control over their earnings, referring presumably to poorer women. While she acknowledges that one improvement has been 'the small means of education provided for women' she stresses its inadequacy because career opportunities are still restricted in the main to teaching. The profession will become overcrowded and wages low. Middle-class women suffer from boredom and a sense of uselessness because, paradoxically, as their families' prosperity expands they are excluded from more and more fields of action.

Their alternative to domestic tasks, the incursion into philanthropic activities is not an expression of disinterested charitable motives but a desperate means of self preservation.

> Now surely [t]his hard-pressed, suffering mass must make itself room somewhere. It has already found some queer outlets. The young ladies who cannot do any such vulgar thing as buy and sell for a living, can do both, and beg besides – for charity. The crème de la crème that cannot walk out alone, has of late years

taken to visiting in the lowest slums and talking to the lowest outcasts. Which is more likely? that charity for these unknown people tempted them forward, or that their own misery drove them out? In this way, and in this way only, could they get out. Had they tried any means of improving their own position, propriety would have stood in their way. With this plea of charity they could go round the obstacles.[350]

One small gain is an increasing concern for the improvement of women's health and Taylor believes that physically stronger women will evince more courage in fighting for their rights. Young women are still, however, under enormous pressure to marry even if it is against their real interests.

Counter-balancing her opinion in the early part of the article that there has been an improvement in manners towards women (though she is uncertain of its continuing), she cites Adam Smith to the effect that new immorality 'is the vice of the rich'. People are becoming richer, she says, and morals are in decline, men's morals now seriously threaten women's happiness in marriage. She challenges the view, still prevalent she claims, that young women ought not to know about the vices indulged in by men. In general, there is more concern about young women having knowledge of men's vices than about the prevalence of vice itself.

'Girls are not to know the real lives of men; such knowledge is degrading to them.' There is no doubt about the degradation. But if such stupid ignorance as these men advocate were possible, it must be under such compression as would almost destroy the faculties of a human being. No, the two halves of humanity improve or deteriorate together.[351]

She has reached the conclusion that voluntary celibacy is the most moral basis for women to achieve independence even though their social influence is thereby diminished. Despite older women advising their daughters to resist unsatisfactory marriage she believes that few young women can 'brace themselves to celibacy', but that if they marry 'for bread' they lay themselves open to oppression and insults. The only other hope she sees is in the growing protest against what she terms 'this advancing profligacy' with the concomitant demand for a higher level of morality in men and within marriage, but she seems doubtful if the protest will engage the attention of most women. The demand that they know nothing of men's vice, necessarily precludes them from fighting against it.

It is a thing to pray for, but – is it a thing we may reasonably hope for? Strange to say, feminine morality does not include even a wish on the subject. They have to profess not to be aware of the existence of the struggle.[352]

Taylor's stress on moral reform seems to reflect the influence of the moral purity movement which, in alliance with some women's rights campaigners such as Josephine Butler, was engaged in the struggle against the Contagious Diseases Act.

At one level Taylor's estimate that very little progress had been made was correct. The scale of personal effort extended during two decades in the women's campaigns would seem out of all proportion to the modest achievements actually registered by 1877, but with hindsight we can see that important foundations were laid for some successful future developments. Mary Taylor was among those many women who made an important though largely unrecognised contribution to the successes that were to come. Even if Taylor had thought it worthwhile continuing with her journalism she would have produced little more for the *Victoria Magazine*. This remarkable achievement in the history of women's journalism and publishing, closed in 1880, symptomatic perhaps of the stagnation which appeared to be afflicting the women's movement.

Taylor wrote well, logically, trenchantly and vividly. She exercised conscious art in her efforts to persuade, varying her methods from straight exposition to dialogue and the creation of lively cameos of imaginary situations to illuminate her ideas and arguments. She drew on a wide range of knowledge of literature, economics, politics and philosophy. Before her association with the *Victoria Magazine* ended in 1877 she had published, in addition to articles, two short stories. The novel was probably still not completed but these two short pieces show that in her fiction, as in her journalism, she hoped to serve the women's cause.

Chapter 7

Brontë Biography: The Taylor Family

Mary Taylor's entry into public debate as a vigorous advocate of the women's cause would further alienate her from Ellen Nussey, who remained much more within the confines of conventional West Yorkshire life than Taylor. Ellen continued to dedicate her energies to what was to be her own cause – the defence and promotion of her dearest friend's memory and reputation. In the process she was contributing to the creation of an ideal image of Charlotte – Charlotte as saint – Charlotte as noble and self-sacrificing – Charlotte as the model daughter of a Church of England clergyman – Charlotte as the perfect lady.

In 1876, almost twenty years after the appearance of Gaskell's *Life,* she succeeded in encouraging work on a new biography and incidentally giving further offence, not only to Mary Taylor but to other members of the family. The author Wemyss Reid, who was to become a distinguished editor of the *Leeds Mercury,* describes in his *Memoirs* how, after delivering a public lecture in Leeds on the Brontës, he was invited by Nussey to visit her. She criticised Gaskell's work and to Reid's astonishment proposed that he should be the one to write a new biography. His initial view corresponded to what we can surmise of Mary Taylor's. As a warm admirer of Gaskell's achievement he considered there was no need for another but, eventually, he compromised with articles which were published by a somewhat reluctant editor in *Macmillan's Magazine,* based on letters provided by Nussey.[353] As they turned out to be highly successful with readers, the articles were collected, expanded and published as *Charlotte Brontë: A Monograph.*

Among the letters that Ellen showed to Reid were those from Charlotte giving an account of the difficulties and anxieties arising from Nicholls's proposal of marriage. Reid declined to use them. He believed that such intimate details of Charlotte's personal life should not be made public.

> ... I was not in sympathy with the public curiosity which aspired to know everything that there was to tell about the Brontës without regard to its intrinsic interest, or to that decent reticence which even the dead have a right to expect from us.[354]

Ellen pressed Reid to write in detail about Charlotte's time in Brussels but like Gaskell before him he had suspected the real situation and confined himself only to discussing Heger's intellectual influence on her.[355]

Like Mary Taylor, Nicholls the widower kept silent and wanted Ellen to do the same. By tenaciously exercising his rights as owner of the copyright of Brontë manuscripts and letters, he was able to frustrate a succession of initiatives that Ellen tried to launch. He complained to Reid when the original *Macmillan* articles appeared. Though Reid's *Monograph* was a success he published no further work on the Brontës, perhaps because of the controversies around privacy in which he came to be involved later, though he actively supported the Brontë Society founded in December 1893. His Preface to the *Monograph* acknowledges Nussey's help and in his *Memoirs* he says that he gave her part of the £100 which he was paid by Macmillans; it was probably one third of the sum.

Wemyss Reid indicates his sensitivity to the perennial problem of biographical writing of how far the public has the right to know about the intimate details of the life of the subject. Like him, Mary Taylor did not believe the public had such a right and she thought they would refuse to believe the full truth about Charlotte's life even if they were to be presented with it. Mary was herself reserved, a very private person, and it was as a result of Ellen's success in persuading Reid to undertake another biography of Charlotte that aspects of her own life were to be made public and those of some other members of the Taylor family. Though she was not above gossiping in her letters with both Charlotte and Ellen, it was surely on the assumption that they, like herself, would respect confidences. It was to protect confidences that she had destroyed Charlotte's letters and guarded her knowledge of Charlotte's feelings for Heger even from Ellen.

A significant cause of Mary's feelings of anger towards the Brontë 'industry' was the interpretation placed by contemporary biographers and critics in their accounts of Charlotte. Where they lauded Brontë's self-sacrifice as noble, Taylor regretted a tragic waste of opportunity, deplorable self-suppression and sacrifice to the selfishness of others. What they approved as a model of the way women should live, she saw as the undermining of women's rights to happiness and individual self-realisation. The reception of Gaskell's biography had already in the 1850s brought to Mary the only too-painful realisation that the concepts of womanhood which inspired Gaskell and the critics conflicted with her own. She had despaired then of influencing the prevailing opinion, a pessimism further intensified as she grew older and came to doubt the possibilities of meaningful progress in winning new rights for women.

With the growth of interest in Brontë biography and the use being made of letters in Ellen's possession, Taylor must have been aware of the possibility that there might be interest in publishing her own letters to Ellen for what they might add to knowledge about Charlotte. This was another potential source of conflict. If Ellen was uninhibited about the publication of Brontë's private letters, she might be willing to collaborate in attempts to publish Mary's. The copyright of her letters was of course owned by Mary herself and she was in a position to obstruct Ellen. Her general policy of refusing to give interviews reflected a determination to frustrate if possible any publishing projects which Ellen might wish to promote.

Discussion of Charlotte's marriage crisis and the time in Brussels apart, Wemyss Reid was clearly in sympathy with Ellen's image of Charlotte, his view probably reinforced by Margaret Wooler, whom he also interviewed. Reid's work exemplifies how Mary was being virtually written out of the Brontë story, and how influential Ellen's view of Charlotte and their friendship was becoming. Charlotte is represented by Reid as having one close friend only 'a solitary friend to whom she clung with such passionate affection throughout her life': 'Charlotte Brontë kept up the closest and most confidential intercourse with her one life-long friend'. While there are references to 'Mary' and to 'M' there is no explanation of who she was. Though we learn that at Roe Head Charlotte made two special friends, only Ellen Nussey is named. In the brief references to *Shirley*, while Ellen is said to be the original of Caroline Helstone and Emily of Shirley herself, and Patrick Brontë is offered as, partially, the model for Helstone, there is no reference whatever to Rose Yorke or to the well-rehearsed parallels between the Taylors and the Yorke family.

Reid tried to respond to Ellen's desire to have Charlotte depicted as happier and more spirited than in *The Life* but, as Gaskell had been, he was anxious also to present her and her sisters as models of womanly nobility.

> Alas! those who knew her and her sisters well during their brief lives are few in number now. The Brontës who plucked the flower of fame out of the thorny waste in which their lots were cast survive in their books and in Mrs. Gaskell's biography. But the Brontës, the women who lived and suffered thirty years ago, and whose characters were instinct with so rare and lofty a nobility, so keen a sensitiveness, so pure a nobility, are known no longer.[356]

He summarises Charlotte's life as:

> ... a life that was made sacred and noble by the self-suppression and patient endurance which were its most marked characteristics.'[357]

The final paragraph of the work returns to this theme.

> ... we see that the artist is greater than her works that the woman is nobler and purer than the writer, and that by her life, even more than by her labours, the author of 'Jane Eyre', must always teach us those lessons of courage, self-sacrifice, and patient endurance of which our poor humanity stands in such pressing and constant need.[358]

This was just the sort of estimate which angered Mary Taylor as the expression of values which she regarded as oppressive and which she had already attacked in her published articles.

Though Reid had declined to reprint the correspondence about Charlotte's engagement and marriage to Nicholls and the crisis provoked by Patrick Brontë's opposition, the Taylors, including Amelia, were not similarly spared. He reprinted parts of Charlotte's letters which refer to members of the Taylor family, thinly disguising them by initial letters. For those readers who already knew something about Brontë's life and the parallels between the Yorkes in *Shirley* and the Taylor family, the 'disguise' would be somewhat transparent.

Charlotte's comments about Joe's engagement to Amelia Ringrose, accusing him of mercenariness, of being 'a cold and unloving suitor' and her melodramatic declaration 'Nature and justice forbid the banns of such wedlock', became public. The world, as well as Mary herself, could now read about Charlotte's appreciation of Mary's 'original and vigorous cast of [her] mind', but there were the criticisms too.

> [a] certain tendency to flightiness . . . Perhaps *flightiness* is not the right word; but it is a devil-may-care tone which I do not like when it proceeds from under a hat, and still less from under a bonnet.[359]

There are also comments about the household at Hunsworth where Joe and John are depicted as living comfortably while their sister in New Zealand is existing in hard conditions, though Mary had been at pains to stress to Charlotte the comfort of the house she and Ellen Taylor occupied in Wellington.

Mary's resentment of Ellen's Nussey's activities was shared by the rest of the Taylor family, though Ellen in a letter of 1882 claimed that they had been 'professing annoyance more than feeling it', and was confident of being able to approach them with a request for a photograph of Red House to send to her American friend Mrs. Cortazzo.[360] The Taylor family, nevertheless, seem to have passed on their poor opinion to the younger generations of the family. Susan Taylor claimed, as late as 1930, that Ellen was silly and likely to fancy herself in love with almost any young man of her circle.

Any concern in the Taylor family in 1877 about the effect of the Reid *Monogram* was quickly overshadowed by a serious and extraordinary upheaval in their lives. For more than forty years Mary's eldest brother, Joshua, had pursued his business interests, raised his children, attended the Moravian Church, and was regarded as a respected member of local society, when suddenly, in 1879 he abandoned wife, home and business, giving up the mill to his two eldest sons and taking up residence in a London hotel. He had become interested in spiritualism and passed under the influence of bogus mediums who had extorted money from him. Indifferent to the problems of the business which he had left in a chaotic state, he seems to have become obsessed by a determination to retrieve his money. His sons were facing bankruptcy but it was only with great difficulty that they got a little help from him, despite the pleas of his wife who visited him in London. Mary Taylor had to come forward to act as one of six guarantors for her nephews. The domineering temperament and uncertain temper, referred to by Susan Taylor and suggested in Charlotte Brontë's characterisation of Matthew Yorke, seem finally to have overwhelmed Joshua's reason. In his diary the family solicitor William Carr referred to him as 'a perverse and shortsighted old man'. Still unreconciled to his family Joshua died alone in 1880, a day before his 68th birthday, a sad and baffling figure, henceforth tactfully described as 'difficult'.

Three years later Richard Taylor, one of Mary's nephews who had been left by his father to try and salvage the business, also died. He had fallen in love with and married his cousin Anne Taylor from New Zealand, the daughter of Waring. His death was attributed by William Carr to the effects of diphtheria, the early death in 1878 of his wife aged twenty-three, after only three or four years of marriage, and the shame of 'the scandalous life and miserable death of his father'. Richard and Anne left one young son, Waring, named after his New Zealand grandfather and thus perpetuating one of the family names. He was cared for by his grandmother at Red House.

Mary Taylor's refusal to be associated with Brontë biography can only have been further reinforced when public controversy involving Ellen resurfaced in 1883. Mary Robinson, who had consulted Ellen, published a biography of Emily Brontë which was reviewed in the *Athenæum* by the poet Algernon Swinburne. He praised the book generally but deplored the space given to Branwell Brontë whom he described as 'that lamentable and contemptible caitiff', and accused of 'common debauchery', 'lying pretensions' and 'nerveless cowardice'. He declared:

> ... it is inconceivable how any one can have put into a lady's hand such a letter as one which defaces two pages of the volume, and it may be permissible to regret that a lady should have made it public.[361]

Francis Leyland, who had known Branwell personally (he subsequently published a book on the Brontës), came to his friend's defence to be answered on Ellen's behalf by Reid, asserting that information about Branwell in Gaskell's *Life* had appeared against Ellen's express wish but with Patrick Brontë's agreement.

> What I wish to make clear is that the responsibility for the publication of Branwell Brontë's history must be divided between his father and Mrs. Gaskell, and that no part of it whatever belongs to Miss Nussey, whose warm memory of her illustrious friend led her to resent the introduction of Branwell's shameful story into the biography.[362]

Ellen tended to look to others to speak on her behalf in public controversy. The resentment others felt at her activities led her to feel that her only reward for her efforts was hostility and malice and her letters are often self-pitying. She persisted, nevertheless, in her self-appointed mission.

Unwelcome news for the Taylors came from Wellington, New Zealand, in the summer of 1884. Waring Taylor was declared bankrupt. William Carr, catching Mary Taylor's crisp and incisive manner of speaking, reports:

> Mary Taylor told me that her brother Waring had failed in New Zealand — a circumstance which she attributed to the extravagance of his numerous family and to the fact that he had lost all control over them.[363]

Mary, who had already had to act as a guarantor for her nephews, now found herself a creditor of her bankrupt brother. She had even more cause to be sharply critical when the following year he was imprisoned for five years for fraud, having misappropriated a variety of funds for which he was a trustee.

After Joshua's death his widow, Mary's sister-in-law, continued to live at Red House. Her marriage to Joshua had taken place against the wishes of his parents. Jane Lister Charlesworth was the daughter of a grocer from Hightown, a village on the hill opposite Gomersal, overlooking the Spen Valley. The Charlesworths were Moravians, and Joshua and Jane were prominent members of the Moravian Church at Gomersal. Jane, though not highly educated, seems to have been a very shrewd and hardworking woman and for a long time succeeded in concealing family troubles from the world at large.[364]

These family troubles and poor health may have contributed to a period of depression for Mary; even her friendship with Grace Hirst appeared to be threatened. Grace considered that Mary was unduly influenced by the Imsengs, the Swiss family she had befriended, and that Euphrosyne, who worked for her in the 1880s, was rude to visitors and even to Mary. Moreoever the maid failed to keep the house clean and this deterred friends from visiting High Royd. At this period too, Mary seemed more than usually negligent of her personal appearance. We know that she despised over-emphasis on housekeeping and household work, that she placed little significance on clothes and personal appearance and she probably stubbornly resisted interference in her personal affairs, but the coolness must have caused her some unhappiness. It was in the late 1880s, Grace thought, that Euphrosyne, the second of the Imseng sisters to work for Mary, died, and after this the two friends became fully reconciled. Grace found a maid for High Royd, Martha Sharpe, who was initially quite bewildered by Mary's system of leaving her to use her own initiative in the domestic arrangements. Again Grace intervened and helped mistress and maid to come to an understanding which lasted for the rest of Mary's life.

Despite the economic slumps of 1875, 1880 and 1884, Mary continued to manage her own affairs competently though the family business eventually fell victim to a combination of changes in the economic situation of the locality and Joshua's poor management, the effects of which Mary's two nephews were unable to overcome. The business at Hunsworth was finally wound up in 1890 by Joshua's son, who became manager for another firm. His wife pre-deceased Mary, dying quite unexpectedly in 1891.

While the Taylors were adjusting to family difficulties, Ellen's devotion to Brontë's memory remained unwavering. If Mrs. Gaskell had, as Mary forecast, put her head into a wasp's nest when writing the biography, Ellen too found herself in further difficulties. She lent Charlotte's letters to enquirers from time to time but failed to keep careful records of her 'treasures', as she termed them, and consequently she sometimes accused quite innocent people of not returning them. She was also, undoubtedly, cheated. Her anxieties were intensified because she was the main source of published information about the Brontës and would be implicated in anything which reflected badly on the them as had indeed been the case when Mary Robinson's work on Emily appeared.

Mary continued generally to resist enquiries. Her decision had its effects. She herself receded yet further into the background, virtually written out of the developing Brontë story, her part in it appearing but rarely. Given her own journalistic abilities Taylor could easily have exploited her knowledge of Charlotte and published her own account but despite her ambitions as a writer she remained silent. Her withdrawal from the field of Brontë biography both deprived posterity of an alternative intimate view of Charlotte's life, as well as any systematic account of Charlotte's reactions to Mary's feminist views.

With the passage of time Ellen's devotion to the memory of the Brontës, especially Charlotte's, seems to have become obsessive. She continued to stress that she was Charlotte's closest friend, even her only friend, her sole confidante. In 1885 when William Scruton interviewed her, Ellen was still taking care to establish a unique claim on Charlotte, to stress how important her collaboration had been for Gaskell, as it undoubtedly was, but also to minimise Gaskell's own personal knowledge of Brontë, as well as Mary's, whose contribution to *The Life* was specifically downgraded.

> It was evident that Charlotte Brontë could unbosom herself to her 'Dear Ellen' as she could not to anyone on earth. The one other early friend besides Miss Nussey, Miss Mary Taylor, went out to Australia [sic] soon after Charlotte's return from the Brussels school. She was not with or near her, as Miss Nussey was, during the most vivid and trying experiences of her life . . . [365]

As late as 1892, when Shorter and T. J. Wise (who thought Mary had died) were pressing her for more information, Ellen represented Mary as eccentric and obstructive.

Mary Taylor the 'Rose Yorke' in *Shirley* is living, but has always proved herself *dead* to any approach on the Brontë subject, and it is understood that long ago she destroyed her letters. She is so peculiar she might prove much otherwise than helpful.[366]

Mary's firm rebuffs to enquirers, expressed in her abrupt and incisive manner, must have been extremely alienating: small wonder they tended to ignore her, but she was not immoveable. In 1878 or 79, she was approached by a clergyman, Altheus Wilkes, who was preparing to write about the Brontës. In a letter of thanks to Ellen for her co-operation he indicated that Mary had been helpful. He never actually proceeded with his project and he was one of those accused by Ellen of not returning letters.[367]

More significantly Taylor agreed in 1887 to talk to a local Methodist New Connexion minister, the Reverend W. Matthews, about Methodist associations with the *Shirley* country. *The Methodist New Connexion Magazine* published his six articles in consecutive issues two years later. Matthews refers to the school at Roe Head and identifies both Ellen Nussey and Mary Taylor as Brontë's 'life-long friends'. He also interviewed Ellen Nussey and describes her as still, in her middle years, recognisably a model for the pretty Caroline Helstone. He mentions her assiduous attendance at church and hints at her hostility to Nonconformism.

He discusses Mary as the prototype for Rose Yorke. Clearly, she made a powerful impression on him.

> After Jessie's death and burial Rose left school and went to Australia [sic]. Her schoolmate and friend asks in *Shirley* 'Will she ever come back?' Yes she came back. Her home is still Gomersal: her natural force of mind strong, her judgment still clear, her intellect penetrative, and her living soul still shining with lightning flashes through her grey eyes. She talks like her father in crisp, vigorous sentences as if they were polished for service as the need arises.
>
> I had the honour of conversing with her on Tuesday morning August 22, 1887, when she talked to me freely about her father and mother and her schooldays at Roe Head and Brussels, with Miss Brontë and other friends.[368]

There are in fact no specific references in the articles to any information provided by Taylor about Charlotte Brontë herself. What she seems to have discussed was her father Joshua, and his sympathies with the Methodist New Connexion, his support for a new chapel for them at Gomersal and donations to the Leeds circuit. There is a reference to Joshua Taylor having taken into Red House and 'hospitably entertained for some weeks' a young clergyman of the New Connexion Methodists who was ill. Perhaps this was the young foreigner to whom Mary refers in her letter to Charlotte about *Shirley* and the nursing of Robert Moore by the Yorkes at Briarmains.

Matthews added to this picture in a further article about characters in *Shirley* in the *British Weekly* shortly after Mary Taylor's death. He repeated his description of Mary's manner of speaking but added:

> Her ivory face, lighted up with a soul restless as quicksilver, shining and flashing through grey eyes, presided over by a noble and cultivated intellect, is a picture photographed on the memory today. But she is gone.[369]

Matthews adopted an over-elevated and enthusiastic style, but even allowing for this his account of Taylor could scarcely be further from the picture given by Ellen of an eccentric and reclusive woman, or Clement Shorter's dramatic and wildly inaccurate statement, probably exaggerating comments by Ellen, that on her return from New Zealand, Taylor 'lived out the remainder of her days in complete seclusion'.[370]

Mary was seventy years old when she was interviewed by Matthews. For thirty years successive census returns record her living at High Royd and always with a resident servant in the house. She is variously described as an 'annuitant' or 'living on her means'. Susan Taylor remembered her as a formidable old lady, who, much to Susan's relief, paid little attention to the children. They, in intervals of playing in her garden, were fascinated by her typewriter which she allowed them to look at but forbade them to touch!

Though she herself was no longer travelling to Pontresina, there were links with the Krone and the Gredig family which kept memories alive. Relatives and friends continued to visit the hotel; Mrs. Joshua Taylor and a nephew's wife were there in 1882. The Richardson family visited from time to time as did the Hassés, leading members of the Moravian church. Madeline Hassé had married Mary's nephew Edward Taylor and was Susan Taylor's mother. Susan, herself a keen Alpinist, is recorded as visiting the Krone in 1900.

Alone of her generation, Mary remained living in Gomersal throughout the 1880s until her death in 1893, having outlived all her siblings but John and Waring.

Though she had come to despair of progress for women, a number of reforms was achieved in her lifetime, though women were still being excluded from the successive extensions of the Parliamentary franchise to men. There was a slow growth of higher education for women but as Taylor had predicted, they were destined mainly for teaching. After 1869 women householders were able to vote in municipal elections; in 1870, after the passage of the Elementary Education Act, they could vote and stand as candidates in the elections for local school boards. The Act provided women with opportunities of teacher-training. In 1875 they could be elected to local Boards of Guardians.

There were changes, too, in Taylor's own immediate locality. Despite developments in the municipal status of the small towns in the Spen Valley, the area was becoming economically subordinated to larger towns nearby. The woollen textile industry was increasingly dominated by Huddersfield and Bradford while commercial activity continued to develop in Leeds. Working people were still employed predominantly in textiles, mining and engineering. The leading families were local manufacturers, many of whom, like the Taylors themselves, were becoming economically less secure.

The early radicalism of the nonconformists declined, as did the political militancy of working men, and local politics became dominated by the new Conservatism. Richard Taylor, Mary's nephew, had been president of the Hunsworth Conservative Working Men's Association.[371] New cultural activities – art galleries, theatres, public concerts – were established in the major towns nearby. The Hallé orchestra's Bradford subscription concerts were initiated in 1865 and the Leeds Triennial Music Festival in the late 1870s. The Spen Valley itself had few such amenities. Though it was natural that she should have gone back to Spen Valley on her return to England, there were not many there who shared Taylor's interests. She nevertheless retained her ambition to publish and to advocate the cause of women's rights. In the years after she had severed her association with the *Victoria Magazine* she reverted to her early ambition to publish her novel. In 1890 *Miss Miles* appeared.

Chapter 8

A Doctrine to Preach

In her review of Eugénie de Guérin's journal Mary Taylor had praised the prose style and commented that good writing is the product of much practice. She herself achieved a clear, trenchant, even, when appropriate, dramatic style. In a number of her articles for the *Victoria Magazine* she had pushed at the boundaries of the periodical article, moving away from exposition alone, testing new possibilities for the form with imaginary dialogues and situations and cameos of individual character. The reviewer of *The First Duty* in *The Englishwoman's Review*[372] appreciated Taylor's potential as a writer of fiction and urged her to develop it. Mrs. Gaskell admired Taylor's style, describing it as 'distinct and graphic in expression' and in the revisions of *The Life* after the threat of libel actions, drew extensively and verbatim on Taylor's second letter.[373]

The article 'An Old Dispute' is structured as a dialogue between 'Gentleman' and 'Lady', 'The Shah on English Laws' is a satirical vignette, as the Shah with remorseless logic interrogates the increasingly embarrassed British Ambassador in an exchange which exposes British practice to ridicule. In 'Our Feminine Respectability' she considers the actual, tragic case of Rosa Easthorpe, constructing around it an imaginary picture of a dreary marriage of convenience, the man 'probably took a wife, as she took a husband, not because she was such a one as he wanted, but such a one as he could afford', producing all the disastrous consequences of aiming to appear 'respectable' without the means actually to be so. In 'What Am I To Do?' there is the young, frustrated and fearful middle-class girl constrained by her family's genteel views of how she should live, imposing on her a way of life which she recognises might condemn her to poverty when she is older. In this persona we see the early elements of the situation and character of Amelia, an important protagonist in Taylor's novel, *Miss Miles*.

Letters had always provided an opportunity to practise good style and Taylor's correspondence from Brussels, Hagen and Wellington reveals her as a shrewd observer and vivid writer with a talent for dialogue. Her section of the letter written jointly with her sister and the two Brontës in Brussels creates an amusing picture of students toiling not very intelligently over their languages. She addressed her correspondents in a relaxed, idiomatic style: 'Read away Ellen books of all sorts and all characters'; 'Now the Dr.'s arrival has determined me to flit' (West Yorkshire word for moving house); 'I have set up shop'. Her letter from Hagen to Ellen describing her piano lessons with Herr Hallé is a brilliant piece of affectionate comedy.

She was not very self-confident, however, either about her style or her staying-power in composing polished prose. While congratulating Charlotte Brontë on her achievement in *Jane Eyre* she was mistrustful of her own gifts:

You have polished to some purpose. If I were to do so I should get tired, and weary everyone else in about two pages.[374]

She tried for acceptance by periodicals back in Britain entrusting articles to her brother to place with *Tait's Magazine* and *Chamber's*. One was an account of the earthquake disasters of 1848. Her efforts were rejected: there were already correspondents established in Wellington sending their reports of events and developments in the colony.[375] As she reported from time to time to Brontë from New Zealand she worked intermittently on the material which was to become *The First Duty of Women* and *Miss Miles*.[376]

Taylor had always hoped to join the ever-expanding number of women who looked to literature and journalism as their profession, but by the time her articles began to appear she was financially independent. No doubt she went on with her writing because she felt a sense of pride at having her work published and she also wanted to make some contribution to the women's cause. Fiction regularly appeared in the *Victoria Magazine* and it was this journal which published Taylor's two short stories.

Though Mary like most of her contemporaries believed that literature should carry a message, hers was by no means typical. She created her fictions, as she did her journalism, as important vehicles for winning sympathy for her feminist convictions. In her comments on *Jane Eyre* she had taunted Brontë:

You are very different from me in having no doctrine to preach. It is impossible to squeeze a moral out of your production. Has the world done so well with you that you have no protest to make against its absurdities ... Once more, have you written through three volumes without declaring war to the knife against a few dozen absurd doctrines, each of which is supported by 'a large and respectable class of readers'?[377]

She later attacked Brontë as 'a coward and a traitor' for advocating in *Shirley* the right to work only for unmarried women.[378]

Taylor's first short story, with the non-committal title of 'A Tale', appeared in September 1873.[379] The narrator is a 70-year-old working woman looking back on her young womanhood, her marriage and its tragedies. Her tone is stoical, disillusioned and bitter. Conforming to one of the most important features of the short story form, Taylor takes us immediately into the heart of the matter, establishing the background with only the minimum of necessary information. We are given no set descriptions of place, character or appearance and indeed it seems as if the narrator herself is going to remain anonymous. We are half way through her account before we learn her name, Mrs. Sorrell, and that, as it were, by chance. The woman's language is economical, her sentences short and simple. The matter-of-fact, unembellished tone lends a certain objectivity to the story, implying that

Mrs. Sorell's story is not hers alone but reflects the socially determined experiences of countless other nameless women. The main theme, society's injustice to women, is announced at the outset. 'I was cruelly used; and it was, so to say, nobody's fault'.[380]

The orphaned girl is taken into their home by poor relatives who are eager to marry her off. When she is nineteen years old they introduce her to a young man, encourage her to imagine herself in love with him and marry him, even though they know he is a drunkard.

She sees her wifely duty as running the household as economically as possible and expects to enjoy companionship with him. He, however, seeks his amusement elsewhere and resolutely keeps friends away from the house. It is very soon clear that he drinks heavily and she is terrified of the ruin she is convinced they face. She seeks help from her relatives who evade their responsibilities by blaming her and refusing to interfere. The husband (as was Branwell Brontë), is a railway clerk. He becomes careless even about doing his work and she takes to going with him to the railway office to try and keep him at work. Eventually she does the work herself.

> He knew that that my eager industry was all in vain; that he was
> deep in debt, and all my efforts to keep a house over our heads
> would come to naught.[381]

The husband disappears, she continues to do his work but soon all the furniture of the house is distrained to pay his debts. She is left, through no fault of her own, in an empty house stripped of all the furnishings. They are her husband's property, she has neither any claim on them nor control over them. When she tries to collect her husband's wages the clerk refuses to give her the money, though he knows the husband has disappeared. She is closely questioned by him and then by the manager. In this scene Taylor expresses the familiar, painful sensitivity of women embarrassed by a collective male gaze. The questioning takes place in full public view of the other workers, men who are there to collect their own wages and who have made way for her to go to the head of the queue. To all the questions put to her she can only honestly reply that she does not know; the woman's ignorance of the facts of her own situation demonstrates her powerlessness. By this stage of the story Taylor has vividly enacted through the situation of this one character the pressures on young women to marry and once married their helplessness and subordination both within the marriage and in society generally.

The manager offers her the husband's job, but at a much lower wage, which she accepts as she has no alternative. From this point she saves slowly what she can, and lives in virtual isolation from other human beings, dreaming that he might come back 'in his right mind'. Return he does, confiscates her earnings which are legally his, and again disappears. She gathers furniture together, is rebuffed when she asks for more wages, and then to pay her husband's debts, creditors once more seize what she passionately believes to be her property by right of her labour but which legally belongs to him. When she asks him to get her possessions back, her uncle trenchantly summarises the situation: '"My things are my own" he said "yours are not"'.[382] She contemplates in deep terror the social degradation which seems to be closing in around her: 'Again and again I watched myself sinking, sinking, starving, starving'.[383]

She is rescued by her uncle and the manager of the railway office They buy back her furniture and remain as its owners while her wages are paid to the uncle to protect them from the husband and his creditors. Once more he returns but it is to die.

> Then I was told my goods and my earnings were my own. I never settled in my own mind whether to believe it or not. I act as if it were true, but to this day I turn cold now and then with the thought that this or some other injustice may at any time turn me out of house and home. I am told that no forsaken wife can be treated so now. It may be so, but I for my part, have found the justice of men as wanting as their chivalry. Their laws made me helpless, and their indifference let me be plundered.[384]

Her bitterness obscures the help she received from the two men and she reiterates her theme of the 'consequence of social arrangements' which operate independently of individual inclinations or benevolence. She deplores the custom of hurrying women into marriage but recognises that in her case, half-educated as she was, she had no trade and marriage was her only 'career'. In such situations:

> Friends on both sides combine to keep silence and clear their conscience by saying 'She can do no better.' If men were guided by either justice or goodwill in their treatment of women this could not be their position.[385]

The other short story, *A Servant Girl's History,* is almost as neutral in its title as Taylor's first. Published in October 1876, it concerns the young working girl trapped in a cycle of under-privilege and desperate poverty.[386]

Elderly ladies are engaged on their favourite topic of 'each other's servants'. The hostess has tried to dismiss her maid but the girl refuses to leave: 'she told me when I gave her notice that I *must not send her away*'.

> It was agreed that the girl shou'd be summoned into the drawing-room, as we were all very curious to see the strange creature that had said 'must' to her mistress.[387]

Fear of destitution and homelessness had spurred the thin, badly-clothed girl into using the word 'must'. Her mother is dead, she has no skills, but has taken advice from her next-door neighbour to 'get a place'. The narrator takes pity on her and offers to employ her. Sheer nervousness completely undermines the girl's self-confidence and makes her appear stupid. The narrator's early reactions to her sound very much like Taylor herself, impatient but capable of regretting hasty comments.

> I spoke harshly, for it is in the nature of stupidity to be as provoking as deliberate malice; still I felt reproved and resolved at the first opportunity to try a little praise.[388]

The girl has virtually no possessions and no money.

> The disgrace of poverty unconcealable had evidently come so often that its sting was always rankling. She was so used to being ashamed that she took the position at a moment's notice, and the recoil to a more natural state of feeling was so strong that she almost went into hysterics when she was praised. I took to praising her for the pleasure of it.[389]

Encouraged by kindness the girl begins to develop into 'a vigorous, capable, willing servant'. The narrator begins to wonder what she will do when the girl finds a young man though she is clear that she would not forbid 'followers' as some employers did. A man does, indeed, appear, ugly, and apparently disreputable, not a 'follower' but the girl's father, demanding to take her away, intending to benefit from her earnings. Moved by the girl's distress the narrator on impulse defies him and to her surprise the father immediately capitulates and disappears. The narrator guards Alice's wages so that she can be immune to threats and demands to hand over her money to the father, who eventually ceases to harass them.

Alice had no skills, she was not even competent at first as a maid of all work and she would have been left to destitution and death if the narrator had not rescued her.

> She would have died of hardship; she might probably have spent two or three years in dying; but if her one hope had failed her, as it was on the point of doing, where could she have turned to get a living by her labour?[390]

This carries an echo of Taylor's account in *Swiss Notes* of her conversation with a poor peasant woman who wished she had died in childhood.

Alice's situation was not unique, Taylor reminds her readers. She refers to the textile areas where, exceptionally, women earn a good living but that is the spontaneous by-product of industrialisation, not the result of conscious provision to help women get skills and well-paid work. She concludes by asking when the constraints on women working will be lifted and when married women will be able to control their own earnings.

> Is it really only ignorance that stands in the way? Does the phrase, one so often hears, 'We don't want women to be the money-

makers', never mean, 'We don't want women to be secure against poverty? We want some to honour and some to dishonour. Their proper position is in the service of men.'[391]

Taylor's most ambitious work was her novel, *Miss Miles,* but success eluded her. In a sad letter to Charlotte Brontë written in 1852 shortly after the death of her cousin, Taylor had announced her decision to remain in business but to live entirely alone.[392] Though she was working successfully at her trade, her hopes and imagination were turned on England and the arrival of letters, books and newspapers, which were vital to her, providing, as she said, 'the best part' of her daily life. A source of comfort in sad moments, consolation for loneliness and homesickness, was the reading of old letters and, also, the writing of her novel.

Taylor had herself always been an avid novel reader with access from her childhood to a wide range of books. Novels, including French novels, went on loan from Red House to the Haworth Parsonage. In *Shirley*, Rose Yorke is seen deeply absorbed in Mrs. Radcliffe's *The Italian*, the bookshelves in Hunsden's room in *The Professor* include works by Eugène Sue and George Sand and it is the influence of the great Frenchwoman's novel *Consuelo* that can be seen in some of the characterisations and developments in *Miss Miles.*

Mary Taylor was not alone in her enthusiasm for Sand whose work gripped the imagination of thousands of English readers and was admired by numbers of English women writers, including Charlotte Brontë, Elizabeth Gaskell, Elizabeth Barrett Browning, Geraldine Jewsbury and George Eliot.[393] Barrett Browning addressed two sonnets to Sand and named the novelist heroine of her poem, a novel in verse, 'Aurora', after Sand, one of whose names was Aurore.

Sand's work was highly regarded in the English movement for women's rights. The *Victoria Magazine* reprinted an obituary from the *Examiner* which declared:

> ... the whole agitation which has stirred our times so profoundly with regard to the position and subjection of women is due to her inspiration.[394]

It reminded readers of Sand's earlier scandalous reputation. 'People under thirty can have no idea of the vehemence of hatred and denunciation with which George Sand and her works were once assailed'.[395]

Ellen Moers, referring to Sand's novel *Consuelo* claimed: 'It was the most famous treatment of the opera singer in nineteenth-century fiction, and every woman of more than ordinary distinction read *Consuelo* or at least knew it was there'.[396] Alexander MacMillan (1818-96), the great publisher, considered *Jane Eyre* 'a sort of English *Consuelo*'.[397]

Sand based the character of Consuelo on her close friend Pauline Viardot

MISS MILES

OR

A TALE OF YORKSHIRE LIFE 60 YEARS AGO

BY

MARY TAYLOR

(of High Royd, Spen, Gomersal,
near Leeds,
"Rose Yorke"
the ~~friend~~ of Charlotte Brontë fame.)

London

REMINGTON & CO PUBLISHERS

HENRIETTA STREET COVENT GARDEN

1890

Brontë Parsonage Museum.

125

the great operatic singer, and when the novel appeared in book form in 1854 Sand dedicated it to her.[398]

In *Consuelo*, Sand explored the nature of the woman artist's vocation and its demands. She treats music as symbolic of morality, and Consuelo's artistry and dedication are aspects of her heroic integrity and independence. Taylor had read the novel in French as the serial was appearing during 1842-3, enthusiastically recommending it to Ellen Nussey. To read and admire the scandalous George Sand as early as 1843 was to confess implicitly to holding advanced, possibly original, views and when Taylor claims for her novel 'original views of life' she was referring to the 'doctrine' she advocated in her journalism and imaginatively embodied in her fiction.

While Sand ranges ambitiously over a broad, cosmopolitan canvas, exploiting elements of the picaresque novel, Taylor's focus is deliberately narrowed on one small community. Drawing on nostalgic memories of Spen Valley society she recreates it in the fictional Repton of the late 1820s and 30s. She described the novel as 'full of music, poverty, disputing, politics, and original views of life', a description which neatly describes *Miss Miles*.[399] She confessed that her pleasure in re-reading the one-and-a-half volumes already completed, impeded progress.

Taylor began the work when the condition-of-England novel, reacting to the impact of industrialisation, was enjoying success. Frances Trollope (1780-1863) had already published her *Michael Armstrong, the Factory Boy* in 1840, Charlotte Elizabeth Tonna (1790-1846) published *The Wrongs of Woman*, during 1843-4, while Mrs. Gaskell was to achieve fame with *Mary Barton* in 1848, the year before *Shirley* was published. Tonna and Trollope attacked the effects of the factory system on women and child workers. Gaskell was deeply concerned about the dangers of class conflict and in representing the plight of the working class was pleading for middle-class understanding and action to heal class divisions and ensure social peace. Brontë's *Shirley*, a romance in a setting of industrial unrest and class conflict, carries a plea for single women to be allowed to work. It places hopes for the amelioration of the effects of industrialisation and the ruthless drive for profit, on the benevolent influence of women and an alliance of gentry and industrial interests.

Taylor's class sympathies lie with the industrial workers and small shopkeepers of Repton and she depicts their way of life with great sympathy through characters who seek to live their lives honestly and face difficulties with dignity and integrity. She depicts them as sturdily independent, quick to exercise mutual solidarity, determined to enjoy their own culture and whatever good things of life come their way and showing the same quality of sympathy and respect expressed by Sand in her novels of peasant life.

Pastoral nostalgia has no part in Taylor's outlook. She sees industrialisation as offering better wages to workers than agriculture did, though she is aware of their suffering during economic crises.

Repton is a divided society marked by tensions between 'land' and 'industry'. The Anglican church is identified with the gentry and with Tories, while the Dissenting chapels command the support of workers and those connected with them, in the local textile industry. Some of them are politically radical, even Chartist.

The Chapel, 'large, bare, ugly, and defiant before the eyes of the vicar of the parish', is their focus for worship and their social and cultural life. In hard times the solidarity of the chapel members has helped many of the poorer brethren to survive, in good times it has provided support for new entrepreneurial ventures.

Though class conflict and class relationships are features of the social context in which Taylor sets her narrative, her aim was to embody in realist fiction her doctrine already theorised in journalism, that the first duty of women was to develop their skills and courage and achieve economic independence.

Taylor situates three of her four young women, Sarah Miles, Maria Bell, and Amelia Turner, firmly in the world of Repton. Dora Wells from the nearby countryside remains an outsider though Repton provides the happy solution to her problems. The ambitions of the four and the possibilities of achieving them, ebb and flow as the local economy fluctuates. The cultural and moral values of the various social and religious groups in the village and nearby town affect their standing and self-confidence as they seek a way out of crises which impede their self-development.

In the course of the narrative the experiences and development of the women are set against the situations of other women characters whose fates and personalities are likewise moulded by the conventions constraining them because they are women. Amelia is tragically destroyed by them while in their various ways Sarah, Maria and Dora confront and finally overcome difficult obstacles. They build their self-confidence, acquire the means to economic independence and win recognition of their own worth. It is this rather than the conventional theme of love, courtship, marriage and happiness-ever-after which constitutes the three happy endings of the work

In structuring a narrative with four centres of interest, Taylor set herself a difficult problem of offering coherent accounts of the progress of each individual while not allowing any of the rest to drop out of the picture and ensuring that they remain sufficiently close to the action to move back as needful, each in turn, to centre stage. She achieves this in the main successfully, by establishing links between principal characters. Maria Bell and Dora Wells are friends from childhood. Letters, a familiar narrative device, maintain their friendship when they are separated. In giving the name Bell for a heroine raised in a moorland parsonage Taylor is covertly celebrating her friendship with Charlotte Brontë and reflecting the importance of letters in the nurturing of their friendship. Maria and Sarah Miles are linked by their teacher-pupil relationship, while later Sarah temporarily goes out to service in the Turner household, observing and vainly trying to help Amelia, the youngest daughter. The Miles family, at Maria's pleading, lend their influence in ensuring Dora Wells's success.

It is not only young women who feature. Taylor creates the character of an older, unmarried women, Miss Everard. Genteel and poor, she fears virtual pauperisation. Her ignorance of practical affairs has left her a victim of systematic cheating by Amelia's father, whose textile business is facing imminent collapse. The Bells are related to but estranged from the Turners, who become even colder to Maria when she decides to earn her living by establishing a school.

It is with Sarah, the Miss Miles of the title, that the work opens. A true daughter of Repton, she is deeply embedded in its life, customs and culture, speaking the local dialect and sharing the values of her loving, pious, chapel-going parents whom she in her turn loves and respects.

Sarah's parents keep a shop which serves as one of the gathering points of the working-class neighbourhood. They share the times of prosperity and poverty of their customers. Their religious and cultural life revolves around the Chapel. There is a heart-warming picture of family relationships, Sarah loving and respecting her parents while they gently exert discipline, guidance and loving care but with any expression of their deepest feelings under firm control.

Sarah's friends are the young people of the Chapel where, as the novel opens, there is a schism. The young men are determined to build a new chapel and appoint a minister who is as convinced as they that fine music has its part to play in their worship and their leisure activities. Sam Sykes, in love with Sarah, is a leader of the faction, and a skilled woolsorter (a highly skilled prestigious trade in the West Yorkshire textile industry), working in a small business with his father. With his friends he practises the music he dreams will be heard in the new chapel. Sarah is drawn in and enthuses them with the power and beauty of her voice. Encouraged by the one highly skilled musician among them, she begins to sense the possibilities of her own talents and develops the ambition to be professionally trained.

Sarah wants to be educated and demands to be allowed to attend Maria's school, seeing it as a means of ultimately earning a good living. Her aunt, a skilled cloth-mender, voices the complaint Taylor frequently expressed in her articles, that women's work is always underpaid, and warns Sarah, 'never you listen to them that tell you you'll ever get rich'.[400]

Taylor creates in Sarah a forceful, intelligent heroine, honest, blunt of speech, occasionally rebellious and intolerant. Mrs. Miles is a wise, tolerant and patient mother, so different from Taylor's own!

At school Sarah learns quickly, assured by Maria that she will get wisdom 'By reading wise books and thinking for yourself', an echo of Taylor's advice to Ellen Nussey. She is disturbed by the lack of seriousness of some of the other pupils, their reluctance to bend their minds to difficult problems and their triviality; a situation repeated when she comes to train as a singer.

The end of Sarah's childhood comes when Miles's customers cannot buy goods or pay debts and she decides to go out to service to earn money.

> She has reached the age, or at least the time, when she stood face to face with the great problem of existence, how was she to live?[401]

When Sam Sykes explains to her that it is possible for good singers to gain a good income she plans to use her earnings to buy singing lessons.

It is not only her own affairs which concern her. As discontent mounts Sarah hears the talk of the men like the young Sam Sykes and like her own father who believe that the Government serves only its own people and that working men like themselves should have the vote to elect a Government to heed their interests. She follows a great Chartist demonstration and identifies with the demands of the working people for work and the suffrage. She rejects her mother's reproach for following the demonstration all day when it has 'naught' to do with her, insisting that when there is suffering, 'It is summat to me!'.[402]

Hard times come to the district and Sarah resolves to go out to work as a servant. Now a little further out in the world, though still the world of Repton, she observes what it is to lead a 'lady's life' as she works in the Turner household, and is appalled by its vapidity and uselessness.

Once, therefore, that aspects of Sarah's character, her ambitions to go to school and her growing interest in singing have been established, Maria Bell takes centre stage, with a chapter bearing the epigraph from Wordsworth, 'Heaven Lies About Us In Our Infancy'.

In a sheltered hollow on the moors, ten miles from Repton, Maria has been brought up by her loving and cultivated parents. Her father is the incumbent of the parish, Dora the daughter of a neighbouring widow. Maria extends a calming influence on the rebellious Dora whose ferocity suggests Taylor's own moods when Martha described her as 'looking as fierce as a tiger'. Dora's frustration and search for a way out of the confines of her situation are also reminiscent of aspects of Taylor's own search for personal independence. The friendship of Maria and Dora exemplifies Taylor's definition of genuine friendship in *The First Duty of Women*. Friends are those:

> . . . who keep up our faith in mankind by giving proof of their goodness, and rouse the ever-returning wish for their welfare, and liking for their company. Whatever blunders youth and enthusiasm may commit on this course, it is the wiser one to take. It gives the habit of clinging to our friends from unselfish motives, and prevents our being surrounded by people who are a source of irritation that cannot be got rid of.[403]

When Dora is fourteen her widowed mother marries again, thinking to provide some protection for herself and her daughter. She discovers that her small means have now become the property of her new husband and that Dora has no claim on it.

> Maria admitted the cruelty of the position while recommending patience, and Dora submitted to the teaching while rebelling against the practice of it.[404]

Dora's mother dies, the girl remains in a hostile household of despicable men, afraid of the corruption of their coarseness but with no means of escape.

Death came often in Victorian novels as in Victorian life and the girls have to separate when, in her turn, Maria is orphaned and without any inheritance from her father, whose savings have collapsed. She leaves for Repton to set up her day school.

While Dora remains for much of the story in the moorland village the reader is kept aware of what is happening to her through her correspondence with Maria, a contact as vital to her as Taylor's and Nussey's letters were to Brontë.

Though reluctant to be thought to be making claims on richer relatives, Maria feels obliged to make contact with the Turners. Her visit develops into a tense conflict with Turner himself and the women of the family who feel that having a woman relative who actually works for her living is a threat to their socially superior position in the community. Amelia Turner is soon to find herself in the situation anticipated with dread by the young woman in 'What Am I To Do?'.

At this meeting we also encounter Miss Everard, the sole surviving member of a family of land-owners who leased the land for the mill in which Turner conducts his business. She is now a middle-aged impoverished spinster, ignorant of business matters but a landlady being cheated by Turner. Her friendship with Maria slowly develops into a mutually beneficial relationship between women of different generations such as *Swiss Notes by Five Ladies* actually expresses.

The fictional friendship is based on genuine concern, one for the other in their respective difficulties in which they offer disinterested mutual support and in the process gain self-confidence and a capacity to survive adverse circumstances. As Maria's school flourishes and she is able to live adequately on her earnings, her self-confidence grows.

> A silent change which she never noticed took place in her character and disposition. She got courage and self-confidence, and was braced up to the certainty that she herself was her own best friend.[405]

Taylor describes this development in a way that echoes her own description of how uncertain she and Ellen Taylor felt when they opened their shop but gained confidence as they gathered experience.

Fundamental to Taylor's views on women's psychology was the conviction that only by practice, by actually embarking on action, could they gain the confidence and develop the self-reliance they needed for success. Once elements of character and situation of the four have been set out Taylor steers them through vicissitudes and crises to the achievement of self-reliance and independence, or failure and death. Each in her own way confronts the need for skills and the means of earning a living. Three achieve success, Amelia is destroyed. The stories of each enact important aspects of Taylor's ideas advocated in her journalism about women's need of education and skills, the opportunity for satisfying employment and for self-sufficiency.

Sarah as pupil has led us to Maria Bell; Sarah as maid brings us into the heart of the Turner family and especially, Amelia Turner. The lives of the Turner women embody Taylor's views about the wastefulness and futility of many middle-class women's lives which she frequently deplored in her articles.

The tensions and ill-feeling in the Turner family are in sharp contrast to the warmth and openness of the Miles family and their friends. Sarah finds herself among older women snobbishly obsessed with appearances and with maintaining their genteel social status, and is bewildered by what she perceives as a contradiction between their leisured and relatively luxurious lives and by their ill-temper and boredom.

> They had apparently everything they wanted, though they could only amuse themselves by sitting in a parlour and doing nothing![406]

Baffled by this she turns her attention to Miss Amelia, pretty, lively and newly returned from boarding school; in this way Taylor introduces a new character, the fourth of the young women, Amelia. Taylor's tone is initially ironic; Miss Amelia patronises the maid, Sarah.

> [She assumes] at once the position of instructor, which the more wealthy classes almost invariably take up towards their inferiors.[407]

The trite moral precepts Amelia imparts are so familiar to Sarah that she feels Amelia must be deliberately concealing real knowledge from her. She finally reaches the conclusion that 'the people before her were commonplace and even vulgar souls'.[408] She nevertheless feels drawn to Amelia who is at least hopeful and friendly and who seems to have some purpose in her life, continuing her music practice and serious reading begun at school. Eliza, the 'housekeeper' of the sisters comments:

> Dear me! what a fuss you make over your reading! Why should you read at all?[409]

131

The protagonist of 'What Am I To Do?' laments that:

> ... I found all my friends even more averse to speak of books of
> any kind other than novels, than older people. They all had the
> impression that it was wrong; not morally wrong, perhaps, but a
> sort of solecism in manners like putting your knife in your
> mouth. Not anything that would prevent you getting to Heaven,
> but fatal to your acceptability on earth.[410]

Amelia's knowledge is defective and it is Sarah who informs her that
Coleridge is the author of *The Ancient Mariner*, which she has seen at Miss
Bell's.

The Turners are expecting a guest. Thelwall is actually demanding the
payment of Turner's debts but the servants assume he is a suitor for Amelia
while Mrs. Turner hopes he will become so. To further the 'courtship' she
urges her husband to 'not a grand ball you know, but a little party, with
some dancing' but the following morning Thelwall leaves Repton and the
Turner house, and Sarah is dismissed.[411] As she approaches her home she
sees the neighbours conferring with Mrs. Miles who announces: "'Dunnot
ye know as Turner's is banked?'". Thelwall has proved insistent, Turner
cannot pay. The economy of the whole village is endangered.

Answering Sarah's anxious enquiry, her friend Sam insists that the Turner
women will not be able to help themselves.

> 'What will they do?' she repeated, and Sammy answered with a
> spice of contempt –
> 'Nought'.[412]

Now disillusioned and realistically clear about what it is to be a 'lady',
Sarah concludes another stage of her growing-up into adulthood.

Sam's sympathies are for the many others who will suffer and among
them are Maria Bell who loses pupils and Miss Everard, who loses the rent
still owed by Turner. Sam and his father also face loss of business. As Sam
has predicted the women of the Turner family are virtually helpless. Their
main concern is to maintain a façade of gentility to be shown to the rest of
Repton. Amelia's desire to work and contribute to the family's finances is
firmly suppressed, throwing her into moral confusion which is exacerbated
by her realisation that she had quite misunderstood Thelwall's flirtatious
behaviour towards her. She had interpreted it as genuine friendship and
interest when, in fact, he has emerged as 'the most grasping creditor'.

> She went wearily about her day's work, and sank in the evenings
> into total inertia. Eliza was busy and cross, Matilda whined and
> grumbled, the house-mother watched painfully lest anything
> should be done or said to vex the master, who sat like a stranger
> at his own fireside. They had become a 'fortuitous concourse of

atoms' and the pet, the hope of the family, was the most isolated atom of them all.[413]

Turner finds a possible solution to his immediate problem by proposing a partnership to Sammy and his father, which they accept. The mill re-opens, and Maria's school, denuded of pupils when the crash came, begins to revive.

Taylor's recognition that success or failure hang by the thread of wider social circumstances is pointed up at this stage of the narrative by Maria's recognition that both the loss of pupils and then the improvement in her prospects have come about quite independently of her own will.

> Her prosperity had left her, and it had come back again. No effort of hers had had anything to do with it, and the prospect of a life-long see-saw between want and well-being was still the same.[414]

When Maria is facing the imminent prospects of the failure of the school she pours out her worries to Dora whom she regards as her only friend, though she is about to make another. Invited to a gathering at the Vicarage, she hears gossip about the odd Mr. Branksome, also expected as a guest, who having used his small inheritance to buy a good apprenticeship, is now a practical engineer. Taylor satirises genteel social life in the triviality of the conversation at this soirée, which includes the predictable lament of the prosperous middle classes about the improvidence of working people. Branksome, now arrived, defends them and says what he thinks a working person would say in self-defence:

> Look here I have worked hard all my life and have no hope but to go on working. I have never been able, and I don't expect to be able, to keep starvation from my door with all I can do. All my life, pleasure and comfort and hope and leisure have passed me by. They have been within sight sometimes, and shall I never taste them? – not for one hour before I die?[415]

Here is no ordinary hero. Not only are his sympathies and opinions unusual, so are his ways of wooing. At this gathering he has met Maria face to face for the first time; she is the woman he has been observing from a distance ever since her arrival in Repton and whom he wants to marry. As he escorts her home he asks for her agreement to their getting to know each other better.

Love at first sight is common enough in the nineteenth-century novel but not many heroines actually receive a proposal of marriage at their very first meeting with the hero! Maria vacillates between rejecting Branksome's advances because 'The customs of the country do not allow it', but recognises the force of his argument that she may be rejecting her chances of love and happiness. They conduct their developing relationship through letters, rationally testing each other's opinions and principles. Branksome's wooing succeeds and Maria too falls in love:

> . . . she walked into it with her eyes open. We all know how it's done! Each side dressed up an image deprived of half its earthly nature, of the residue they made a god! And each believed in the homage of the other.[416]

There are illusory elements in this relationship but it also, on Branksome's part especially, has defining elements of rationality which holds the promise of a loving and lasting partnership.

When Taylor was describing the novel to Brontë in 1852 she confesses to problems in creating male characters, not being able to anticipate what they might do or how they might turn out.[417] Perhaps her difficulties arose not so much from lack of knowledge of men but because the love stories in her novel were not characteristically romantic, there are no poetic passages describing sexual passion, characters in love are not swept off their feet into ecstacies of desire. We are not even told what Branksome and Sykes look like! They are not glamorous heroes but young men working hard at their industrial trades. It is their integrity which is intended to recommend them to us, and their attitudes to women. In particular, the quality of their respect for Maria and Sarah respectively are intended to serve as decisive indicators of their moral worth. Sarah's and Maria's love crises are not romantic, not the result of unfounded jealousy or unfortunate misunderstanding; they involve complex questions of genuine esteem on the one hand and self-respect on the other. Branksome has to learn to trust Maria's independent judgment and to understand that she is capable of taking important decisions without relying on him. Sam Sykes has to discard patronising attitudes towards young women, even a certain contempt, before he wins back Sarah's love.

While the village revives with the re-opening of the mill, Sarah alone remains uneasy and discontented, resenting others' assurances that she is well-off where she is. Taylor equates Sarah's feelings to those of a man imprisoned in a dungeon, an echo of her own view of the life that the Brontës faced and that Ellen Nussey was living in Birstall which she described as 'the cage'.

> . . . I think you feel pent up enough where you are to see why they [Charlotte and Emily Brontë] are right in staying outside the cage – though it is somewhat cold.[418]

Sarah embarks on yet a further stage of her life by moving to the neighbouring town to be trained as a singer. At this point of the novel Taylor recycles aspects of *A Tale*. Sarah's landlady, Mrs. Gracehurst is a friend of Mrs. Miles and a former Repton 'chapeller'. Just as the name Maria Bell carries resonances of Charlotte Brontë's *nom de plume*, so Taylor has coined this fictional name from the actual name of her younger friend Grace Hirst! Mrs. Gracehurst who keeps a small dame school, is married to a drunkard who periodically returns to appropriate her goods and earnings (which legally belong to him), to sell for more drink. Poor though she is, she appears even poorer in order to deflect her husband's attention from the little she has.

> This woman's dress was even cynical in its poverty. A black gown so flat in its folds, so ragged in the sleeves, and in the gathers, and round the bottom, and so brown all over, could only be worn by a woman who had deliberately given up the intention of looking as well as she could.[419]

The solidarity of her neighbours helps her to survive. They carry away her furniture and goods, hiding them in into their own houses, until the husband leaves. Anything but gracious, Mrs. Gracehurst is understandably dour and cynical about young men and women and their relationships.

Sarah works hard and is determined to learn, stoutly resisting involvement in the gossip of the young women studying with her as they fantasise about the young men they meet. She is nevertheless disturbed by their behaviour and the hypocritical attitude of the men who pay the girls compliments but sneer at them behind their backs. Mrs. Gracehurst's bleak comments about their foolishness reinforce Sarah's rigid attitudes to affectation and petty deceits. She begins to fear that nobody is to be trusted. Echoing the final lines of *Paradise Lost* and two lines of Wordsworth, Taylor comments:

> Sarah had always believed in good folk and bad folk; those whom she trusted she trusted absolutely, and all others she relegated into the outer world, where it did not matter what they were or what they did. In this warm heaven she had lived since her infancy, and now it was fading into the light of common day. The grey, cold world was all before her, but there was in it no place of rest.[420]

Successive feelings of unease reinforce her growing mistrust. Directly open and honest as she is herself, she is suspicious that Sam wants the new chapel more for musical than religious reasons and she begins also to doubt the genuineness of his friendship for her: 'perhaps the men-folk, as she called them, were not friends, but managers, who spoke fair for purposes of their own'.[421]

Her break with Sam comes as he is about to announce to the choir the musical programme for the opening of the chapel. Sam is rather embarrassed and takes refuge in joining in the jokes at the expense of the young women present, behaving to them as the young men in Baumforth had behaved to her fellow students. Sarah sees this as betrayal. Without explanation she walks out on the group. Sam follows her, puts his arm round her waist, to be answered by a fierce blow between the eyes which leaves him stunned. How unlike the love stories of the conventional heroines of Victorian fiction!

Sarah sings at the chapel opening and begins through engagements to earn money including at the local Anglican Church much to the dismay of her chapel-going friends, with the exception of Sam who defends her. Invited by Mrs. Overton, the banker's wife, to stay in her house and teach her singing, Sarah witnesses the futility, restlessness and petty deceits of what has quickly degenerated into a loveless marriage.

Amelia Turner, disappointed in her illusory prospects of marriage, then suffers from being forbidden to work for money, despite the collapse of Turner's business. Taylor in her article 'Feminine Honesty' had discussed at length the convention which regarded the employment of a middle-class woman for money as declassing herself and disgracing her male relatives, and she identifies this as one reason for women's poverty.

> It is the belief of most men who can maintain their daughters without their working for wages that they ought not to work for wages. Not merely when he can provide a sure income both for the present and the future, but when he has only a life income, and even that uncertain, a father will frequently object to his daughters earning money, and neglect to teach them any means of doing so . . . Of this large class a considerable proportion must, either from death or misfortune, leave their children penniless, and a larger number must be unable to provide them a living on the scale to which they have been accustomed. The girls are doomed to remain in this poverty, however pitiable it may be, because it has been thought kinder not to teach them any means of getting out of it.[422]

Frustrated and unoccupied Amelia begins to fail in health and strength of will. After having appealed to Sarah to help her find work she turns down the opportunity offered, falls irretrievably into a decline and dies.

Maria Bell's crises are first, her near despair as her school suffers the effects of the mill closure, and then, the disagreement with Branksome which arises from her sense of responsibility and obligations to Dora Wells. The narrative picks up the theme of women's friendships, intertwining Maria's and Dora's lives more closely when Dora, in desperation, leaves the Woodman household to seek shelter with Maria.

At the house of a neighbour Dora has met an agent who engages public lecturers and readers, a popular form of education-cum-entertainment in the nineteenth century, and she sees a way of earning money. She asks Maria's help in giving a public lecture on *Measure for Measure*.[423]

Maria faces the most serious test of her loyalty to Dora. She realises that if she cannot persuade the villagers to accept the propriety of Dora's appearing in public she will share the ostracism and her school will sink yet deeper into failure. Taylor's own objective and warm-hearted narrative voice addresses the reader at this point.

> We each of us think of our little private struggle as the thing of the most importance, but it is only when it is ennobled by fellow-feeling that it kindles into enthusiasm. And enthusiasm in spite of the cynics, is the only thing that brings forth our best strength and noblest nature.[424]

Miss Everard, suprisingly enough, is sympathetic to the venture, a clue to the change in her outlook, the result of her growing friendship with Maria. Taylor catches the sense of the mixed fear and exhilaration of the three women as they first rather doubtfully contemplate the difficulties of the project and then decide to launch out on it nevertheless: they laugh! Maria decides first to consult Mrs. Dodds, the Vicar's wife, as a leader of the community.

> 'Lectures! Mechanics' Institutes!' Mrs. Dodds looked as if something improper were being enacted before her eyes.[425]

Thus Mary Taylor satirises the 'uneasy virtues' she had mocked from New Zealand.[426] Mrs. Dodds can only recommend the abandonment of the whole idea and 'patience'; she feels that Miss Bell is 'getting into a state of rebellion'.[427]

In describing the problems of this project for establishing a profession for Dora, Taylor draws on her intimate knowledge of Dissenting psychology. Rejected by the Anglican Mrs. Dodds, Maria turns to Sarah's parents, leading members of the 'chapellers' community. Though shocked and disapproving at first they are nevertheless willing to debate the problem and listen carefully, if sceptically. As they appear about to reject her proposal for Dora to give her performance at the chapel, Maria becomes desperate and angry.

> You have spoken of right, Mr. Miles. When you refuse a helping hand to a friendless woman fighting for an honest living, does the action approve itself to your conscience?
>
> He stood up. Maria had thought that as the case was hopeless she might as well give vent to her feeling, but he took it as an honest argument. In case of conscience he was accustomed to be thought in the wrong, and to have to maintain his point.
>
> 'I cannot say it does,' he said deliberately, to Maria's astonishment. 'If the lass has no notion but of gaining summat to live on,' he added slowly, 'I think she has a right to try.'[428]

Miles the Dissenter is moved by the power of his own conscience and, as an independent working man, by his conviction of the individual's right to strive to make a living. The Miles couple promise their help, the young men are enthusiastic and especially as the Church people have expressed opposition.

Paradoxically, the launching of Dora's project precipitates Maria's personal crisis. Branksome deplores her initiative in forwarding the scheme and foresees only failure and disgrace. In a bitter letter Maria breaks off their relationship. Everard Branksome was as much astonished with his 'setting down' as Sammy had been with his blow on the forehead.[429] He has, however, met with an aspect of Maria's character, confidence in her own judgment, which he had not before suspected 'prompt, passionate, scornful' and his admiration and love for her deepen. Unknown to her he proceeds to go about encouraging support for Dora's public appearance and helping to ensure its success.

On the day of the public performance, Dora, carefully advised by Miss Everard and Maria, delivers her lecture not on *Measure for Measure* in fact but on 'Justice', ending with the peroration:

> If we wish for justice we must each one stretch forth his arms to help his neighbour. For so it is decreed, that no man can stand alone.[430]

Dora's career develops not as a lecturer but as a reciter or *diseuse*. She soon has 'a good repertoire of poetry and prose fit for declamation'.[431]

Maria, still disillusioned with Branksome, rejects his attempts at reconciliation.

It remains for Taylor to conclude the novel by reconciling the lovers. Sarah, having witnessed deceit and dishonesty in the Overton household, begins to appreciate the honesty and plain-dealing of her family and friends and recognises her love for Sam. Sam himself is in deep trouble, deceived by Turner about the extent of the indebtedness of the business and harried by Thelwall who suggests a way of their going bankrupt which would cheat other creditors. Sam rejects Thelwall's dishonest proposal and the business is broken. As neighbours meet to discuss Sam's difficulties and commiserate with him, they are joined by Sarah, he uninvited, sees her home and the scene is set for frank discussion of their problems. He denies he showed contempt for her and declares his intention of waiting for her until she is convinced of his honesty and his respect for her. Sarah, accepting him, places their relationship on a new and unconventional footing, reminding him that she is earning good money.

> She laid hold of both sides of his coat collar, and looked up in his face.
>
> 'Sammy, I believe ye're an honest man and a good one, and I should like to help you!
>
> . . . Never mind being a bankrupt, Sammy. I can add ten

shillings i't week mysen,' at which Sammy nearly fell on the floor with laughing.[432]

As all this takes place, Turner, after travelling in a snowstorm melodramatically, arrives at Maria's to ask for shelter and is taken in. Maria and Miss Everard, who has been brought by Maria to live with her in the wake of the business collapse, nurse him but he dies. As his business affairs are being finalised it transpires that one of the creditors whose interests Sammy has honestly, if unwittingly, protected is Miss Everard, who remains still the owner of the mill and the house which Turner had leased.

Happy endings accumulate as the novel draws to a close. Dora arrives, buoyant, working and earning money. She tries to give Maria a present of £5, evoking the gift sent to Mary in New Zealand by Charlotte Brontë from her *Jane Eyre* earnings. The money was used to buy a cow – 'your cow', as Mary called it to Charlotte. Taylor ends this penultimate chapter with a dialogue between Miss Everard and Dora and a comment, which register the changes which have taken place in them and express her belief that women gain the capacity to act through engaging in action and that women's salvation will come through self-reliance and working for a living.

> A victory won increases the strength, as, indeed, we go on in any way we have begun, be it for good or evil.[433]

The happy ending for Sam and Sarah is not only their new understanding, but the invitation by Overton's bank for Sam to continue running the mill.

As Turner's and Sammy's creditors are paid, the big house is restored to Miss Everard and there Maria establishes her school. Branksome freely acknowledges that he had been wrong to try to discourage Maria in her project for Dora, but it takes more time to convince her to accept his renewed overtures. Like Sarah, Maria's resentment lies in her suspicion that Branksome does not really respect her.

> 'You wanted me,' he said, 'and I failed you! My poor girl! you did not know how ready I was to help you!' . . .
> 'Good God, Maria! Do you suspect me of despising you? I was wrong in my advice, and you were wiser than I! . . . you have won Maria![434]

Taylor brings reconciliations about through honest protest, self-criticism and explanation, leading to mutual understanding. Each of the lovers has up to a point been wrong; the young women, while admirably defending their right to independent action, learn the need to be willing to discuss their grievances and not to be unrealistically rigid in their judgments and demands on their men. Both men concede their mistakes and recognise the women's strengths and capacities for autonomous action. They are all changed and matured by their experiences. They are in sight, says Taylor, in closing, of 'that paradise which never comes but at the end of a novel', thus ironically and characteristically subverting the conventions to the very end.

Unable to achieve publication for many years, Taylor seems to have paid for the novel to appear in 1890. She cannot have been any longer ambitious to establish herself as a writer but she would have been justified in believing that her doctrine still needed advocacy. The very nature of this novel and its publication at any time during the thirty years after her return from New Zealand would have militated against its success. As realist fiction it is not untypical of the times either in its narrative method or in having a cause to advocate. It is the message which is untypical. Imaginatively embodied in fiction are the theories Taylor had set out in her journalism. She recreates in terms of individual characterisation and situation her views on the social and psychological stresses women faced in challenging their subordinate social and economic status, the moral effects of dependence and its impact on relationships between men and women and, more positively, the value of women's friendships and the exhilaration of women's successful struggle to achieve their goals.

By 1890 the condition-of-England novel was out of fashion. *Miss Miles* was out-moded for an *avant-garde* readership interested in new forms of novel-writing, more complex modern psychology and open discussion of sexual relationships; neither was it for the reader looking for romance and escapism. The heroines were neither 'New Women' conscious of the needs of their own sexuality, nor were they seeking their happiness in love and marriage alone.[435] Taylor's milieu is the unglamorous world of work, not of leisured aristocracy, which with the liberal use of dialect could also have militated against its success. The women's movement by 1890 had registered some successes, but though campaigning for further rights went on, neither the cause nor the doctrine commanded wide support. Taylor's political message was still not generally acceptable and sadly, failed, as one of her obituarists said, 'to find favour with the public'.

Chapter 9

Epilogue

With the appearance of her novel achieved after a very long period of gestation, Mary Taylor wrote no more for publication. In February 1890 she wrote to her cousin Mary Doublet to whom she had sent a copy of her book and who had asked for translations of the 'mottoes' which head chapters and which she provides. At the same time she gently disclaims any suggestion of having merely depicted the Spen Valley.

> There is no reality in it, nor a single person taken from life . . . There is no such place as Repton but many Yorkshire valleys with a lane and a beck running down them. All the hills between Yorkshire and Lancashire have such valleys with moorland above them. So you may find a Repton a dozen times over.[436]

In implicitly laying claim to a generalising imagination at work in the creation of the book, she echoes Charlotte Brontë's rebuke to Ellen Nussey forty years before when the latter attempted to identify which actual people appeared as fictional characters.

Mary's typewritten letter is characteristically brief, but carefully, even elegantly, composed and she is clearly grateful for the interest shown in the book. The remainder of the letter deals not with her novel but with the gift of flower seeds she is enclosing, with its careful specifying of the Latin names of the plants and suitability for the climate. It suggests a quiet way of life and an interest in her garden maintained into old age when she was no longer travelling but remaining more or less permanently at home.

Mary Taylor died suddenly on March 1st 1893. She was dressing in preparation for going to Leeds and the coach was waiting to take her to the station but as the time arranged for her to leave passed and she failed to appear, Martha Sharpe, knowing how punctual her mistress normally was, became alarmed. She found her mistress fallen on the floor of her bedroom, unconscious. She never recovered consciousness; some accounts say she died on the same day she collapsed, Grace Hirst thought she had fallen ill three or four days before. She thought that Taylor feared dying and that her death 'came so mercifully'. Jealously guarding her independence as she did, Taylor probably feared a lingering end with the consequent dependence on others.

Alerted by a telegram from Ellen Nussey and provided with information by her, Clement Shorter published an obituary in the *Illustrated London News* on March 18th.[437] It draws on the reminiscences of schooldays published in Gaskell's *Life* with the anecdote of Mary's rebellion at school in defence of Charlotte and echoing Ellen's suggestion that this was symptomatic of the eccentricity 'which was not unnoticeable in later years'.

It also refers to 'capriciousness and kindness' but, careful not to be seen critical of the dead, concedes that 'she was a true and good woman'.

The *Athenæum*, the previous week had included a brief notice of Taylor's death in its announcement of a new edition of Brontë novels in preparation by Clement Shorter and Dr. Robertson Nicoll.[438] Her death went unremarked by the *Englishwoman's Review*, which had warmly commended *The First Duty* and urged Taylor to write fiction. The older generation of women's rights activists were in danger of being forgotten: even Emily Faithfull's passing two years later was to merit only a short paragraph.

Shorter, ever on the alert for Brontë material, contacted Mary's nephew Joshua almost immediately after Mary's death had been announced and obtained permission to print her letters. Extracts from them appeared in 1896 in his *Charlotte Brontë and Her Circle*. Many of the letters are badly edited. There are also the inaccurate statements that following her return from New Zealand Mary had been 'living in complete seclusion', and that she had built a house for herself. The book acknowledges the help she gave to Mrs. Gaskell, and refers to her contributions to the *Victoria Magazine*, *The First Duty of Women* and *Miss Miles* along with a brief description of her 'gospel'.

> This novel strives to inculcate the advantages as well as the duty of women learning to make themselves independent of men. It is well, though not brilliantly written, and might, had the author possessed any of the latter-day gifts of self-advertisement, have attracted the public, if only by the mere fact that its author was a friend of Currer Bell's. But Miss Taylor, it is clear, hated advertisement, and severely refused to be lionised by Brontë worshippers.[439]

Like most people who have referred to Mary Taylor's 1870 collection of *Victoria Magazine* articles, he does not seem to be aware that she continued to write more articles for the magazine after the publication of *The First Duty of Women*. In his 1900 edition of Gaskell's *Life* which appeared after Ellen Nussey's death, he pays tribute to Taylor's intellectual abilities while dismissing her writing:

> All her letters show remarkable intellectual powers, and indeed it would not be too much to say that until Miss Brontë attained to literary fame Mary Taylor was the only human being of a high order of intelligence with whom she had come into contact apart from her own family circle. Miss Taylor's two books, however, published upon her return to England, had no special significance.[440]

In 1908 Mary reappeared in the story of Charlotte Brontë with some of her letters reproduced more fully by Shorter in *The Brontës; Life and Letters*.

There Mary is described as a great friend and the intellectual equal of Charlotte but there is silence about her feminist opinions.

> The reader will have discovered that one of the most attractive personalities in Charlotte Brontë's life was Miss Mary Taylor, the 'M–' of Mrs. Gaskell's biography and the Rose Yorke of *Shirley*. Mary Taylor will always have a peculiar interest to those who care for the Brontës.[441]

Taylor's passing was noted by a number of obituaries in newspapers of the immediate locality and in others which covered wider areas of the West Riding, such as the *Yorkshire Post*. Reflecting the growing prestige of the Brontë novels these newspapers were always eager to rehearse the local links of the sisters with the district. The Taylor family's association with Charlotte as well as the intrinsic interest of their various personalities provided good copy. All the obituaries, as was to be expected, described Mary's friendship with Charlotte Brontë with its origins in their schooldays and, of course, the relationship of the Taylor family to *Shirley*. In addition her emigration and return to Spen Valley were generally commented on. A further and important element of the tributes however was the treatment of Mary as a well-respected member of a family in good standing in the area and as a woman of vigorous intelligence, an occasional author and a good businesswoman.

Further accounts of the family, of Mary especially, and the Taylor connections with the Brontës, were stimulated by the announcement of her brother Waring's death, in Wellington in 1903. The *Yorkshire Daily Observer* described Waring's disreputable proceedings on December 18th but three days later printed an article, 'Rose Yorke in Real Life' submitted by a correspondent. It repeats the, by now familiar, stories of her schooldays and emigration but adds:

> Miss Taylor spent her latter days in quiet retirement at her home in Gomersal, and it seems but yesterday that her carriage driven by a staid coachman and drawn by an equally staid animal, was a familiar sight in the district. Quiet but very self-possessed, she was an admirable businesswoman, with a way of going straight to the point that was at times disconcerting.[442]

This, almost certainly by her own solicitor, was adapted as an item for the newspaper of the immediate locality.[443]

In her will Mary left over £4,000. She remembered Clementine Imseng, leaving her £100 and £50 to each of her two other servants, Josiah Mortimer and Martha Sharpe (to whom she left all her clothing). After the trust fund for John Taylor in New Zealand to yield £40 a year 'if he becomes bankrupt', the residue, after all necessary expenses had been paid, was bequeathed to her two nephews, Joshua and Thomas. Her money, some of which had come to her directly as assistance in New Zealand and inheritance on her return, was returned to the family, increased by the fruits of her own enterprise and careful management.

Among members of the next generation, three of Mary's great nephews moved out of the textile trade to become medical practitioners; Richard's son, Waring practised from Red House. Despite the succession of business failures, the family still owned considerable properties near Gomersal as well as in London, South Wales and Cornwall, which were finally sold in 1920 by private auction within the family, a considerable part being bought by Waring.[444]

Mary Taylor's way of life was guided by those principles to which she had been passionately committed from young womanhood. In search of economic and intellectual independence she developed the courage and self-confidence to overcome obstacles and even the disapproval of friends and acquaintances. In harmonising her principles and her practice she achieved a considerable degree of fulfilment, albeit at the cost of the frustration of not being able to share her most cherished ideas with those around her and discouragement at the lack of progress of the women's cause.

Rather more than most women, however, she was able to realise many of the hopes and dreams of her youth, self-supporting and independent, with the leisure to read, write and travel. There were nevertheless ambitions which eluded her. She failed to achieve literary success, her considerable journalistic skills went largely unrecognised even within the relatively small circle of women's rights activists into whose society she never became absorbed.

Her uncompromising temperament, forthright speech and her refusal to attract publicity may have exacted a price, but it was not only her personality which contributed to her relative obscurity but the times and the place in which she lived. She was born too early to take advantage of opportunities for the higher education and intellectual life for which she was so clearly fitted, and after her return from New Zealand she took the decision to return to her birthplace and family, to a cultural and political environment which was narrow, conservative, and losing the dynamism of its earlier stages of development.

Mary Taylor's grave lies in Gomersal churchyard, tended by local admirers. While ever the works of the Brontë sisters are read and their lives retold, her name and aspects of her career will feature but her life has more significance than as a footnote to Brontë studies. She was in that 'second echelon of advocates for women's rights' who have gone largely unhonoured and unsung, but whose lives and ideas remain a vital part of women's history. They made important pioneering contributions both to the achievement of practical social advances for women and to the enrichment of the ideology which permeated the debates around their demands and still remain, though in differing forms, a feature of 'the Woman Question' of our own times.

Appendix 1

Contributions by Mary Taylor to the *Victoria Magazine*
Articles collected in *The First Duty of Women* are indicated by an asterisk.
The frontispiece of the collection states that the articles appeared from
1865-70 but a careful check has revealed no article earlier than December
1866.
Except where indicated articles were signed 'T'.
The list includes two short stories.

Volume VIII
★ 'A Philistine's Opinion of Eugénie de Guérin', December 1866; p.162.
Unsigned.
'Co-operation and Competition', January 1867; p.215.
'Drifting', February 1867; p.297.

Volume IX
★ 'Feminine Honesty', May 1867; p.7.
★ 'Feminine Knowledge', June 1867; p.99.
★ 'Feminine Work', September 1867; p.403.

Volume X
★ 'Feminine Idleness', November 1867; p.1.
★ 'Feminine Character', December 1867; p.97 .
★ 'Marriage', January 1868; p.193.
★ 'Feminine Earnings', March 1868; p.385.

Volume XI
★ 'Feminine Respectability', May 1868;p.1.
'Feminine Suffrage and the Pall Mall Gazette', July 1868; p.211.
'Memoirs of Baron Bunsen', August 1868; p.346.

Volume XIII
★ 'An Old Dispute', July 1869; p. 239.Unsigned.
★ 'Crystallised Morality', September 1869; p.406.

Volume XIV
★ 'Plain Living and High Thinking', February 1870; p.331.

Volume XV
★ 'Redundant Women', June 1870; p.97.
★ 'What Am I To Do?', July 1870; p.215.
'Feminine Profitable Labour', October 1870; p.555.

Volume XVII
'The Revolt and the Revolters', July 1871; p.193. Signed 'Mary Taylor'.
'Notes of A Swiss Tour', August 1871; p.289.
'Domestic Economy', August 1871; p.345.

Volume XIX
'Plain Sewing', September 1873; p.385. Signed 'Mary Taylor'.

Volume XXI
'The Shah on English Laws', August 1873; p.359. Signed 'Mary Taylor'.
'A Tale', September 1873; p.395.

Volume XXIII
'Liberal Tyranny', September 1874; p.398 Signed 'M.T'.

Volume XXVII
'A Servant Girl's History', October 1876; p.503 .Signed 'M.T.'

Volume XXIX
July 1877 'Once More the Woman Question', July 1877; p.209. Signed 'M.T'.

Appendix 2

Ellen Nussey and Brontë Biography

Some of the material in this Appendix appeared in 'Mary Taylor, Ellen Nussey and Brontë Biography', *Brontë Society Transactions*, Volume 21, Part 7, 1996. It indicates the extent of Ellen Nussey's persistent initiatives for developing Brontë biography and the difficulties she met; a situation from which Mary Taylor distanced herself.

Ellen Nussey and Arthur Nicholls

Ellen's relationship with Nicholls was fraught with tension and hostility. She had considered Nicholls a poor match for Charlotte, while he in his turn had tried after the marriage to interfere in the correspondence between the two women. He thought Charlotte's letters to Ellen were indiscreet and threatened to censor them unless Ellen promised, in writing, to 'fire' them.[445] Ellen seems to have asked for some undertaking from Nicholls in return. Charlotte, the mediator, informed her friend:

> On my asking him whether he would give the pledge required in return he says 'yes' we may write any dangerous stuff we please to each other.[446]

What 'the pledge required' was is not known but Ellen briefly comments in pencil at the foot of the page of one of the two aborted volumes of letters (see below) 'he never gave the pledge'.[447] The other volume has 'conditional not complied with'.[448] This was her justification for not 'firing' Charlotte's letters. Relations had been made worse when Nicholls, who had strong reservations about a biography of Charlotte, tried to exclude Ellen from any part in Gaskell's work by suggesting that only Patrick should see the manuscript.

Nicholls, as owner of the copyright of Charlotte's letters, was able to obstruct some of Ellen's efforts for further publications and as she grew older her hostility to Nicholls intensified. When Shorter told her in 1895 that he had arranged to visit Nicholls she replied:

> He had better show himself even thus late a man of honour.[449]

According to Shorter, Nicholls denied any knowledge of letters from Ellen to Charlotte.

Ellen Nussey, Biographers and Editors

Clement Shorter was only one of[450] a number of biographers and editors with whom Ellen co-operated. Among others who published work on the Brontës with her help were William Scruton,[451] Horsfall Turner[452], Mary Robinson[453] and Wemyss Reid. As well as publishing biographical material and editing the Brontë novels and Gaskell's biography, Shorter, along with

T. J. Wise,[454] collected letters and manuscripts. Her assistance to Altheus Wilkes came to nothing. After Ellen's death, Shorter, who had energetically exploited Ellen's dedication and knowledge, commented:

> Miss Nussey was probably from the first an ardent hero-worshipper of her more gifted friend – her senior by a year. In the period that succeeded Charlotte Brontë's death this hero-worship became little less than idolatry, and Miss Nussey in her later years received numerous visitors who were anxious to learn something of the Brontë sisters. To these visitors she was always ready to give courteous consideration, although she was able to add but little to the information which in the days when memory was most acute she had imparted to Mrs. Gaskell.[455]

Initially Nussey seems to have had one disinterested motive, the defence of Charlotte's reputation, but as the years passed she enjoyed the prestige of being the Brontë authority and she also became aware that in Charlotte's letters she was in possession of a financial asset. She seems to have developed some resentment that she had received no share of the money paid to Gaskell for *The Life*.[456] Feeling increasingly financially insecure as she grew older, she made efforts to realise the monetary value of the letters while at the same time being genuinely anxious to see them deposited in a secure archive. She sought the help of both Wemyss Reid and George Smith in an attempt to sell them to the British Museum and she seems later to have been under the impression that T. J. Wise would ensure their safe-keeping in the South Kensington Museum, (the Victoria and Albert).

Though she often found herself in difficulties and even conflicts, Ellen's concern about Charlotte's reputation was not negligible. Women writers were under some pressure to exercise caution in the way they treated certain topics in order to avoid charges of immorality, irresponsibility and coarseness. There were areas of human experience, especially sexual experience, which the truly refined woman was supposed not to know about, or reveal her knowledge if she did. Critical response to Currer Bell's novels was mixed. Some reviews recognised a new and important voice in fiction, but others detected coarseness and rebelliousness, even 'moral Jacobinism'.

Ellen's desire to defend the reputation of the Brontës was also affected by specifically local factors. In the circles she mixed in there was some resentment at the depiction of West Yorkshire society as brutal and savage, by Charlotte herself in *Shirley*, and by Mrs. Gaskell in the biography. There was defensiveness about the possible depiction of actual local personalities under fictional names. Mary Taylor's mother was angered. Soon after the publication of *The Life* there was an article by a nephew of the Reverend Hammond Roberson (regarded as a partial model for Helstone in *Shirley*) attacking Gaskell and Brontë and defending his uncle. Ellen made sure a letter was written to the local newspaper defending Charlotte.[457] According to Wemyss Reid the Brontë novels in the 1860s were not popular, neither was there sympathetic interest in their lives and personalities, despite the success of Gaskell's *Life*, published three years earlier. Paying his first visit to Haworth in 1866 he had been surprised by a feeling there that was 'nothing less than positive antipathy', and he sensed hostility, even beyond the village itself.[458] He claims that the novels of the three sisters were explained as the vindictive revenge of impoverished governesses resentful at their exclusion from polite West Riding society.

Nicholls's concern to prevent publication of Charlotte's letters appears to have been an understandable sensitivity to anything relating to his courtship of Charlotte and the crisis precipitated by their engagement and marriage. By respecting Nicholls's privacy on the grounds of principle Reid also avoided provoking him in the exercise of his ownership of copyright but he must have felt sufficiently confident of Nicholls's indifference to the susceptibilities of the Taylors to make public the comments Charlotte had made about them. Ellen was always nervous about the treatment of Branwell's reputation, one of the most difficult and contentious topics in Brontë biography. Mrs. Gaskell had soon found herself in difficulties in relation to her treatment of Branwell and his employer Mrs. Robinson. Twenty-five years later, as Mary Robinson was working on her biography of Emily Brontë, she had to write to Ellen, reassuring her that nothing in the book would reflect on Ellen herself.

Swinburne's review of Robinson's book drew both Francis Leyland and Wemyss Reid into controversy (see Chapter 6). Leyland asserted that Branwell's behaviour was not so different from that of many other young men; it was Branwell's frail health which was undermined by his indulgences while others who did the same were unaffected. It was the narrow views of the Brontë family that led them to exaggerate and dramatise Branwell's conduct. The attack on Ellen came in his comment that though Charlotte discussed Branwell with 'a particular friend', she had never intended her letters to be made public.[459]

Reid replied on Ellen's behalf, transferring any blame for the revelations about Branwell to Patrick Brontë and to Mrs. Gaskell, stating that Nussey had not wanted any references to Branwell's story. It was Mrs. Gaskell, needing sufficient material to produce two volumes for *The Life*, who had drawn on the letters which revealed Branwell's situation.

> I have the best authority for saying that it was at the urgent request of Mr. Brontë that Miss Nussey placed Charlotte's letters in the hands of Mrs. Gaskell, and she did so on the express stipulation that no painful revelations should be made with regard to Branwell.[460]

Reid also claims that Mrs. Gaskell went ahead despite Nussey's objections but with Mr. Brontë's agreement, even though the father later regretted it.

In 1889, still determined to see the publication of the letters, Ellen placed them at the disposal of J. Horsfall Turner, but when they were already edited, printed and about to be published, Nicholls intervened to suppress the book. All but a handful of the volumes were burned.

Successive setbacks and criticisms produced acute anxiety and self-pity in Ellen:

> It is sad now to think that Miss Nussey's long and faithful attachment to the members of the Brontë family brought with it many pains and penalties, and that in taking up cudgels in their defence she estranged herself from some whom she had once reckoned amongst her friends . . . Someone has said that Miss Nussey was a lady who had strong likes and dislikes. I can quite believe it . . . Can we wonder that during the forty years she was privileged to survive her dearest of friends she should have so jealously guarded her fair name against the imputations and reflections cast upon her by her numerous detractors, most of whom were, alas, those of her own sex? This Miss Nussey has done, though at the cost of many sleepless nights, and the sacrifice of her own peace of mind. In speaking now of some of her 'dislikes', I do so all the more readily because I am committing no breach of confidence, and because it was her own expressed wish to be put right with the world, as far as possible, on several points concerning which there was much ignorance and misapprehension.[461]

In 1895 Clement Shorter broke through Nicholls's resistance.

> An examination of Charlotte Brontë's will, which was proved at York by her husband in 1855, suggested an easy way out of the difficulty. I made up my mind to try and see Mr. Nicholls. I had heard of his disinclination to be in any way associated with the controversy which had gathered round his wife for all these years; but I wrote to him nevertheless, and received a cordial invitation to visit him in his Irish home.[462]

It is not clear what the loophole was in Charlotte's will but Shorter certainly used the argument that some copies of Horsfall Turner's edition of the letters had survived the bonfire and were in the possession of some other people. As a safeguard he argued that rather than be suppressed, the letters should be edited properly. Nicholls yielded and received £400 for Brontë manuscripts, letters and copyrights. Around the same time Shorter was promising to send Ellen a cheque for £300, presumably for the ownership of the letters of which Nicholls had now sold the copyright. In acknowledging the promise, Ellen expressed her deep sense of isolation and even persecution.

> I have quite enough [trouble] in other ways – envy and jealousy are always at work among a few weak-minded aspiring women in social life, however quiet and unassuming, just a target to shoot littleness at.[463]

By October, however, she was complaining about both J. T. Wise and Shorter and 'unscrupulous grabbing men in literary London'.

Ellen was not wise in the ways of literary entrepreneurs, cheating collectors and ruthless editors. She was too trusting and not very efficient in keeping control of the letters. Brontë studies are nevertheless deeply indebted to her despite her mistakes.

There is a rather sad epitaph on all Ellen's activity and concern and worry, from the old friend who had been asked by her to destroy the sheets of the aborted Horsfall Turner book.

> Poor old lady! The last years of her life had many disappointments, most of them arising entirely from her warped views of life. She had a kind heart, and she was an interesting companion, with many memories of things local and otherwise.[464]

Notes

Despite errors and omissions the major source of Charlotte Brontë's correspondence has been T. J. Wise and J. A. Symington, *The Brontës: Their Lives Friendships and Correspondence*, 4 volumes, Oxford, 1932, The Shakespeare Head Brontë (referred to here as W&S). Joan Stevens (referred to here as Stevens) provides correction of some details in *Mary Taylor, Friend of Charlotte Brontë: Letters from New Zealand and Elsewhere*, Auckland and Oxford University Presses, 1972, as does Margaret Smith, *The Letters of Charlotte Brontë, Vol. One 1829-1847, Vol. Two 1848-51*, Clarendon Press, Oxford, 1995-2000 which will ultimately completely supersede Wise and Symington. Reference is made to significant corrections in the footnotes.

1.   Q. D. Leavis, Introduction to *Jane Eyre*, Penguin Books 1977.
2.   Ellen Moers, *Literary Women,* The Women's Press, London, 1980, p.139.
3.   Elizabeth Gaskell, *The Life of Charlotte Brontë*, p.129, ed. Alan Shelston, Penguin, 1975.
4.   C.B. to E.N. January 3rd 1841; W&S 107.
5.   See e.g. Sharpe's *London Magazine of Entertainment and Instruction,* June 1855 vol.v, p.339, 'A Few Words about "Jane Eyre".'
6.   For a discussion of the letters and the accounts from Nussey and Taylor see Elizabeth Gaskell, *The Life of Charlotte Brontë*, ed. Alan Shelston, Penguin, 1975, p.21.
7.   W&S letter 966, April 19th 1856.
8.   C.B. to Gaskell, September 20th 1851; W&S 708.
9.   July 30th 1857; W&S 987.
10. March 17th [1858] letter 387, p.495 in *The Letters of Mrs. Gaskell,* ed. J.A.V. Chapple and A. Pollard, Manchester, 1966.
11. p.314, vol.3 no.75, April 4th 1857.
12. Letter to Ellen Nussey; W&S 994, January 28th 1858.
13. Gaskell, p.170.
14. see Pat Hudson, *The Genesis of Industrial Capital: A Study of the West Riding Wool Textile Industry c.1750-1850*, Cambridge University Press, 1968.
15. *Leeds Mercury,* December 9th 1826.
16. Frank Peel, *Spen Valley: Past and Present,* Kirklees Historical Reprints, Kirklees Leisure Service 1987.
17. Peel, p.226.
18. Peel, p.239.
19. Peel, p.309.
20. See below, M.T.'s letter to C.B. about *Shirley* and Waring's denial that his father spoke dialect, p.29.
21. July 30th 1857; W&S 987.
22. Peel, p.397
23. July 30th 1857; W&S 987.
24. W. Gérin, *Charlotte Brontë: The Evolution of Genius.* Oxford, 1967, p.65.
25. Gaskell, p.133.
26. C. Shorter, *Charlotte Brontë and Her Circle,* Hodder and Stoughton, London, 1896, p.235.
27. Gaskell, p.132, 'Mary Taylor's Narrative'; W&S vol.1, p.91.
28. Gaskell, p.130, 'Mary Taylor's Narrative'; W&S vol.1, p.90.
29. A letter from C.B. to Mary Dixon between January 30th and June 1843; unpublished; in Berg Collection in New York Public Library; cited Stevens pp.41-42 and Gérin, p.219. Smith has 'early 1843', p.313.
30. Gaskell, p.132, 'Mary Taylor's Narrative'; W&S vol.1, p.91.

31. See Christine Alexander, *The Early Writings of Charlotte Brontë*, Basil Blackwell, Oxford, 1983. Sue Lonoff 'Brontë's Belgian Essays: The Discourse of Empowerment' in *Victorian Studies* vol.32, no.3, Spring 1989, p.399 draws attention to the scene in *Shirley*, chapter 22, where Shirley herself withdraws into a 'trance' after reading a book which 'has set her brain astir, furnished her mind with pictures'.
32. C.B. to E.N. July 4th 1849; W&S 453.
33. W&S 47, May 28th 1836, C.B. to E.N.: 'When you see her [Miss Taylor] in church . . . '.; W&S 101, July 14th 1840, C.B. to E.N.: ' . . . give a note to Martha in church'.; W&S 130, March 1842, M.T. to E.N.: 'too wet to go to church'.; W&S 135, June 22nd 1842, Martha Taylor to E.N.: 'I shall be in church on Sunday'. Other members of the family adhered to the Moravians who were strong in the district.
34. Gaskell, p.131: 'Mary Taylor's Narrative'; W&S vol 1, p.90.
35. March 13th 1835; W&S 35.
36. C.B. to E.N. June 20th 1833; W&S 27.
37. A Taylor employee, Thomas Porritt of Dewsbury, recalled driving Charlotte Brontë from Roe Head to Red House in the Taylor's carriage. *The Reporter* December 20th or 26th 1896.
38. C.B. to E.N. April 15th 1839; W&S 74.
39. Letter to E.N. June 9th 1838; W&S 68.
40. W&S 64, give August 24th [1837], but for a discussion of the dating of Charlotte Brontë's letters about this visit and the Taylor's tour see Edward Chitham & Tom Winnifrith, *Brontë Facts and Brontë Problems*, Macmillan, London, 1983, pp.26-28.
41. ' "What's the matter with you now?" as my mother used to say, as if it were the twentieth time in a fortnight.' M.T. to C.B. after December 1851; W&S 763. See also the interview by Susan May Taylor with Grace Hirst, *Mary Taylor* ms Notebook, Brontë Parsonage Library, p.13.
42. Postmark November 21st 1840; W&S 106. Smith gives the date as November 20th and a fuller version of the letter, p.232.
43. Stevens, p.17, Joan Stevens reproduces more of this letter than is in; W&S 106. What remains of the censored passage after 'her attainments are of the very highest standard' is as follows: 'your destiny has . . . *thought* her doubts . . . the fact that she would . . . really marry . . . merely brought to a pitch of great intensity seldom equalled . . . did not value her the less for it because I understand, yet I doubt whether Mary will ever marry. Branwell was identified in this letter in an article by C. W. Hatfield, cited in Gérin pp.167-8'. Though writing nearly a century later, Mary's niece is indignant at Charlotte's idea and attributes it to her 'sisterly jealousy', that everyone who met Branwell must lose her heart to him, or to a 'diplomatic warning' from Charlotte to Ellen Nussey 'for E.N.'s empty little head seems to have turned very easily in the direction of any young man in her circle . . . ' ms letter to Dr. M. Edgerley, June 22nd 1930, Brontë Parsonage Library.
44. Gaskell, p.577.
45. C.B. to E.N. August 20th 1840; W&S 103. Smith has 'sophistical'.
46. *The Professor*, Dent Everyman Library, 1975, chapter 4.
47. C.B. to E.N. January 3rd 1841; W&S 107.
48. In her interview with Susan Taylor, Grace Hirst remarked that Joshua's wife had had a very sad life. 'I asked in what way? She said that she had lost her daughter Emily and that Susan was always delicate. I felt that she really meant something else and was hedging . . . perhaps grandfather's rather trying ways!' Susan Taylor, *Mary Taylor*, ms Notebook, Interview with Grace Hirst, December 5th 1931, Brontë Parsonage Library, p.14.
49. C.B. to Emily Brontë, April 2nd 1841. W&S 112. Smith has 'peculiar' circumstances.
50. Joan Stevens, ' "Her Own Landmarks" . . . Mary Taylor's Shop in New Zealand.' *Brontë Society Transactions*, part 79, 1969, p.315.
51. C.B. to E.N. September 13th 1846; W&S 267, cited Stevens, p.59.
52. I am indebted to Joan Stevens for this information about conditions and also to Charlotte Godley, *Letters from Early New Zealand*, 1936, intended for private circulation only.

53. See M.T. to C.B. Wellington August 13th 1850; W&S 583 & 584
54. *The First Duty of Women*, The Victoria Press, London, 1870, p.242.
55. *First Duty*, p.96.
56. *First Duty*, pp 95-6.
57. Charlotte Brontë, *Unfinished Novels*, Sutton, Stroud, 1993, p.45. Introduction T. Winnifrith.
58. *Unfinished Novels*, p.105.
59. *Unfinished Novels*, p.106.
60. Gaskell, p.378.
61. September 21st 1849; Gaskell, p.382; W&S 474.
62. Gaskell, p.388; C.B. to E.N. November 16th 1849; W&S 492.
63. Gaskell, p.379.
64. M.T. to C.B. August 13th 1850; W&S 584.
65. *Shirley*, chapter 9.
66. *Shirley*, chapter 9.
67. These volumes were bequeathed to New Zealand relatives by his daughter Susan Taylor (b.1876) on her death in 1955 and made available to Joan Stevens to whose work I am indebted for some of the material in this discussion: see her article, 'Sidelights on "Shirley"': Brontëana in New Zealand', *Brontë Society Transactions*, part 79, 1969.
68. *Shirley*, chapter 3.
69. *Shirley*, chapter 3
70. *Shirley*, chapter 4.
71. *Shirley*, chapter 4.
72. Stevens, 'Sidelights on "Shirley"', *Brontë Society Transactions*, part 79, 1969, p.307.
73. *Shirley*, chapter 4.
74. Postmarked July 24th 1848; W&S 382.
75. Stevens, 'Sidelights on "Shirley"', *Brontë Society Transactions*, part 79, 1969 p.306.
76. Stevens, 'Sidelights on "Shirley"', *Brontë Society Transactions*, part 79, 1969 p.311.
77. Gaskell, p.170.
78. M.T. to C.B. August 13th 1850; W&S 584.
79. *Shirley*, chapter 9.
80. Stevens, 'Sidelights on "Shirley"', *Brontë Society Transactions*. part 79, 1969 p.308.
81. July 28th 1848; W&S 383.
82. November 20th 1845; W&S 219.
83. M.T. to E.N. March 11th 1851; W&S 647.
84. M.T. to E.N. March 11th 1851; W&S 647.
85. Susan Taylor, *Mary Taylor*, ms Notebook, Interview with Grace Hirst, December 5th 1931, Brontë Parsonage Library, p.13. There is a slip of memory here; Mrs. Taylor's family name was Tickell; it was Mary's grandmother who was a Waring.
86. M.T. to C.B. August 13th 1850; W&S 584.
87. *Shirley*, chapter 9.
88. *Shirley*, chapter 9.
89. Stevens, 'Sidelights on "Shirley"', *Brontë Society Transactions*, part 79, 1969 pp.308-9.
90. *Shirley*, chapter 9.
91. August 13th 1850; W&S 584.
92. *Shirley*, chapter 9.
93. Stevens, 'Sidelights on "Shirley"', *Brontë Society Transactions*, part 79, 1969, p.303. Stevens points out that the notes in each of the editions were written some years after the actual dates of their publication.
94. Stevens, 'Sidelights on "Shirley"', *Brontë Society Transactions*, part 79, 1969, p.311.
95. *The Brontës ; The Critical Heritage*, ed. Miriam Allott, Routledge & Kegan Paul, London & Boston, 1974, p.415.
96. June 7th 1851; W&S 675.
97. *Shirley*, Chapter 9.
98. M.T. to C.B.5 April 1850; W&S 542

99. *Shirley*, chapter 9.
100. Susan Taylor, *Mary Taylor*, ms Notebook, Interview with Grace Hirst, December 5th 1931, Brontë Parsonage Library, p.15.
101. C.B. to E.N. June 10th 1841; W&S 115.
102. The Victoria Press, London, 1870, p.94.
103. August 7th 1841; W&S 119.
104. C.B. to E.N. January 30th 1843; W&S 152.
105. August 7th 1841; W&S 119.
106. August 7th 1841; W&S 119.
107. September 9th; cf. Martha's letter to E.N. September 9th 1841; W&S 120.
108. C.B. to E.N. October 17th 1841; W&S 122. (Smith has 'to this step'.)
109. In her quotation from C.B.'s letter to Miss Branwell, September 29th 1841; W&S 121, Mrs. Gaskell (p.219) is in error. It is not Mary but Martha who is at Koekelberg at this time. Martha's letter to C.B. of September 9th 1841; W&S 120, would seem to confirm this. Mary would be hardly likely to leave Brussels on the 9th and be back by the 29th. C.B. to E.N. January 20th 1842, W&S 129 saying she regrets missing Martha by going to Lille, which was being considered as an alternative to Brussels. Mary's own letter from Château Koekelberg, March -April 5th 1842 W&S 130 giving an account of her school routine, reads like a first letter from Brussels.
110. C.B. to E.N. November 2nd 1841; W&S 123. Smith has ampersand.
111. Gérin, p.199.
112. George Dixon became a Liberal MP and educational reformer.
113. *hallack*: In a letter to E.N. June -July 24th 1848.; W&S 382 Mary uses this West Yorkshire dialect word which is a form of 'hollock' meaning to idle away time; to loiter; to loaf; to play; *The English Dialect Dictionary* ed. Joseph Wright, Oxford University Press, 1961.
114. Gaskell, p.586. See also: 'Prodigious was the amount of life I lived that morning. Finding myself before St Paul's I went in. I mounted to the dome. I saw thence London, with its river, and its bridges, and its churches; I saw antique Westminster and the green Temple Gardens, with sun upon them, and a glad, blue sky of early spring above.' (*Villette*, Collins, London and Glasgow, 1972, chapter 6.)
115. Gaskell, p.586.
116. For discussions of its location see Gérin, pp.202-3 and Stevens, pp.171-6.
117. March-April 5th 1842; W&S 130.
118. March-April 5th 1842; W&S 130.
119. March-April 5th 1842; W&S 130.
120. March-April 5th 1842; W&S 130.
121. Smith has ampersand.
122. W&S 138, undated, probably around July 1842 and certainly before end of October 1842.
123. W&S 138, undated, probably around July 1842 and certainly before end of October 1842. Stevens and Smith have 'where'; Smith has 'mentioned'.
124. Letter to E.N. September 24th 1842; W&S 142.
125. Letter to E.N. September 24th 1842; W&S 142.
126. Letter to E.N. September 24th 1842; W&S 142.
127. *The Infernal World of Branwell Brontë*, Gollancz, London, 1960, p.142.
128. Hale, London, 1974, pp.82-3.
129. Hodder and Stoughton, London, 1975.
130. Smith has ampersand.
131. October 30th 1842; W&S 145. Smith gives October 30th & November 1st 1842.
132. Letter to E.N. June 25th, 1843; Stevens letter 11, previously unpublished.
133. Letter to C.B. April 5th 1850; W&S 542.
134. *The Professor,* chapter 19; *Shirley,* chapter 9.
135. February 16th 1843; W&S 153.
136. March 6th 1843; W&S 154.
137. C.B. to E.N. April 1st 1843; W&S 155.

138. Letter to E.N. June 25th, 1843; Stevens letter 11, previously unpublished.
139. Letter to E.N. June 25th, 1843; Stevens letter 11, previously unpublished.
140. Winter 1843; Stevens letter 12, previously unpublished.
141. For a discussion of Sand's impact on and influence in England see Patricia Thomson, *George Sand and the Victorians: Her Influence and Reputation in Nineteenth Century England*, Macmillan, London, 1977.
142. Winter, 1843; Stevens letter 12, previously unpublished.
143. C.B. to E.N. October 13th 1843; W&S 165.
144. Gaskell, p.589.
145. Gaskell, pp.588-9.
146. C.B. to E.N. November 15th 1843; W&S 166. According to Stevens this is wrongly dated. Mildred Christian dates it shortly after October 13th. Smith has no italics on 'prudent' and has varied punctuation.
147. December 30th 1843. Abraham Dixon to Mary Dixon. Leeds City Museum.
148. A letter of E.N.'s to Mary Gorham May 21st in a transcription by C.V. Hatfield at the Brontë Parsonage Library.
149. *The Letters of Mrs. Gaskell*, letter 256.
150. Gaskell, pp.548-9.
151. C.B. to E.N. September 16th 1844,; W&S 183. Smith gives October 26th.
152. For discussion of the friendship of Mary Taylor and Charlotte Brontë see also Pauline Nestor, *Female Friendships and Communities: Charlotte Brontë. George Eliot. Elizabeth Gaskell*, Clarendon Press, Oxford, 1988.
153. *First Duty*, 'Feminine Character', p.166.
154. Rebecca Fraser, *Charlotte Brontë*, Methuen, London, 1988, p.128.
155. M.T. to C.B. August 13th 1850; W&S 584.
156. M.T. to C.B. April 5th 1850; W&S 542.
157. M.T. to E.N. April 19th 1856; W&S 966.
158. See for example her letter to Gaskell, *The Life*, p.458, re. J.S. Mill, September 20th 1851; W&S 708 and also her letter to W.S. Williams re. girls' employment, July 3rd 1849; W&S 452.
159. Gaskell, p.580.
160. M.T to C.B. April 5th, 1850; W&S 542.
161. Gaskell, p.131; letter of January 18th 1856.
162. C.B. to E.N. January 20th 1842; W&S 129.
163. C.B. to E.N. September 13th 1846; W&S 267.
164. C.B. to E.N. April 2nd 1845; W&S 194.
165. For some of the information relating to aspects of life in Wellington and some of the area's residents, I am indebted to the work of Joan Stevens.
   For interesting accounts of these aspects of settler life in New Zealand see Charlotte Godley, *Letters From New Zealand*, and *New Zealand Letters of Thomas Arnold, The Younger*, edited J. Bertram, University of Auckland, London & Wellington, 1966.
166. See 'Advice to Intending Colonists' in *Life in a Young Colony*, Selections from Early New Zealand Writing, ed. Cherry A Hankin, Whitcoulls Publishers, Christchurch, Sydney, London, 1981.
167. C.B. to E.N. September 18th 1845; W&S 214.
168. Philip Henderson, *Samuel Butler*, Cohen and West Ltd., London, 1953, p.54.
169. Cited in Keith Sinclair, *A History of New Zealand*, Penguin, Harmondsworth, 1973, p.101.
170. *First Duty*, p.95.
171. Letter to E.N. 11th March 1851; W&S 647. Stevens letter 23, has 'wd.'
172. Cited Philip Henderson, *Samuel Butler*, p.45.
173. M.T. to C.B.; W&S 382, postmark July 24th 1848. Stevens letter 16 has 'June to July 24th 1848'.
174. M.T. to E.N. March 11th 1851; W&S 647. Stevens letter 23 has 'every where' [sic],' - &; no comma after 'while'.
175. M.T. to C.B. (postmark) July 24th 1848 but started before 1st July; W&S 382. Stevens letter 16 has *'middle classes'*.

176. C.B. to E.N. June 5th 1847; W&S 292.
177. C.B. to E.N. December 24th 1847; W&S 330.
178. C.B. to E.N. March 6th 1848; W&S 355.
179. C.B. to E.N. July 4th 1849; W&S 453.
180. M.T. to C.B. New Zealand postmark July 24th 1848 but started before July 1st; W&S 382.
     Stevens letter 16, has 'shd' and *'inbetweenity'*.
181. M.T. to E.N. January 8th 1857; W&S 977.
182. C.B. to Miss Wooler August 28th 1848; W&S 388.
183. C.B. to Miss Wooler August 28th 1848;W&S 388.
184. M.T. to C.B; W&S 382, postmark, July 24th 1848 but started before July 1st.
185. M.T. to C.B. April 10th 1849; W&S 436, For evidence which tends to refute Mary's opinion
     of Dr. Knox (who was the brother of the notorious Knox of the Burke and Hare scandals)
     see Joan Stevens, *'Brother Fred' and The Two Cultures: New Zealand's First Librarian*, New
     Zealand Libraries, October 1968.
186. C.B. to E.N. September 13th 1846; W&S 267.
187. M.T. to C.B. postmark July 24th 1848; begun before July 1st; W&S 382.
188. *New Zealand Letters of Thomas Arnold,* p.52.
189. M.T. to E.N. February 9th 1849; W&S 422.
190. M.T. to C.B. postmark July 24th 1848 but started before July 1st; W&S 382.
191. M.T. to E.N. February 9th 1849; W&S 422.
192. M.T. to C.B. April 5th 1850; W&S 542. In fact no such marriage took place and Rhodes it
     seems was by no means disreputable; see Stevens, 'Her Own Landmarks', p.317.
193. C.B. to Margaret Wooler August 28th 1848; W&S 388.
194. M.T. to C.B. postmarked July 24th 1848 but started before July 1st; W&S 382.
195. M.T. to E.N. February 9th 1849; W&S 422.
196. M.T. to C.B. April 10th 1849; W&S 436, ms. in Brontë Parsonage Library.
197. M.T. to C.B. April 10th 1849; W&S 436, Stevens letter 18. MS in Brontë Parsonage Library.
198. Dixon Papers, Leeds City Museum.
199. C.B. to E.N. June 26th 1848; W&S 37.
200. His letters in the small collection of Dixon papers in the Leeds City Museum refer quite
     frequently to money and economies and suggest somewhat frequent financial difficulties.
201. M.T. to E.N. February 9th 1849; W&S 422. Given the date of this letter Joan Stevens is
     obviously correct in pointing to the error in W&S who write that the cousins arrived early
     in 1849.
202. Stevens, 'Her Own Landmarks'. For further evidence about their departure see C.B. to
     E.N. February 16th 1849; W&S 423, saying that Ellen and Henry were waiting in London
     for their ship to leave.
203. For a description of this site see Stevens, 'Her Own Landmarks'.
204. M.T. to C.B. April 5th 1850; W&S 542, Stevens letter 19 has 'empl[oy]ment'.
205. M.T. to E.N. August 15th 1850; W&S 585.
206. 'What Can Educated Women Do?' (II) 'The English Woman's Journal', January 1860;
     reprinted in *Barbara Leigh Smith Bodichon and the Langham Place Group*, ed. Candida Ann
     Lacey, Routledge & Kegan Paul, New York & London, 1987, p.164.
207. M.T. to E.N. August 15th 1850; W&S 585.
208. M.T. to E.N. March 11th 1851; W&S 647, Stevens letter 23 has 'when we're quite tired';
     'ham' not 'have'; and D. Copperfield [sic].
209. M.T. to E.N. March 11th 1851; W&S 647.
210. C.B. to Miss Wooler October 21st 1851; W&S 713.
211. M.T. to C.B. April 5th 1850; W&S 542. Stevens letter 19 has 'objec[tion] and 's[o]'.
212. M.T. to C.B. April 5th 1850; W&S 542.
213. C.B. to E.N. January 28th 1850; W&S 522, 'Mary Taylor seems in good health and spirits
     and in the way of doing well.'
     C.B. to E.N. October 14th 1850; W&S 610, 'I have had a letter from Mary lately – she is
     well, happy, and prosperous – her shop thriving, – herself content – I am glad of this.'

C.B. to E.N. February 26th 1851; W&S 645, 'I also received a letter from Mary Taylor written not in high spirits – but still showing hopeful prospects.'

214. M.T. to C.B. 1852; W&S 763, gives what must be an estimated date of April; Stevens letter 24 notes that C.B. sent on the letter to E.N. which bears a postmark 'Keighley' and 'October 27th'.

215. Gaskell, p.469, 'she heard in March' and C.B. to E.N, W&S 754 gives March 4th 1852. Brontë did indeed write 'March' but Stevens notes that it would have been impossible for news of a death on December 27th to arrive by March 4th Her investigation into sailings from New Zealand suggest the more likely date of May 4th.

216. Susan Taylor, *Mary Taylor*, ms. Notebook, Interview with Grace Hirst, December 5th 1931, Brontë Parsonage Library, pp.18-19

217. M.T. to E.N. January 8th 1857; W&S 977. Stevens letter 29 has 'A book is worth any of them and a good book worth them put together. Mamas included.'

218. Susan Taylor, *Mary Taylor*, ms Notebook, Interview with Grace Hirst, December 5th 1931, p.8, Brontë Parsonage Library.

219. *First Duty*, p.156.

220. M.T. to E.N. postmark July 21st 1853 (written May,June, July); W&S 856. Stevens letter 25 has 'abt', 'shd' [pay] /legal/ 'yr' 'wd'.

221. M.T. to E.N. February 24th and March 3rd 1854; W&S 879. Stevens letter 26 has 'yr' 'C's' 'shdn't' 'shd' 'wd'.

222. Gaskell wrote to Smith on the last day of May expressing a wish to write about Brontë. Within the week Ellen Nussey wrote to Nicholls complaining about an article in *Sharp's Magazine* with the suggestion of a biography to put matters straight and Mrs. Gaskell as the obvious writer of it. E.N. to Nicholls June 6th 1855; W&S 954. Patrick Brontë wrote requesting Gaskell to undertake the work on June 16th 1855; W&S 956 (misdated July; see Chapple & Pollard, p.349). Gaskell visited Haworth to discuss the project on July 23rd 1855.

223. Gaskell, p.526.

224. Margaret Wooler to Ellen Nussey; 1857 (no other dates); W&S 992.

225. Stevens, p.71.

226. June 4th 1858; W&S 997,

227. C.B. to E.N. 14th October, 1850; W&S 610.

228. Edward Taylor in the *Shirley* annotations says in the late 1860s, a report in the *Spenborough Guardian* of 18th March 1904 says in the 1870s. Margaret Smith gives 1875/6 but gives no source. White's *History, Gazeteer and Directory of the West Riding* lists him in 1866 in business in Hunsworth with his home in Wike, but he does not appear in the 1870 edition.

229. Population Census, 1851.

230. Susan M. Taylor, ms. Notebook, Interview with Grace Hirst, December 5th 1931, Brontë Parsonage Library, pp.11-12.

231. 'Feminine Idleness', *The First Duty of Women*, p.122. Taylor defines going into society as 'a number of people with nothing to do [can] meet to seek in company for sources of interest that none of them have [sic] got separately.'

232. Moravians moved into Yorkshire from London; a 'love-feast' apparently intended to win converts and establish a local settlement was held at Great Gomersal in 1742.

233. Susan Taylor, *Mary Taylor*, ms. Notebook, Interview with Grace Hirst, December 5th 1931, Brontë Parsonage Library, p.3. There are two factual errors in the document; the family name of Mary's mother was Tickell, not Waring; Mary died 1893 not 1903. See Chapter 1, note 85.

234. Susan Taylor, *Mary Taylor*, ms Notebook, Interview with Grace Hirst, December 5th 1931, Brontë Parsonage Library, p.13.

235. Susan Taylor, *Mary Taylor*, ms Notebook, Interview with Grace Hirst, December 5th 1931, Brontë Parsonage Library, p.4. Grace uses the term 'dinner' in the northern sense of the midday meal.

236. William Scruton, 'Reminiscences of the Late Miss Ellen Nussey', *Brontë Society Transactions*, vol. 1, part 8, p.25 1895-98. Based on an interview of 1885.

237. First published Stevens, letter 33. The date of the publication of the Mendelssohn 1862 supports Stevens' suggestion that the letter was written around 1863.
238. A factor in the formation of the American women's rights movement was the rejection of the credentials of American women delegates to the World Anti-Slavery Convention in London in 1840.
239. William Carr, ms. Diary, West Yorkshire Archives Service, Kirklees Office, Central Library, Huddersfield, pages unnumbered. Richardson died 1879, Isabel 1899 aged 78 or 79.
240. W&S 919 C.B. to E.N. October 11th 1854. I am grateful to Louise Barnard for information regarding this letter.
241 The Visitors' Book, The Krone now Kronenhof Hotel, Pontresina. I am grateful to Herr J. Thommen, Director of the Kronenhof, for making Visitors' Books available to me.
242. Susan Taylor, *Mary Taylor*, ms. Notebook, Interview with Grace Hirst, December 5th 1931, Brontë Parsonage Library, pp.8-9.
243. William Scruton, 'Reminiscences of the Late Miss Ellen Nussey,' *Brontë Society Transactions*, vol. 1, part 8, 1895-8, p.35.
244. *Memorials of Two Sisters*, ed. Margaret J. Shaen, Longmans, Green & Co., London, 1908. A letter of January 16th 1857, p.167.
245. Mrs. Ellis H. Chadwick *In the Footsteps of the Brontës*, Pitman and Sons London, 1914, p.275; see also T. Wemyss Reid, *Charlotte Brontë: Monograph*, Macmillan & Co, London, 1877, p.2.
246. *Memoirs of Sir Wemyss Reid*, 1843-85, ed. Stuart J. Reid, Cassell and Company Ltd, London, 1905, p.232.
247. C.K. Shorter, *The Brontës; Life and Letters*, Hodder and Stoughton, London, 1908 vol.1, p.8.
248. Constantin Heger to E.N. September 7th 1863; W&S vol.IV, letter 1009; cf. *In the Footsteps of the Brontës*, Mrs. Ellis M. Chadwick, Pitman and Sons, London, 1914, p.275.
249. *Hours At Home*, Vol. II June-September 1870. New York.
250. Reprinted in *Brontë Society Transactions*, vol. 2, part 10, August 1899, p.58.
251. *Brontë Society Transactions*, vol. 2, part 10, August 1899, p.58. This is an almost verbatim quotation from Sir James Kay Shuttleworth's letter to Gaskell on the publication of *The Life* in 1857, cited Shorter, *The Brontës: Life and Letters*, vol.I, p.10.
252. *Swiss Notes By Five Ladies*, Inchbold & Beck, Leeds, 1875, p.vi.
253. *Swiss Notes*, p.vii.
254. Susan Taylor, *Mary Taylor*, ms. Notebook, Interview with Grace Hirst, December 5th 1931, Brontë Parsonage Library, pp 6-7.
255. *Swiss Notes*, p.61.
256. *Swiss Notes*, p10.
257. *Swiss Notes*, p.11.
258. *Swiss Notes*, p.28.
259. *Swiss Notes*, p.13.
260. *Swiss Notes*, p.63.
261. *Swiss Notes*, p.132.
262. *Swiss Notes*, p.131.
263. *Swiss Notes*, p.70.
264. *Swiss Notes*, p.116.
265. *Swiss Notes*, p.127.
266. *Swiss Notes*, p.117.
267. *Swiss Notes*, pp 71-2.
268. *Swiss Notes*, p.134.
269. *Swiss Notes*, p.v.
270. I have been unable to trace any information about the Imseng family. *The Athenaeum*, July 31st 1869, in a despatch from Lausanne refers to the death of a man named Imseng, the Vicar of a village called Saas – 'on the left of the the bank of the Vispback, as you advance to the Monte Rosa'; it goes on to say there were nearly 40 persons in the village with the

name of Imseng the 'effects of isolation and intermarriage'. The village referred to may have been Saas-Grund in a valley next to the one where St Nicklaus or St. Nicholas is situated, south of Visp.

271. Signed 'M.T'. in the *Victoria Magazine,* October, vol.XXVII, May-October 1876, p.512.

272. The *Victoria Magazine,* August 1872, vol.XVII, p.304.

273. The *Victoria Magazine,* August 1872, vol.XVII, p.307.

274. The register of visitors at the Hotel Krone, Pontresina.

275. M.T. to C.B. April 25th 1850; W&S 550.

276. *Shirley,* Chapter 37.

277. M.T. to C.B. April 10th 1849; W&S 436.
    Below the *Victoria Magazine* is listed as *V.M.*; *The First Duty of Women* as *F.D.*

278. Faithfull was especially committed to the cause of employment for women and became particularly active in the Society for the Promotion of the Employment of Women. Hers was the main responsibility for the establishment in 1859 of the Victoria Press where women were trained and employed as typographers. This initiative combined the advantages of providing some women with training and employment and making available a press placed at the service of the women's cause. *The Englishwoman's Journal* and *The Proceedings of the National Association for the Promotion of Social Science* were printed there. For an account of the *Victoria Magazine* and Faithfull's direction of it see Pauline A. Nestor, 'A New Departure in Women's Publishing: "The Englishwoman's Journal" and "The Victoria Magazine"' in *Victorian Periodicals Review,* vol.XV, 1982, pp.93-105.

279. Preface to 'Essays in Criticism', *Matthew Arnold, Poetry and Prose,* ed. John Bryson, Rupert Hart-Davis, London, 1954, p.348, pp.395-410.

280. The two editions attracted numbers of reviews in the British periodical press, including, in addition to the Arnold review, the *Edinburgh Review,* July 1864, the *Pall Mall Gazette,* October 1865 and March 1866 and the *Athenaeum,* February 1866.

281. *F.D.,* pp.235, 236-7.

282. *F.D.,* pp.239-40.

283. The women were often abusively attacked in the press for their alleged unwomanliness and some were consequently anxious to demonstrate their womanliness, even piety.

284. For details of dates of Taylor's articles and the form of acknowledgement see Appendix 1.

285. Brussels; W&S 138 n.d..

286. The frontispiece of the volume is inaccurate in dating the publication of the articles from 1865, the earliest, *A Philistine's Opinion of Eugénie de Guérin* appeared only in December 1866.

287. *F.D.,* p.7.

288. *F.D.,* p.13. This may be referring to work like John Ruskin's 'Of Queen's Gardens' in *Sesame and Lilies* (1865) and Patmore's *The Angel in the House* (1854-6).

289. *F.D.,* p.24.

290. 1870, vol.XV, pp.458-9.

291. Greg provoked a number of replies including from Frances Power Cobbe (1823-1904) in November 1862 in *Frazer's Magazine,* from Jessie Boucherett (1825-1905) in *Women's Work and Women's Culture,* ed. Josephine Butler, Macmillan, London, 1869.

292. *F.D.,* p.25.

293. *F.D.,* p.27.

294. *F.D.,* pp.30-31.

295. 'What Can Educated Women Do?' (II) reprinted in *Barbara Leigh Smith Bodichon and the Langham Place Group* and *Woman's Work and Woman's Culture,* ed. Josephine Butler, Macmillan, London, 1869, p.xv.

296. *F.D.,* p.41.

297. See Bessie Rayner Parkes, 'The Balance of Public Opinion in Regard to Woman's Work', reprinted in *Barbara Leigh Smith Bodichon and the Langham Place Group,* p.202.

298. 'Feminine Work', *F.D.,* pp.72-3.

299. *F.D.,* pp. 87-8.

300. *F.D.,* p.94.

301. *F.D.*, p.95.
302. *F.D.*, pp.108-9.
303. Reprinted *Barbara Leigh Smith Bodichon and the Langham Place Group*, pp.305-19.
304. *F.D.*, p.111-112.
305. *F.D.*, p.116.
306. See 'Feminine Suffrage', 1868, where she discusses this.
307. Reprinted in *Barbara Leigh Smith Bodichon and the Langham Place Group*, pp 354-77.
308. *F.D.*, pp.143-4.
309. August 10th 1854; W&S 911.
310. *F.D.*, pp.138-9.
311. *F.D.*, p.140.
312. *F.D.*, pp.154-5.
313. *F.D.*, p.149.
314. *F.D.*, pp.150-1.
315. February 24th-March 3rd 1854; W&S 879.
316. *F.D.*, p.165.
317. *F.D.*, p.180.
318. *F.D.*, p.184.
319. Replies to Linton appeared in *Macmillan's Magazine* and *The Englishwoman's Review*. The *Victoria Magazine* reproduced an article from the *St Paul's Magazine*. In January and February 1870, the *Saturday Review* returned to the attack with articles like *Friendship* and the *Exclusiveness of Women* to which the *Victoria Magazine* replied in October 1871 and still under the impression that 'The Girl of the Period' article was the work of a man. In 1874 it published a series of articles 'Thoughts About Friendship'. The May 1876 number of *Belgravia* carried yet another Linton article, 'Women's Place in Nature and Society', with her characteristic misogynist attacks which the *Victoria Magazine* trenchantly characterised as 'hashed mutton hashed again'.
320. *F.D.*, p.192.
321. *F.D.*, p.194.
322. *F.D.*, p. 206.
323. *F.D.*, p.266.
324. Gaskell, p.577.
325. *V.M.*, vol.XIII, May 1869, p.55 carried a report headed 'Rochdale Co-op and Married Women's Property' referring to a speech of Russell Gurney in the second debate on the Bill on married women's property. 'The Secretary of a co-operative society at Rochdale was examined before the Select Committee. The Society consisted of 7,000 members, who were entirely working people, and a great number of married women, registered as shareholders, received the profits derived from their shares, and so strong was public feeling in Rochdale in support of the payment of those profits to the women that none of their husbands had ventured to enforce their legal claim to them'.
326. *F.D.*, p.270.
327. *F.D.*, p.272.
328. *F.D.*, p.276.
329. *F.D.*, p.277.
330. Vol.V, January 1871, p27.
331. *V.M.* vol.XVI, November 1870, p.96.
332. 'Feminine Profitable Labour', *V.M.*, vol.XV, October 1870, p.556.
333. 'Feminine Profitable Labour', *V.M.*, vol XV, October 1870, pp 562-563.
334. Millicent Fawcett (1847-1929), one of the leaders of the women's movement, a prominent member of the Women's Suffrage Committee and subsequently President of the National Union of Women's Suffrage Societies.
335. *V.M.*, vol.XXVII, October 1876, pp.184-5.
336. Faithfull became associated with the work of the Women's Protective and Provident League founded in 1875 by Emma Patterson, a bookbinder by trade, who had worked at the Victoria

Press. The League represented an important initiative in the establishment of stable union organisation for women workers.

337. Though a Married Women's Property Act had been passed in 1870 it was very restricted and most women's rights reformers regarded it as virtually ineffective. For a discussion of the debates and passage of the Bill see Lee Holcombe, *Wives and Property,* University of Toronto Press, Toronto Buffalo, 1983, chapter 8.

338. *V.M.*, vol.XX1, August 1873 pp.361-2.

339. *V.M.*, vol XX1, August 1873, p.363.

340. *V.M.*, vol XX1, August 1873, p.365.

341. Charles L. Graves, *Life and Letters of Alexander Macmillan*, Macmillan & Co. London, 1910, p.202.

342. 'Fair Play v. Goldwin Smith' concentrated on refuting Smith's claims of the negative effects of the gains of the women's movement in the United States. It may have been by Faithfull herself who had made an American tour the previous year and had regularly sent reports to the *Victoria Magazine* describing her enthusiastic reception. *V.M.*, vol.XX1 September 1873.

343. September 1874, vol.XXX, p.377.

344. *Macmillan's Magazine*, May 1874, vol.XXX, p.139.

345. *Macmillan's Magazine* May 1874, vol.XXX, p.145.

346. *V.M.*, vol.XXIII, September 1874, p.405.

347. *V.M.*, vol XXIII, September 1874, p.405.

348. *V.M.*, vol.XXIX, July 1877 p.211.

349. *V.M.*, vol.XXIX, July 1877 p.209.

350. *V.M.*, vol XXIX, July 1877 pp. 215-16.

351. *V.M.*, vol.XXIX, July 1877 p.217.

352. *V.M.*, vol.XXIX, July 1877 p.218.

353. *Macmillan's Magazine*, May to October, 1876, vol.XXXIV, pp.385 and 481.

354. *Memoirs of Sir Wemyss Reid, 1842-1885*, ed. Stuart J. Reid, Cassell and Company Ltd., London, 1905, p.237.

355. Ellen later complained about Reid gossiping at a dinner party about Charlotte's feelings for Heger; Clement Shorter enquired from Ellen about 'the love affair', see Shorter to E.N. September 3rd 1889, ms. letter, Brontë Parsonage Library. I have been unable to trace any reply.

356. Wemyss Reid, *Charlotte Brontë*, pp.3-4.

357. Wemyss Reid, *Charlotte Brontë*, p.6.

358. Wemyss Reid, *Charlotte Brontë*, p.236.

359. Wemyss Reid, *Charlotte Brontë*, p.68.
     C.B. to E.N. September 18th 1845; W&S 214.

360. E.N. to Mrs. Cortazzo, October 6th 1882, ms. letter, Brontë Parsonage Library.

361. *The Athenæum*, June 16th 1883, pp.762-3.

362. *The Athenæum*, August 4th 1883, p.147.

363. William Carr, ms. diary, West Yorkshire Archives Service, Kirklees, Central Library, Huddersfield, August 30th 1884.

364. William Carr, ms. diary, West Yorkshire Archives Service, Kirklees, Central Library, Huddersfield, August 22nd 1887.

365. William Scruton, 'Reminiscences of the Late Miss Ellen Nussey', *Brontë Society Transactions*, vol. 1, part 8, 1895-98, pp.34-35. Based on an interview of 1885.

366. Ellen Nussey to T. J. Wise, November 18th 1892. ms. Brotherton Library Collection. Wise had been seeking information from Nussey about the possible whereabouts of other letters: ms letter from Wise to Ellen Nussey, November 17th 1892, Brontë Parsonage Museum.

367. MS letter from the Reverend A. Wilkes to Ellen Nussey, February 10th 1879, Brontë Parsonage Museum.

368. *Methodist New Connexion Magazine*, 1889, p.470. There is a curious echo in the question and answer in this passage of Edward Taylor's comment in the 1886 annotated edition of

Shirley.
369. *British Weekly,* July 13th 1893.
370. C.K. Shorter, *Charlotte Brontë and Her Circle,* p.259.
371. Mabel Ferrett, *The Taylors of Red House,* Kirklees Leisure Services, Huddersfield, 1987, p.46.
   References to *Miss Miles* are to the 1890 Remington edition. For ease of access I cite also the chapter numbers.
372. January 1871, vol.V. pp.24-7.
373. Gaskell, pp.128-9.
374. M.T. to C.B. postmark July 24th 1848; W&S 382, Stevens letter 16 'between June to July 24th 1848.'
375. M.T. to C.B April 10th 1849; W&S 436..
376. April 5th 1850; W&S 542.
377. Postmark July 24th 1848; W&S 382, Stevens letter 16 'between June and July 24th 1848'.
378. 25 April 1850; W&S 550.
379. VM, vol.XXI, September 1873, pp.395-416.
380. p.395.
381. p.404.
382. p.410.
383. p.412.
384. p.415.
385. p.416.
386. VM, Vol XXVII, October 1876, p.503.
387. p.503.
388. p.504.
389. p.506.
390. p.512.
391. p.512.
392. n.d. postmarked Keighley, 25th October; W&S.
393. Patricia Thomson, *George Sand and the Victorians.*
394. Also cited in Pauline A. Nestor, 'A New Departure in Women's Publishing: The Englishwoman's Journal and The Victoria Magazine', *Victorian Periodicals Review,* XV, 1982.
395. Vol.XXVII, August 1876, pp.344-5.
396. Ellen Moers, *Literary Women,* p.190.
397. Charles L. Graves, *Life and Letters of Alexander MacMillan,* p.32.
398. As well as possessing a fine voice, Viardot was a highly intelligent musician devoted to her art and, in Sand's view, not only the greatest singer of her day, but an artist of unshakeable integrity refusing to pander to what she regarded as the debased musical taste of some of her audiences. See e.g. a letter to George Sand of 1841, *Lettres inédites de George Sand et de Pauline Viardot,* Notes and introduction by Thérèse Marix-Spire, Nouvelles Éditions Latines, Paris, 1959, p.39.
399. M.T. to C.B. received October 1852; W&S 793.
400. *Miss Miles,* chapter 2, p.26.
401. Chapter 13, p.158.
402. Chapter 14, p.177.
403. *First Duty,* p.165: 'Feminine Character'.
404. *Miss Miles,* Chapter 4, p.38.
405. Chapter 6, p.75.
406. Chapter 15, p.188.
407. Chapter 15, p.188.
408. Chapter 15, p.188.
409. Chapter 15, p.184.
410. *First Duty,* p.2.

411. *Miss Miles,* Chapter 15, p.196 & 201.
412. Chapter 15, p.203.
413. Chapter 17, p.225.
414. Chapter 16, p.212.
415. Chapter 11, p.136.
416. Chapter 16, p.213.
417. W&S 763.
418. September 24th 1842, W&S 142, .
419. *Miss Miles,* Chapter 18, p.229.
420. Chapter 19, p.256: 'The world was all before them, where to choose/Their place of rest', book XII lines 646-7, Milton. Wordsworth's *Intimations of Immortality from Recollections of Early Childhood*, stanza V, also quoted as epigraphs to chapters 3 and 4: 'Heaven lies about us in our infancy' and 'And fade [sic] into the light of common day'.
421. Chapter 19, p.259.
422. *First Duty*, pp.52-3.
423. In 1848 Fanny Kemble took her father's place as a reader: 'Nobody could deny that readings were popular and therefore profitable' (M.N. Armstrong, *A Passionate Victorian; The Biography of Fanny Kemble 1809-1893*, Macmillan, London, 1938, p.304). The *Saturday Review* (April 16th 1859 p.476) carried an advertisement for a series of lectures at the Hanover Square Rooms by Mrs. Holcroft, one of which was on strong-minded women! The *Pall Mall Gazette* (January 16th 1866) reviewed a performance by an American *diseuse*, Miss Hardinge, 'a celebrated contemporaneous orator' who included in her performance 'a short sketch of the history of America'. The *Victoria Magazine* (vol.XXX November-April 1878) carried an article on Miss Ella Dietz, described as a 'Reader'. Dickens reading his own work is perhaps the outstanding example but many nineteenth-century periodicals carry advertisements for and reviews of this type of public event. Emily Faithfull lectured in the United States, the *Victoria Magazine* (vol.XVI November 1870-April 1871, issue of March 1871, p.471) reported her public lecture in York, *The Best Society*; she also gave dramatic readings, a meeting of the Victoria Discussion Society on July 3rd 1871 was given over to dramatic and poetry readings.
424. *Miss Miles,* Chapter 23, p.329.
425. Chapter 23, p.331.
426. M.T. to C.B. April 5th 1850; W&S 542.
427. *Miss Miles,* Chapter 23, p.333.
428. Chapter 23, p.336.
429. Chapter 23, p.342.
430. Chapter 23, p.345.
431. Chapter 23, p.347.
432. Chapter 27, p.407.
433. Chapter 28, p.420.
434. Chapter 29, pp 433-4.
435. *Tess of the D'Urbervilles* was to appear one year after the publication of *Miss Miles* and *Jude the Obscure* five years later.
436. Mary Taylor to Mary Doublet, February 17th 1890. Private collection; photocopy in Brontë Parsonage Library. Mary Doublet was a cousin of the Taylors, born in France in 1826 and probably the daughter of Joshua Taylor's brother who had been interned in France during the Napleonic Wars and settled in that country. In the 1871 census she is recorded as a widow and a naturalised British citizen.
437. *The Illustrated London News*, March 18th 1893, p.326. Clement Shorter was the editor of *The Illustrated London News* until 1902.
438. *The Athenæum*, March 11th 1893, no.3411, p.314.
439. C. K. Shorter, *Charlotte Brontë and Her Circle*, p.259.
440. *The Life and Works of Charlotte Brontë and Her Sisters*, vol.VII, 'The Life of Charlotte Brontë by Mrs. Gaskell', Smith, Elder & Co. London, 1900, p.106.
441. *The Brontës: Life and Letters*, p.428.

442. An anonymous contributor to *The Yorkshire Daily Observer*, December 21st 1903.
443. *The Guardian*, December 24th 1903.
444. Letter from W. Hemingway to Mrs. Shaw, occupant of Red House, October 9th 1952. MS at Red House. Hemingway was the son of the agent for Taylor properties.
445. C.B. to E.N. October 31st 1854; W&S 921.
446. C.B. to E.N. November 7th 1854; W&S 923.
447. Horsfall Turner, ed. *The Story of the Brontës*, Bradford, 1889, p.333. SB 1364, one of the two aborted volumes in the Brontë Parsonage Library.
448. Horsfall Turner, ed. *The Story of the Brontës*, Bradford, 1889, p.333. SB 243, one of the two aborted volumes in the Brontë Parsonage Library.
449. E.N. to Clement Shorter, April 10th 1895, ms. letter, Brotherton Collection.
450. Clement Shorter was the author of a number of books on the Brontës.
451. A founder-member of the Brontë Society, and local historian.
452. Local historian and antiquarian credited as the originator of the idea of the Brontë Society; cf. Herbert Wroot, 'The Brontë Society and Its Work' in *A Centenary Memorial 1816-1916*, edited Butler Wood, Fisher & Unwin, 1917.
453. Mary Robinson was the biographer of *Emily Brontë*, 1883.
454. See *The Two Forgers: A Biography of Harry Buxton Forman and Thomas James Wise*, John Collins, Scolar Press, 1992, pp.117-8.
455. C.K. Shorter, Introduction and Notes to Mrs. Gaskell, *The Life of Charlotte Brontë*, Smith, Elder, & Co., London, 1900, p.100.
456. Mrs.Ellis H. Chadwick, *In the Footsteps of the Brontës*, Pitman and Sons London 1914, p.278; E.N. to Mrs. Flowers, June 29th 1883, ms. letter, Brotherton Collection.
457. Mrs. Ellis H. Chadwick, *In the Footsteps of the Brontës*, Pitman and Sons, London, 1914, p.371 and *The Heckmondwike Herald*, April 7th 1887.
458. *Memoirs of Sir Wemyss Reid*, ed. Stuart J. Reid, p.230.
459. *Athenæum*, July 21st 1883, p.79.
460. *Athenæum*, August 4th 1883, pp.146-7.
461. William Scruton, 'Reminiscences of the Late Miss Ellen Nussey', pp.30-31.
462. C. K. Shorter, *The Brontës: Life and Letters*, p.19.
463. E.N. to Clement Shorter, October 20th 1895, ms letter, Brotherton Collection.
464. J. Ridley, n.d., W&S, vol.V, p.290.

Select Bibliography

Brontë, Charlotte. *Ashworth*. Alan Sutton, Stroud, Gloucestershire, 1993.

Emma. Dent, London, 1969.

Jane Eyre. Preface, Q. Leavis, Penguin Books, Harmondsworth, 1977.

The Professor. Dent, London, 1969.

Shirley, London: Dent, London, 1970.

The Letters of Charlotte Brontë. Vol.1, 1829-1847. Vol.2. 1848-51, ed. Margaret Smith, Clarendon Press: Oxford, 1995, 2000.

Ferrett, Mabel. *The Taylors of Red House*, Kirklees Leisure Services, Huddersfield, 1987.

Gaskell, Elizabeth. *The Life of Charlotte Brontë*. ed. Alan Shelston. Penguin Books, Harmondsworth, 1975.

Greg, 'Why Are Women Redundant?' *Literary and Social Judgments*, Vol.2, 4th edition, Trubner, London, 1877, pp.44-90.

Guérin, Eugénie de. *Journal et Fragments*. G. S. Trebutien, Paris, 1868, 21st edition; first appeared as *Journal et Lettres*, G. S. Trebutien, Paris, 1862.

Lacey, Candida Ann, ed. *Barbara Leigh Smith Bodichon and the Langham Place Group*. Routledge & Kegan Paul, New York and London, 1987.

Moers, Ellen. *Literary Women*. The Women's Press, London, 1980.

Stevens, Joan. *Mary Taylor, Friend of Charlotte Brontë, Letters from New Zealand and Elsewhere*, Auckland University Press. Oxford University Press, 1972.

Taylor, Mary. *The First Duty of Women*, Emily Faithfull, London, 1870.

Miss Miles, or, A Tale of Yorkshire life Sixty Years Ago. Remington & Co. London, 1890.

Swiss Notes by Five Ladies (contributor), Leeds: Inchbold & Beck, 1875.

Wise, Thomas J. and John Alexander Symington, (eds). *The Brontës: Their Lives, Friendships and Correspondence*, 4 vols. Shakespeare Head Brontë, Blackwell, Oxford: 1932.

Index

Arnold, Matthew, 82-83

Arnold, Thomas, dislikes William Couper, 50

Bodichon, Barbara (1827-91), women's leader, 88

Branwell, Miss, Charlotte Brontë's aunt, 97-98

Brontë, Branwell, 38, 51, 74, 118; possible relationship with Mary, 11-12

Brontë, Charlotte, iv-vii, 40, 41, 59, 88, 89

Her life: attends same school as Mary, 6-9; Mary's opinion of her, v, vi, 8, 9, 41, her opinion of Mary, 11, 12, 34-35, 37, 39, 42, 44, 48, 112; encouraged to write by Mary, 8, 41; becomes school teacher at Roe Head, 10; Mary and Ellen Nussey frequent visitors, 10; leaves teaching and returns to Haworth, 16; education in Brussels, 28-30, 33; feelings for Constantin Heger, 35, 69, 109; Mary suggests she join her in Hagen, declines, 36; returns to Haworth, 37; her feminism, contrasted with that of Mary, 40; worries that Mary is in poverty in New Zealand, 50; visited by Joe and Ellen Taylor, 51; rejects, and then accepts Arthur Nicholls' proposal of marriage, 58-59; dies, 59

Her writings: *The Professor*, 13; *Ashworth*, 16; *Emma*, 17; *Jane Eyre*, 43, 46; *Shirley*, 18, 19-25, 43, 81, 111, 126; Ellen Nussey as the possible basis of Caroline Helstone in *Shirley*, 111, 116; Mary as the possible basis for characters in *Ashworth*, 16, in *Emma*, 17, in *Shirley* Mary, 11, 116; others of the Taylor family as possible bases for characters in *Shirley*, 18-25

Brontë, Emily, attends finishing school in Brussels, 28, 30, 34; biography of, by Mary Robinson, 113

Brontë, Patrick, iv, v, 28, 58, 111, 113

Chartists, 4, 81

Contagious Diseases Act (1864), effects, 95

Couper, William, employs Mary as a tutor for his daughter, 50; marries Margaret Knox, 50

Craig, Isa (1831-1903), paper on female insanity, 91

Dixon, Abraham (?-1850), brother-in-law of Joshua Taylor, 2, 28, 33, 51

Dixon, Laetitia (née Taylor) (1780-1842), Mary's aunt, 28

Dixon, Mary, daughter of Abraham, becomes friend of Charlotte Brontë, 28, 34, 35

Doublet, Mary, Mary's cousin, 141

Factories Acts, 81, 100-1

Faithfull, Emily (1835-95), editor of the *Victoria Magazine*, 82; disagrees with Mary over Nine Hours Bill, 100-1

Gaskell, Elizabeth, iv, 90, 124; her biography of Charlotte Brontë, iv-vii, 4, 19, 29, 37, 57, 60, 68-69, 83, 109, 115, 119, 142

Gomersal, Mary's birthplace, iv, 1, 4

Goussaert, Madame, Martha attends her finishing school in Brussels, 15; Mary's opinion of her, 29; visits Mary in Hagen, 33

Greg, W.R., anti-feminist writer, 86-88

Guérin, Eugénie de (1805-48), work reviewed by Mary, 82-83

Hallé, Frederick, gives Mary piano lessons, 34

Heger, Constantin, the object of Charlotte Brontë's affections, 57, 69

Hirst, Grace, friend of Mary, 56, 141; recalls Mary, 22, 64-65, 67; Mary escorts her to school in Germany, 71; visits High Royd, and goes on holiday with Mary to Switzerland, 71-79

High Royd, Mary's home on her return from New Zealand, 63, 71, 114

Hunsworth, 2-4

Knox, Dr. Frederick, 49, marriages of his daughters, 49-50

Knox, Mary, marries Waring, 50

Koekelberg, Château de, Brussels, finishing school attended by Mary and Martha, 15, 28-31

Linton, Eliza Lynn, writer, 95

Luddites, machine breakers, 3-4, 5

Matthews, Rev. W., interviews Mary about Methodist associations in *Shirley* 'country', 116-117

Methodism, in industrial areas of West Riding, 1, 4-6, 116-17; radical influence of declines, 118; in Mary's *Miss Miles*, 127

Mill, Harriet Taylor, wife of John Stuart Mill, v

Mill, John Stuart, v, 104

New Zealand, Waring Taylor decides to emigrate there, 14-15; Mary decides to join him, 38; conditions around Wellington, 38, 43, 44; and on the voyage there, 43-44; difficulties in communications, 38; political conditions in, 43; social conditions in, 44-45

Nicholls, Arthur, proposes to Charlotte Brontë, 58; disapproves of Ellen Nussey's role in biography of Charlotte Brontë, 68, 69, further disapproves of her sponsoring a new biography, 109

Nielson, Minnie, accompanies Mary to Switzerland, 71-80

Nine Hours Bill, disagreement within women's movement over, 100-101

Nussey, Ellen (1817-97), iv, 29, 30, 32, 33, 34, 35-36, 41, 53, 61, 109, 141; her role in Gaskell's biography of Charlotte Brontë, iv-v, 59, 68-69, 109, attempts to have further biographical material published, 68-69, 109-111, 115; attends same school as Mary, 6-9; her opinion of the Taylor girls' dress sense, 7; her sentimental nature, 6; visits Charlotte Brontë, 10; Mary encourages her to read widely, 35-36; thinks that one of Mary's brothers might propose to her, 42; offered a position as a companion, 57; disapproves of Arthur Nicholls, 58; unable to resume friendship with Mary at previous levels of intimacy, 65-70; her conservative opinions, 65-66; dislikes Isabel Richardson, 67; writes an article on Charlotte Brontë for *Scribner's Monthly*, 69-70; engages Wemyss Reid to write new biography of Charlotte Brontë, to Mary's disapproval, 109-112; her friendship with Charlotte emphasized at the expense of Mary's, 111, 115; distances herself from Mary Robinson's biography of Emily Brontë, 113

Nussey, Henry, Ellen's brother, proposes marriage to Charlotte Brontë, 42

Nussey, Joshua, Ellen's brother, 84

Parkes, Bessie Rayner, 53

Plug Riots, 4

Reid, Wemyss, his biography of Charlotte Brontë, 109-112; opposition of Arthur Nicholls to the work, 109; makes little direct mention of Mary by name, 111

Richardson, Rev. George, husband of Isabel, 67; their daughters, 67

Richardson, Isabel (née Nussey) (c.1821-99), Ellen Nussey's half-cousin and friend of Mary, 67

Ringrose, Amelia, wife of Joe Taylor, 58, 62; remarries and moves to Beverley, 62

Roberson, Rev. Hammond (1757-1841), Mary's opinion of him, 5

Robinson, Mrs. (Lady Scott), v

Robinson, Mary, her biography of Emily Brontë, 113

Ross, Marion, accompanies Mary to Switzerland, 71-79

Sand, George, her popularity, 36, 124-126

Schmidt, Frau, offers Mary somewhere to stay in Germany (1842), 31

Sharpe, Martha, Mary's maid, 114, 143

Shorter, Clement, inaccurate statements about Mary, 117; writes Mary's obituary, 141-2; uses extracts from her letters in his book *Charlotte Brontë and Her Circle*, 142; makes further inaccurate statements about Mary and dismisses her writing, 142

Smith, Goldwin (1823-1910), opposes women's suffrage, 103-5

Taylor, Anne (née Tickell) (1781/82-1856), Mary's mother, iv, 2; her stern nature, 14-22; as the possible basis for the character of Mrs. Yorke in *Shirley*, 22, dislikes the novel entirely, 22; dies, 60

Taylor Anne, daughter of Waring, marries her cousin Richard, dies, 113

Taylor, Edward, Mary's nephew, 23-24

Taylor, Ellen (1826-51), Mary's cousin, arrives in New Zealand, 51-52; goes into business with Mary, 52-55; dies of consumption, 55

Taylor, Emily (c.1849-1862), daughter of Joshua, dies, 63

Taylor, Emily Martha, (1851-58), daughter of Joe, dies, 63

Taylor, Jane Lister (née Charlesworth), wife of Joshua III, 114

Taylor, John (1736/37-1805), Mary's grandfather, 1

Taylor, John (1813-1901), Mary's brother, 2, 14, 26, 42, 143; accompanies Mary to Brussels, 26; Mary comes to live with him in England, 62; emigrates to New Zealand, 62

Taylor, Joseph ('Joe') (1816-57) Mary's brother, 2, 23, 25; accompanies Mary and the Brontë sisters to Brussels, 28; accompanies Mary to Austria, 35; marries Amelia Ringrose, 24, 58; has a daughter, 58; dies, 58

Taylor, Joshua II (1766-1840), Mary's father, iv, 1-2, 5, 116-7; bankruptcy, 2-3; gives French language books to Charlotte Brontë, 12-13; dies, 13; a possible model for the character of Hunsden in Charlotte Brontë's The Professor, 13, and of Yorke in Shirley, 20-22, 25

Taylor, Joshua III (1812-80), Mary's brother, 2; inherits business and Red House from father, 14, 62; provides for Mary, 63, abandons wife and family, takes up spiritualism, becomes bankrupt, 112-113, dies, 113; the possible basis for the character of Matthew in Shirley, 23

Taylor, Joshua IV, son of Joshua III, 62, winds up family business, 115

Taylor, Martha (1819-42), Mary's sister, 2; her schooling, 6, nicknamed 'Patty', 6; attends a finishing school in Brussels, 15, 27-36; dies, possibly from cholera, or a complication of pregnancy, 31-33

Taylor, Mary

Attitudes to people: herself, 40, 79; her father, 21; her mother, 11, 21, 26, 30; her sister Martha, 31, and reaction to her death, 58-59; Branwell Brontë, 12; Charlotte Brontë, v-vi, 8, 58-59; Patrick Brontë, v; William Couper, 50; Mary Knox, 49; Ellen Nussey, 65-66, 67; Rev. Hammond Roberson, 5; George Sand, 36; Catherine Wooler, 5

Character: 79-80, 142-143; 'a bit cranky', 65; her 'flightiness', 44; her honesty, v, 8, 31, 39; sense of justice, 7; private and reserved, 32, 110; stoicism and determination, 55; according to others: Charlotte Brontë, 15, 39, 42, 112, Grace Hirst, 72, Rev,. W. Matthews, 116-117, Ellen Nussey, 117, Susan Taylor, 64, 114

Early life: born, iv; her parents, v, 2, 5, 11, 12-13, 20-22; her home (Red House), 1; her schooling, 6-9, nicknamed 'Pag' or 'Polly', 8; returns home, 9, falls ill, 11, reads copiously, 12; moves to Hunsworth after her father's death, 14; wishes to make a living for herself, 15, but not as a governess, 26, 28-31; and goes on to Germany, 34; the possible basis for the character of Rose Yorke in Shirley, 23

In Germany: takes piano lessons, 34; moves to Hagen and lives alone, 35; goes on holiday to Austria with Joe, 35; reads widely, 36; suggests Charlotte should join her, 36; returns briefly to England, 38; goes on holiday to Switzerland, 38; decides to emigrate to New Zealand and takes her leave of Charlotte, 38-39

In New Zealand: arrives, 44; stays with Waring, 48; lodges with Mrs. Knox, 49; earns some money by trading, 50; becomes a tutor and moves to Porirua, 50; returns to Mrs. Knox, 51; goes into business with Ellen Taylor, 52-55; social life, 53-55; sadness at death of Ellen Taylor, 55; determined to carry on alone, 56-57; enjoyment of reading, 56-57; mentions returning home, 59; replies to requests for information on Charlotte Brontë from Mrs. Gaskell, iv, vi, 8, 59; decides to return to England, 60

In England: lives with brother John at Hunsworth, 62; moves to High Royd, 63; acquires an eccentric reputation, 63-

64; attends Church of England services, 64; disapproves of the 'Brontë industry', 69, 110, 115; travels widely, to Germany, with Grace Hirst, 71, to Switzerland, with Grace Hirst and three other women, 71-78,; finds work for Swiss friends in England, 79; acts a guarantor for nephews following Joshua's bankruptcy, 112-13, a creditor of Waring, 114; declines to co-operate with further Brontë biographers, 115, but helps Altheus Wilkes, 116, and Rev. W. Matthews, 116-117; dies, 141; obituaries, 142-143; will 143-144

Friends and acquaintances: Branwell Brontë, 11-12; Charlotte Brontë, v, 6-7, 34, 38-39, encourages her to write, 8, 41, encourages her to come to Brussels, 28; Grace Hirst, 71-79; Imseng family, 79, 143; Ellen Nussey, quarrels and then breaks with her, 65-70, 110-111

Health: 48, 49, 91, 114

Opinions: derived from experience, 88; on Female Middle Class Emigration Society, 88; on friendship, 39; on holidays, 78; on Jane Eyre, 46, 50, 116-117; on men, 94-95; on New Zealand, 30, her fellow colonists, 45-48; on Nine Hours Bill, 100-103; on political reform, 7, 10; on poverty, 75, 85-88, 90, 91, 103, 126; on reading, 35-36, 55, 56-57; on religious beliefs, 40-41, 75; on Shirley, 116-117; on slavery, 66; on social conventions, 72, 85; on the Swiss, 80; on trade unions, 100-103; on women, importance of education for, 92-94; incidence of mental problems amongst, 91-92, their conversation, 21, 46-48, their health, 92-93, their 'natural role' rejected, 84-87, 96, their passivity rejected, 83, 96, and the necessity for change, 98-99, 106, the validity of their opinions, 84, 93-94, their right to happiness, 58, their right to vote, 103-105

Writings: style of, 108, 119; Victoria Magazine articles, 60, 66, 79, 82; The First Duty of Women and Victoria Magazine articles, Chapter 6; Miss Miles, 124-140; Short Stories, 120-124; Swiss Notes by Five Ladies, 77-86, 134

Taylor, Richard, son of Joshua III, marries Anne his cousin, dies, 113, 118

Taylor, Susan, daughter of Edward, 64, 67; childhood memories of Mary, 113

Taylor, Waring, son of Richard, brought up by grandmother, 113, 144

Taylor, William Waring ('Waring') (1819-1903), Mary's brother, 2, 43; decides to emigrate to New Zealand, 14-15; supports his mother in disliking Brontë's Shirley, 22; marries, 43; living in Wellington, 48, in Wanganui, 61; daughter Anne marries and dies, 113; bankrupt, 114; dies, 143

Tonna, Charlotte Elizabeth, 126

Trollope, Frances, 126

Waring, Anne (1739-1817), Mary's grandmother, 2

Weightman, William, dies, 31

Wilkes, Rev. Altheus, is helped by Mary in a work on the Brontës, 116

Wilson, Rev. Carus, v

Women's rights movement, 82, 84, 88, 106-108, 140

Woollen industry, 2-3; industrial relations in, 3-5

Wooler, Margaret (1793-1885), 10, 60, 61, 111; her school attended by Mary and the Brontës, 6-9; gives away Charlotte Brontë at her wedding, 58